The Weight of All Flesh

The Berkeley Tanner Lectures

The Tanner Lectures on Human Values were established by the American scholar, industrialist, and philanthropist Obert Clark Tanner; they are presented annually at nine universities in the United States and England. The University of California, Berkeley became a permanent host of annual Tanner Lectures in the academic year 2000–2001. This work is the tenth in a series of books based on the Berkeley Tanner Lectures. The volume includes revised and extended versions of the lectures that Eric L. Santner presented at Berkeley in April of 2014, together with expanded responses from the three invited commentators on that occasion—Bonnie Honig, Peter E. Gordon, and Hent de Vries—and a final rejoinder by Professor Santner. This volume is edited by Kevis Goodman, who also contributes an introduction. The Berkeley Tanner Lecture Series was established in the belief that these distinguished lectures, together with the lively debates stimulated by their presentation in Berkeley, deserve to be made available to a wider audience. Additional volumes are in preparation.

MARTIN JAY
R. JAY WALLACE
Series Editors

Volumes Published in the Series

The Weight of All Flesh:
On the Subject-Matter
of Political Economy

Eric L. Santner

With Commentaries by
Bonnie Honig
Peter E. Gordon
Hent de Vries

Edited and Introduction by
Kevis Goodman

OXFORD
UNIVERSITY PRESS

OXFORD

Oxford University Press is a department of the University of
Oxford. It furthers the University's objective of excellence in research,
scholarship, and education by publishing worldwide.

Oxford   New York
Auckland   Cape Town   Dar es Salaam   Hong Kong   Karachi
Kuala Lumpur   Madrid   Melbourne   Mexico City   Nairobi
New Delhi   Shanghai   Taipei   Toronto

With offices in
Argentina   Austria   Brazil   Chile   Czech Republic   France   Greece
Guatemala   Hungary   Italy   Japan   Poland   Portugal   Singapore
South Korea   Switzerland   Thailand   Turkey   Ukraine   Vietnam

Oxford is a registered trademark of Oxford University Press
in the UK and certain other countries.

Published in the United States of America by
Oxford University Press
198 Madison Avenue, New York, NY 10016

Library of Congress Cataloging-in-Publication Data
The weight of all flesh : on the subject-matter of political economy / Eric L. Santner ; with
commentaries by Bonnie Honig, Peter E. Gordon, Hent de Vries ; edited and introduction by
Kevis Gooman.
pages cm. — (Berkeley Tanner lectures)
Includes bibliographical references and index.
ISBN 978-0-19-025408-7 (hardcover : alk. paper)   1. Political theology.
2. Collectivism.   3. Kings and rulers—Philosophy.   I. Gooman, Kevis, editor.
II. Honig, Bonnie, writer of added commentary.   III. Gordon, Peter Eli, writer of added
commentary.   IV. Vries, Hent de, writer of added commentary.
V. Santner, Eric L., 1955– Speeches. Selections.
BT83.59.W45 2015
201'.72—dc23
2015005148

Contents

THE WEIGHT OF ALL FLESH: ON THE SUBJECT-MATTER OF POLITICAL ECONOMY

ERIC L. SANTNER

COMMENTS

REPLY TO THE COMMENTATORS

Acknowledgments

A number of people have been involved in the life of this project. I am deeply indebted to the participants in various seminars in which my thinking on the "subject-matter of political economy" took shape. The members of my core classes, "Self, Culture, and Society," in which we read Smith, Marx, and Weber together, helped me to deepen my relationship to these thinkers. The students in my seminar "Symbolic Economies" contributed to my thinking about the links between Freudian and Marxist conceptions of value, drive, and desire. The participants in my DAAD summer seminar, "Political Economy and Libidinal Economy in German Culture and Thought," were genuine collaborators in the development of the arguments presented in this volume. I am, finally, very grateful to the contributions made to this project by the participants in the seminar on the history of avarice. I owe a special debt of gratitude to my remarkable co-instructor in that seminar, Mladen Dolar, whose work and friendship are ongoing sources of inspiration for me. I also want to thank some key interlocutors: Anna Kornbluh, Adam Kotsko, Kenneth Reinhard, Robert Buch, Florian Klinger, Marcia Klotz, Paul Mendes-Flohr, Moishe Postone. I am no doubt forgetting others who have in some way or another helped me to articulate the thoughts in this volume. I am deeply grateful to the Tanner Committee at the University of California at Berkeley, above all Martin Jay and Jay Wallace, for making the occasion of these lectures possible and for helping to give it the right shape and tone. I am, of course, deeply in debt to the three respondents to the lectures, Bonnie Honig, Peter Gordon, and Hent de Vries, for taking the time and having the patience to think with me even across barriers of disagreement and contestation. I am extremely grateful to Julia Lupton and John Hamilton, whose careful and critical reading of the manuscript helped to bring it to its final form. Finally, I owe more than I can say to Kevis Goodman, the editor of this volume; she has been a true collaborator from start to finish. She has made every voice in this volume speak more clearly and precisely. None of this—not the lectures, not the responses, not the volume—would have come about without her care and concerted efforts.

—Eric L. Santner

Contributors

ERIC SANTNER, a leading cultural theorist and scholar of German literature, cinema, and history, is the Philip and Ida Romberg Distinguished Service Professor in Modern Germanic Studies at the University of Chicago, as well as a member of the University's Center for Jewish Studies. He has been a visiting fellow at various institutions, including Dartmouth, Washington University, Cornell, and the University of Konstanz (Germany). He works at the intersection of literature, philosophy, psychoanalysis, political theory, and religious thought.

Santner's many publications include: *Friedrich Hölderlin: Narrative Vigilance and the Poetic Imagination* (Rutgers, 1986); *Stranded Objects: Mourning, Memory, and Film in Postwar Germany* (Cornell, 1990); *My Own Private Germany: Daniel Paul Schreber's Secret History of Modernity* (Princeton, 1996); *On the Psychotheology of Everyday Life: Reflections on Freud and Rosenzweig* (Chicago, 2001); *On Creaturely Life: Rilke, Benjamin, Sebald* (Chicago, 2006); *The Neighbor: Three Inquiries in Political Theology* (Chicago, 2006, with Slavoj Zizek and Kenneth Reinhard); and *The Royal Remains: The People's Two Bodies and the Endgames of Sovereignty* (Chicago, 2011). He edited the German Library Series volume of works by Friedrich Hölderlin and co-edited, with Moishe Postone, *Catastrophe and Meaning: The Holocaust and the Twentieth Century* (Chicago, 2003). His work has been translated into German, Spanish, French, Korean, Hebrew, Polish, Italian, and Portuguese.

HENT DE VRIES is the Russ Family Chair in the Humanities and the Director of the Humanities Center at Johns Hopkins University, where he is also Professor of Philosophy. He is, furthermore, the Director of the School for Criticism and Theory at Cornell University (through 2018). He has held multiple visiting faculty positions or research stays in Europe and the United States, including the University of Amsterdam, where he was a co-founder of the Amsterdam School for Cultural Analysis, the Collège de Philosophie in Paris, Hebrew University, Princeton, Chicago, Harvard, Brown, and elsewhere.

His principal publications include: *Philosophy and the Turn to Religion* (Johns Hopkins, 1999, 2000), *Religion and Violence: Philosophical Perspectives from Kant to Derrida* (Johns Hopkins, 2002, 2006), and *Minimal Theologies: Critiques of Secular Reason in Theodor W. Adorno and Emmanuel Levinas* (Johns Hopkins, 2005). He is the co-editor, with Samuel Weber, of *Violence, Identity, and Self-Determination* (Stanford, 1997) and of *Religion and Media* (Stanford, 2002). He is also the co-editor, with Lawrence E. Sullivan, of *Political Theologies: Public Religions in a Post-Secular World* (Fordham, 2006), the editor of *Religion: Beyond a Concept* (Fordham, 2007), and the co-editor, with Willemien Otten and Arjo Vanderjagt, of *How the West Was Won: Essays on Literary Imagination, the Canon and the Christian Middle Ages* (Brill, 2010). He is also the co-editor, with Ward Blanton, of *Paul and the Philosophers* (Fordham, 2013) and, with Nils F. Schott, of *Love and Forgiveness for a More Just World* (Columbia, 2015).

Currently de Vries is completing several book-length studies, including a trilogy on the subject and politics of global religion in the age of new media. He is the editor of the book series, Cultural Memory in the Present, published by Stanford University Press.

PETER E. GORDON is the Amabel B. James Professor of History and Harvard College Professor at Harvard University, where he is also a Faculty Affiliate of the Department of Germanic Languages and Literature and the Department of Philosophy. His scholarship focuses on modern European intellectual history from the late nineteenth to the late twentieth century. His primary area of expertise is Continental Philosophy and modern German and French thought. He has written extensively on Martin Heidegger, phenomenology, and, most recently, secularization and social thought in the twentieth century.

Gordon's highly regarded first book, *Rosenzweig and Heidegger: Between Judaism and German Philosophy* (2003), was awarded the Morris D. Forkosch Prize, the Salo W. Baron Prize, the Goldstein Goren Prize, and the Koret Foundation Publication Prize. His most recent book on the 1929 debate between Martin Heidegger and Ernst Cassirer, entitled *Continental Divide: Heidegger, Cassirer, Davos* (Harvard, 2010), was awarded the Jacques Barzun Prize from the American Philosophical Society in 2010. Gordon is the co-editor of several books, including *Weimar Thought: A Contested Legacy* (Princeton, 2013); *The Modernist Imagination: Intellectual History and Critical Theory* (Berghahn Books, 2008); *The Cambridge Companion to Modern Jewish Philosophy* (Cambridge, 2007); and *The Trace of God: Derrida and Religion* (Fordham, 2014). Additionally, Gordon serves on the editorial boards for *Modern Intellectual History, The Journal of the History of Ideas, Jewish Social Studies*, and *New German Critique*, and he has written reviews for *The New Republic* and *The New York Review of Books*.

Peter Gordon received his B.A. from Reed College in 1988, and his Ph.D. from the University of California, Berkeley in 1997. A recipient of both an honorary Harvard College Professorship and Harvard's Phi Beta Kappa Prize for Excellence in Teaching, Gordon has been on the faculty of the History Department at Harvard University since 2000, and was appointed Amabel B. James Professor of History in 2011. He is the co-founder and co-chair of the *Harvard Colloquium for Intellectual History*. He is currently working on a new book on secularization and social thought in the twentieth century. His newest book, forthcoming, will be entitled *Adorno and Existence: Five Lectures*.

BONNIE HONIG is Nancy Duke Lewis Professor in the Departments of Modern Culture and Media (MCM) and Political Science at Brown University. She is also Affiliated Research Professor at the American Bar Foundation in Chicago. She works at the intersections of political theory, law, cultural studies, feminist theory, and literary theory.

She is the author of several prizewinning books and articles, including *Emergency Politics: Paradox, Law, Democracy* (Princeton, 2009; co-winner of the David Easton prize) and *Political Theory and the Displacement of Politics* (1993; winner of the 1994 Scripps Prize for best first book in political theory). Her most recent book is *Antigone, Interrupted* (Cambridge, 2013), which explores the politics of gender, law, grief, and the human through a reading of Sophocles's tragedy and its many prior interpreters. She is currently working on a new book based on her lectures in the *Thinking Out Loud Series* in Sydney, Australia, in 2013.

Bonnie Honig received her B.A. in political science from Concordia University, Quebec, in 1980. She received her M.S.C. with Distinction from the London School of Economics in 1981, her M.A. in political theory from the Johns Hopkins University in 1986, and her Ph.D., also from Johns Hopkins, in 1989. Until 2013 she was Sarah Rebecca Roland Professor of Political Science at Northwestern University and senior research professor at the American Bar Foundation in Chicago. Prior to joining the faculty at Northwestern in 1997, Honig was Assistant and Associate Professor at Harvard University. Honig has received fellowships from the National Endowment for the Humanities, the Center for the Advanced Study in the Behavioral Sciences, and, most recently, the American Philosophical Society.

KEVIS GOODMAN is Associate Professor of English at the University of California, Berkeley, where she writes about and teaches British literature from Milton through the Romantic period. She is the author of *Georgic Modernity and British Romanticism: Poetry and the Mediation of History* (Cambridge, 2004, 2008). Her articles on topics in literary history and literary criticism have appeared in several book collections, as well as in such journals as *English Literary History, Studies in Romanticism, European Romantic Review, South Atlantic Quarterly, The Wordsworth Circle,* and others. The book she is currently completing, entitled *Pathologies of Motion*, studies Enlightenment medicine and Romantic aesthetic theory and practice, primarily in Britain, as forms of knowledge that found overlapping ways to register and represent the historical present unfolding in the body.

Goodman is the recipient of an American Council of Learned Societies Fellowship for *Pathologies of Motion*. At Berkeley, she has won the campus's Distinguished Teaching Award and Faculty Award for Outstanding Mentorship of Graduate Student Instructors.

The Weight of All Flesh

Introduction

KEVIS GOODMAN

Oh! What's the matter? What's the matter?
—William Wordsworth, "Goody Blake and Harry Gill" (*Lyrical Ballads*)

Over the course of three days in April 2014, Eric L. Santner delivered the Tanner Lectures on Human Values at the University of California, Berkeley. Those attending on the first day heard Lecture 1, "On the Subject-Matter of Political Economy," and the first of three response papers, this one by Bonnie Honig. The next day, Lecture 2, entitled "Paradoxologies," was followed by response papers from Peter Gordon and Hent de Vries. The third day consisted of a seminar and discussion, with follow-up comments from Professors Santner, Honig, Gordon, and de Vries, as well as questions from the audience. During the months that followed, the debates of those three days were extended by the circulation of documents: first, Santner added a preface and extended his two lectures into their current form in this volume (Preface, Lecture 1, Lecture 2); these texts next went to Honig, Gordon, and de Vries, who read them before expanding their commentaries. These three pieces in turn went back to Santner, who wrote the Reply to the Commentators. Although titled "In Response," it amounts to a third essay, for, in a pattern that has marked his career, Santner's retrospective gaze propels him forward. The result is a sequence of mutually referring chapters and, as I think readers of this book will discover, a remarkable and often passionate exchange of views.[1]

The Weight of All Flesh: On the Subject-Matter of Political Economy is Eric Santner's latest installment in an ongoing critical project. Positing origins is questionable business, of course, but the project clearly took shape in Santner's third book, *My Own Private Germany: Daniel Paul Schreber's Secret History of Modernity*; it continued through *On the Psychotheology of Everyday Life: Reflections on Freud and Rosenzweig* (2001) and *On Creaturely Life: Rilke, Benjamin, Sebald* (2006); and it crested in *The Royal Remains: The People's Two Bodies and the Endgames of Sovereignty* (2011), where Santner announced the need for a "science of the flesh," whose theorization he continues here. Each of these books picks up one or more threads from the previous books, partly rehearses them, and then advances them in new directions and with renewed impetus, in an intellectual investigation that resembles the technique of exploration that Freud called "Remembering, Repeating, and Working Through"—a process whose larger cultural and historical implications, beyond the treatment situation, have long interested Santner and continue to do so here. Santner takes considerable pains in this volume to orient us in this sequence, and one does not have to know the earlier books to be engaged by this one. Nonetheless, some background does help, and so I want to provide a glimpse of the prehistory, within what I am tempted to call the Santner Cycle (along the lines of such literary cycles as the Oedipus, Arthurian, and Ring Cycles), to this scholar's fascination with the element that he calls "the flesh." For when he describes it, as he will several times in the course of this book, as a "spectral" substance that "forms *at* and *as* the unstable jointure of the somatic and the normative dimensions of human life" (238, emphasis added)—as the stuff that constitutes the "gap" between our biological being and "the historical forms of life" (84) in which human communities unfold—these formulations and their implications have been gestating for some time.

Santner's acute awareness of the instability of this jointure developed in his work on the peculiarly representative case of

Daniel Paul Schreber, whose *Memoirs*, together with Freud's famous study, formed the center of *My Own Private Germany* and parts of *On the Psychotheology of Everyday Life*. Schreber's mental breakdown occurred at the moment when he was nominated by the Ministry of Justice to the Supreme Court of Saxony as its *Senatspräsident* (presiding judge). He experienced this call not as an elevation or authorization but as physical decomposition: in his delusions, his body was converted into a *Luder*, a word whose meanings range from "wretch" to "carrion," the rotting flesh of an animal.² Santner argued that Schreber's was a crisis of "symbolic investiture," the performative act that endows an individual with a new social status within a shared space of representation—one that, when matters progress smoothly, he can, in turn, invest his energies in or "cathect" (Freud's term is *Besetzung*, "to occupy"). However, as Santner argued, Schreber did not "metabolize his investiture": the title did not fit (he did not feel addressed by it), and as a result the citation returned in the form of an invasive excitation, a disturbing mental and corporeal intensification.³ A word (*Senatspräsident*), we might say, made Schreber flesh—but a flesh, as we will see, of a very specific and peculiar kind.

Santner, who has always been sensitive to the ways in which culture-wide crises can be registered in the most intimate core of our being ("fantasy," he once remarked, "can be grasped as what is least 'proper' to oneself"⁴), followed Schreber's own intuition that his condition had something to do with larger historical transformations, arguing that Schreber's symptoms were symptomatic in the larger sense, at once reflecting and disclosing the general attenuation of social bonds and traditional sources of authority afflicting *fin de siècle* Europe. Schreber's illness, in other words, led him into the heart of the "secret history of modernity." Modernity's secret (or one of them), as Santner has argued by drawing on Walter Benjamin's "Critique of Violence" in earlier work, and in this volume on Slavoj Žižek, is the ultimate arbitrariness of the rule of law insofar as it is founded and thereafter sustained by a dimension of force and violence. Consequently, as Santner put it in *On the Psychotheology of Everyday Life*, "every call to order addressed to a human subject—and a symbolic investiture is such a call—secretes a 'surplus value' of psychic excitation that, as it were, bears the burden, holds the place, of the missing foundation of the institutional authority that issued the call." The "fundamental restlessness or unsettledness of the human mind," or what Santner likes to call its "too-muchness," thus pertains "to the constitutive uncertainties that plague identity in a universe of symbolic values"—values that cannot absolve themselves from their groundlessness. As a result, "these values are filled with a surplus charge that can never be fully diffused or discharged" (*Psychotheology*, 50–51). With the retreat of transcendent supports for the juridical order, moreover, this paradoxically dearth-generated surplus becomes all the more insistent. No longer referred to a life or power beyond this one, it exerts its force in the fabric of everyday life, creating there a pressure that Santner has in recent writing, including this volume, called a "surplus of immanence." The outward manifestation of this surplus immanent charge in both psychic experience and representations of the outer world is a troubling and perverse animation, whose quasi-mechanical insistence makes it more like "undeadness" than anything resembling true life. In *On Creaturely Life*, Santner adopts Walter Benjamin's term "petrified unrest" for this ghastly animation, and—in a turn that briefly but precisely anticipated this volume's significant engagement with Marx and political economy—located it, among other sites, in the phenomenon of the commodity and our life among commodities.[5]

Beginning with *On the Psychotheology of Everyday Life* and *On Creaturely Life*, Santner characterized and explored this disturbance, this "too-muchness," as "biopolitical animation"—biopolitical because it begins "not with biological life but rather where biological life is amplified and perturbed by the symbolic dimension of relationality at the very heart of which lie problems of authority and authorization."[6] The life exposed to the lack of foundation for the historical forms of authority, to the paradoxical lawlessness at the origin of the law, Santner came by 2006 to call "creaturely," where creaturely existence is, for him, emphatically *not* something we share with all living things both great and small, but a "specifically human way of finding oneself caught in the midst of antagonisms in and of the political field" (*On Creaturely Life,* xix). The vulnerability that *creaturely* "flesh is heir to" consists less of the "thousand natural shocks" of Hamlet's famous soliloquy than the unnatural ones that come with radical subjection to a sovereign authority. For Santner as for others, one salient instance of this exceptional authority in the historical record is the political theology of sovereignty of the sixteenth and early seventeenth centuries, a topic that, having hovered at the peripheries and interstices of his work,[7] came to the fore in *The Royal Remains,* this volume's immediate precursor.

Santner's fascination with the political theology of sovereignty and with the famous study of its medieval origins, Ernst Kantorowicz's *The King's Two Bodies,* seems inevitable in retrospect, given Santner's earlier and ongoing interest in Schreber's crisis of symbolic investiture. For the legal doctrine whose history *The King's Two Bodies* traced—"the fiction of a royal super-body conjoined in some mysterious way to the king's natural and individual body," as Kantorowicz explained it—was formulated by sixteenth-century jurists precisely to ward off the arrival of an investiture crisis with the death of every monarch. [8] This doctrine protected the integrity and persistence of the state by conceiving the migration of the more-than-human part of kingship, this virtual super-body, from one mortal incarnation to another. Its roots were christological: "We need only replace the strange image of the [King's] Two Bodies by the more customary theological term of the Two Natures" of Christ, Kantorowicz argued, "to make it poignantly felt that the speech of the Elizabethan lawyers derived its tenor in the last analysis from theological diction, and that their speech itself, to say the least, was crypto-theological" (16).

Taking his cue not only from Kantorowicz but also from Michel Foucault and Hannah Arendt, Santner's *The Royal Remains* explored the question of what happened to this crypto-theological logic after the end of sovereignty, following the English and French revolutions, as the power and office of the ruling monarch was shaken (England) or dissolved (France), and disseminated into social space over the course of an increasingly secularized modernity. What happens to that "super-body" (Kantorowicz) or "virtual reality" (Santner)—whose crucial function is not only to secure the principle of sovereignty but also (and just as importantly) to bind subjects to each other and to help them feel both invested and represented in a larger polity—when it floats free of the person of the king? "The flesh of the social bond," Santner argued, "found its new locus of representational corporeality in the national community," the nation-centered polity.[9] The result was a new doubling, or "gemination" (Kantorowicz's word for the two natures of Christ and for the Christ-impersonating king), resulting in the People's Two Bodies. One body, corresponding to that fiction of the royal super-body, is a no less fantasmatic ideal than its precursor in the divinely ordained royal flesh; this is the idea of the nation's capital-P People, who are given or assumed to bear a putatively somatic dignity—something that, ominously and disastrously, has been given the name "race." The other body, corresponding to the abject subject ruled by an absolute sovereign, or the equally abject figure of the deposed Richard II in Kantorowicz's remarkable reading of Shakespeare's play, is the creature, as Santner's earlier work had explored it.[10] This is, in other words, an extension of the condition of the *Luder* Schreber, at the moment that his somatic being was unable to bear the title and normative role conferred upon him. One of Santner's crucial claims in *The Royal Remains*, therefore, was that biopolitics, the management of life as an administrative function of the state, "assumes its particular urgency and expansiveness in modernity precisely because what is at issue in it is not simply the biological health of populations" but, rather, that first fantasy: "the 'sublime' life-substance of the People, who, at least in principle, become the bearers of sovereignty, assume the dignity of the *prince*"—that is, his symbolically charged, super-body flesh (xi–xii, emphasis in original). If the true entity to be managed is the virtually real stuff of a supersensible super-body, then programs of health and hygiene are not likely to be of much use.

We are now in the position to ask of "the flesh," as Santner explicates it, the double questions posed by the only *apparently* tautological, only apparently doggerel, first line of Wordsworth's poem in the epigraph above: "What's the matter? what's the matter?"[11] These are, in fact, two questions. First, what is its *material*—what is it made of? And second, what is *wrong* with it such that it recurs, with all the force of a repetition compulsion, in different sites and formations: political theology, biopolitical administration, and (in this volume) political economy? What is the matter with it such that, in all of these distributions and redistributions, it needs to be managed, whether liturgically, juridically, biopolitically, or economically—but in all cases laboriously?

In response to the first question, the first and obvious point is that, in Santner's analyses, the flesh—whether in its sublime or its abject creaturely versions—is not the physical body, not the corporeal matter beneath our skin that we gain and shed over our life span. It is, as Santner has put it on several occasions, "something in the body that is more than a body yet is not simply spirit."[12] In other words, it is a fantasy construct, charged with shared human desires, fears, and values, a virtual reality that has often gathered around bodies, whether individual or corporate, yet remains abstracted from them, like some enigmatic halo—with the crucial qualification that it cannot be seen. As such, it is above all a *social medium*, binding together social and political communities in a way that merely physical matter cannot, and like all mediums, it is most apparent when it fails to function, when it starts registering static. It is at least in part for this reason that, in his first lecture here, Santner takes brief but polemical aim at the movement that, since the mid-1990s, has been called the "new materialism[s]"—scholarship that is post-humanist in its orientation and tends to conceive nonhuman and even inorganic matter as lively and full of agency.[13] Although Santner has always been the first to emphasize the riven condition of the human psyche and its "internal alterity" (no psychoanalytically inclined theorist could do otherwise), the category of the subject, in all of its self-division—and indeed because of it—remains crucial to him.[14] The new materialisms are, in his view, too quick to dispense with it, and they fail to recognize the creaturely dimension that distinguishes human beings from other kinds of life. And it is at least in part as a riposte to this post-humanist materialism that Santner introduces in this book a new keyword, a new fellow-traveler with the flesh that accompanies and further defines it: "subject-matter" (hyphenated to distinguish it from the conventional sense of subject matter, or topic). Subject-matter denotes the inscription of subjects and their social relationships into matter by way of their work upon, and libidinal investment in, the material objects that circulate among them.[15] I will return to this concept briefly later.

Therefore, although it may be tempting to associate Santner's use of the term "flesh" with Maurice Merleau-Ponty's idea of the "flesh of the world"—especially because Santner likes to praise Merleau-Ponty's comment that Freud is our "only philosopher of the flesh"—the connection is, to my mind, potentially misleading.[16] For while Merleau-Ponty, like Santner, insists that "flesh is not matter, in the sense of corpuscles of being which would add up or continue on one another to form beings," Merleau-Ponty's notion of "intercorporeity" fuses human and nonhuman worlds, and it therefore has been cited by new materialist scholars as a source of inspiration.[17] While Kantorowicz remains the proximate influence on Santner's use of "flesh," it is also helpful to reach further back: to Saint Paul's important distinction between the body (*soma*) and the flesh (*sarx*). Where *soma* describes the existence of all creatures, *sarx* denotes fallen temporal existence, historical entanglement in the world and one's relationship to other fallen creatures.[18] For Santner, who touches on Paul in *The Royal Remains* and in this volume, what is crucial about the role of the flesh in Pauline doctrine is its centrifugal threat to the principle of corporate integrity: to organic conceptions of the *corpus mysticum* of the Church and later to the secular entities that modeled themselves after its corporate and organic ideal.

By this point at least a preliminary answer to the second sense of "what's the matter?"—that is, what is wrong with the flesh such that it recurs in different historical instantiations and requires such management?—may be clear. (The full answer, of course, resides in the arguments that are the main acts of this volume.) Whether in its form as the fantasmatic physiology that attends the king's empirical body, or the equally fantasmatic concept of the unity of the polity—or, as we will see in the lectures that follow, the mystical character of the commodity and surplus value generated by labor—the virtual reality that Santner calls the "flesh" is not just an imaginary abstraction: it is an abstraction charged with the impossible task of securing and indemnifying an order founded upon a core groundlessness and an inaugural violence. As such it functions, or can function, as a defense against the contingency of the normative order, its institutions, and the "symbolic investitures" and identities that order offers. Ever since his early work on the fetishistic use of narrative among German historians intent on salvaging an intact national identity in the aftermath of the Final Solution and the defeat of Germany in World War II, Santner has worried about various forms that fetishism, and particularly narratives designed to preserve the fiction of intact identity, can take.[19] This book, with its exploration of what it calls the "fetishistic disavowal of *what does not work* in human life" under capitalism is no exception (101).

And so it is that now, in *The Weight of All Flesh*, Santner moves from the fetishism of persons (King, People) to the fetishism of the commodity, turning from the King's two bodies to focus on a new "gemination": "the dual character of the labor embedded in commodities," as Marx described it in *Capital*. [20] More generally, Santner explores the complex trajectory leading "from the political theology of sovereignty to the political economy of the wealth of nations" (30). [21] The process of abstraction now under consideration is not the production of the fantasmatic flesh of the royal super-body shadowing its empirical double, nor the sublime substance of "the People," but the double abstraction that first turns the specific sensuous object for use into a commodified object for exchange (but still visible) and then, crucially, dissociates value from the material commodity to yield an invisible or virtual network of exchange, one that comprises, as Marx put it, the "social relation between commodity and commodity," in which "all its sensuous characteristics are extinguished" (*Capital*, 139 and 128). We can see how Santner's notion of "subject-matter" may function not only as a response to the new materialisms but also as a way of engaging Marx. For, in Marx, commodity exchange involves a nightmare intensification of precisely the inscription of subjects into matter—so much so that they appear, fantastically, to vanish into the invisible network in which commodities interact with each other. Marx famously represents this scenario with one of his darkly brilliant personifications, in a passage that neither Santner nor Peter Gordon (whose response examines Marx in more detail) quotes directly, but which bears on both of their divergent arguments. As long as a table is considered in terms of its usefulness, Marx argued, it "continues to be wood, an ordinary, sensuous thing. But as soon as it emerges as a commodity, it changes into a thing which transcends sensuousness. It not only stands with its feet on the ground, but, in relation to all other commodities, it stands on its head, and evolves out of its wooden brain grotesque ideas, far more wonderful than if it were to begin dancing of its own free will" (*Capital*, 163–64). Santner has long worried, as I noted above, about the perverse animation or "undeadness" of creaturely life subjected to normative pressures. In Marx, as subjects are occluded by the things they make, and things appear person-ified (made into persons), they acquire precisely that "surplus of immanence," the "spectral materiality" (*die gespenstische Gegenständlichkeit*) that becomes Santner's subject here. They form a new, but no less virtual, flesh. Santner's hyphenated "subject-matter," that is, asks us to recall the subjects and human labor that might otherwise vanish into the weirdly animated, acrobatic commodity.

Of course, the argument by which Santner tracks the movement from political theology to political economy is far more intricate and detailed than this rapid preview. For the genealogy that leads from one to the other—as well as for the different reasons that both Hent de Vries and Peter Gordon question this genealogy—one cannot do better than to read this book. I will not be a spoiler. There you will find much else. Santner will take up Kantorowicz's comment that, in medieval political theology, the Two-Natured King (who is *christomimētēs*, or "Christ-impersonating") is "an effluence of a sacramental and liturgical action performed at the altar" (*King's Two Bodies*, 59). Noting the etymology of liturgy (from *laos*, "people," and *ergon*, "work"), he will probe the question of what kind of neoliturgical or quasi-liturgical action produces value, the new flesh of the twenty-first century world of neoliberal capitalism. What, moreover, is the quality of creaturely life now exposed not only to the force of the law but also to the exigencies of an economic machine that has us all plugged into our computers, "vibrating" around the clock? Lastly, Santner will pose the question of what forms intervention into, and resistance to, this vast web of busy-ness might take. What could be a counter to doxology—or, in his terms, a para-doxology? (The prefix, *para*, "to one side," also denotes a movement that runs amiss of or aslant its object, drawing near it in order to alter it, as in the act of parody.[22]) This is a difficult challenge, but one that Bonnie Honig will take up as she explores a third way of negotiating the gap between the somatic and the normative, one that is neither (just) political theology nor (just) political economy, but entails democratic and, crucially, nonpathological ways of mobilizing the flesh.

Before concluding, however, I want to say something about Santner's method, for it is important to understand what it is and especially what it is not, and does not try to be. Although he is interested in the specificity of (a long) modernity, Eric Santner is not primarily a historian. There is no thick contextualization, and his genealogy of the flesh does not aim to be exhaustive. He does not here, for example, take up Adam Smith in any detail, nor does he touch on other eighteenth- and early nineteenth-century political economists who were crucial influences on Marx. It seems more precise to say that he is interested in *historical "constellation,"* to use Benjamin's key term, rather than *historical chronology.*[23] However, he is everywhere concerned with the *experience of historicity,* by which I mean the condition of bodies caught up or defined by a history that lies beyond their immediate experience but everywhere affects and seeps into their everyday life. The experience of historicity is, after all, one way of describing "the jointure between the somatic and normative." To be creaturely, Santner writes in this volume, "is to exist in forms of life that are, in turn, contingent, contested, susceptible to breakdown—in a word, *historical*" (84). This is an existence that, as Derrida writes about haunting in *Specters of Marx,* "is historical, to be sure, but it is not *dated.*"[24]

One question that has frequently been raised about Santner's previous work, and that recurred several times in the questions asked of this project during the seminar following the lectures, has to do with the role of association and analogy in his work. One member of the audience resisted the "tapestry of texts" provided by the lectures, wondering if one can associate and build analogies between thinkers, often of different eras, whose systems diverge in significant ways—for example, analogies between Freud and Foucault, or Freud and Marx, or Kantorowicz and Agamben (and so forth). This is one of Peter Gordon's concerns as well, when he here describes the alliance between political theological analysis and Marxian critique as "perturbed." Santner has not himself been perturbed by what he once called "my tendency to reconcile conflicts and tension among my 'team' of co-thinkers and interlocutors," and indeed he has embraced it.[25] In *The Royal Remains* he identified his own method with the literary work of Rainer Maria Rilke and, in particular, with Walter Benjamin's notion of constellation:

> For Benjamin, too, the task of reading, of the critical engagement with history and with cultural texts of any kind, involves the seizing of a moment in which a constellation of what he refers to as "nonsensuous similarities" comes into focus.... For Benjamin it is language itself that provides what he refers to as "the most perfect archive of nonsensuous similarity." Benjamin goes on to characterize language as "the highest application of the mimetic faculty—a medium into which the earlier perceptual capacity for recognizing the similar had, without residue, entered to such an extent that language now represents the medium in which objects encounter and come into relation with each other."[26]

This belief in language as a medium for hearing and drawing out family resemblances that are consequential or whose consequences need exploration—and may, in fact, point to a real historical connection yet to be articulated—is, among other things, one feature of *literary* thinking. Santner is committed to the possibility that literary analysis may yield a truth not available by other means, even when this analysis means yoking together heterogeneous ideas (as Samuel Johnson famously said of John Donne). To my mind, his method is literary in this sense, and not only because he turns to literary texts (Shakespeare, Kafka, Rilke, and many more) as materials for his argument, although he often does, and does well.

Of course, association is also the method of psychoanalysis—Freud frequently called free and uncensored association "the fundamental rule of analysis."[27] Therefore, when at the end of the seminar of the third day Santner answered one version of the question about associational method by saying that he was "allowing these various theorists to free-associate together," and joking (but only partly) that if they cannot talk to each other, "perhaps they can fantasize together," it was hard not to think of psychoanalytic technique as well as literary analogy.[28] Santner is obviously a psychoanalytic thinker, but he is one in very particular ways and not, perhaps, as that designation is usually understood (and usually with disapproval). As Julia Lupton and C. J. Gordon have noted, Santner is not interested in " 'scaling up' individual psychology as a matter of mass formations." Rather, he conjoins psychoanalysis with social theory and religious thought "by locating the social nucleus of psychoanalytic thinking and linking these insights to sea changes in the theological and juridical structures of the *ancien régime* as they pass into the life forms of liberalism, capitalism, secularism, and totalitarianism."[29] "Libido theory," Santner wrote in *The Royal Remains*, "is a special kind of *social theory*"; it can "show how individuals get initiated, drawn into, 'seduced' by, the ways in which historical forms of life have—always precariously and provisionally—come to terms with fundamental impasses plaguing human flourishing more generally" (*Royal Remains*, 73).

There is another interesting effect of psychoanalysis on and in Santner's thought, one that is evident in this volume and was raised by the cluster of questions during the Tanner seminar that, in one way or another, amounted to: So what do we do? How do we resist or respond to the twenty-first-century doxology of everyday life, which has us worshiping and vibrating all day and night at the temple of value? This effect, which also lies at the core of Santner's response to Gordon here, appears in Santner's skepticism about the *sufficiency* of critique that limits itself to cognition and conceptual analysis (that such analysis is necessary he does not dispute). As a cultural critic, he has taken to heart Freud's experience that interpreting the causes or meaning of a patient's symptoms and informing him or her of them did very little to stop the symptoms themselves and indeed often strengthened the patient's resistance to understanding the roots of the illness. Freud concluded that "one must allow the patient time to become conversant with this resistance with which he has now become acquainted, to *work through* it, to overcome it, by continuing, in defiance of it, the analytic work according to the fundamental rule of analysis"—that is, free association.[30] But what exactly "working through" our resistances to change might involve in the rather different situation of confronting and critiquing the manic 24/7 busy-ness of late capitalism is hard to describe, and Santner has so far seemed hesitant in detailing it. This tentativeness is certainly not because he doesn't seek an answer (quite the contrary, as should be apparent in this volume). It results from his sense of the limits of ideology critique and conceptual analysis when what one is dealing with are not (or not only) *ideas* or concepts but, rather, what Bonnie Honig describes, in her concluding sentence, as the "unconscious and enigmatic registers of human existence" (162) that Santner has made it *his* business to track. And perhaps it is also fair to say that he is still working through the question. No doubt he will continue to do so with his signature creative constellations—that is, precisely "according to the fundamental rule of analysis." There will undoubtedly be a fuller answer, for which we will have to stay tuned, if not vibrating, for the next stage of the Santner cycle.

Notes

1. Because of their structure and sequential emergence, Berkeley-Tanner volumes can be tricky to produce, and so I am all the more grateful to the four scholars who have given us this one: to Eric Santer especially, whose brilliance had to be matched by considerable patience as four others serially worked with his texts and his ideas over a protracted period of time. It has been an honor to work with him. I owe great thanks, too, to Bonnie Honig, Peter Gordon, and Hent de Vries for their graciousness and support—in particular, Bonnie Honig's wise and rapid-fire responses showed me how "24/7" can bear an

entirely generous and happy aspect. Two others must be named as well: Jordan Greenwald and C. F. S. Creasy, who helped prepare the manuscript and its index for the press with skill, intelligence, and good spirits.

2. Eric Santner, *My Own Private Germany: Daniel Paul Schreber's Secret History of Modernity* (Princeton, NJ: Princeton University Press, 1996), 41.

3. Eric Santner, *The Psychotheology of Everyday Life: Reflections on Freud and Rosenzweig* (Chicago: University of Chicago Press), 49.

4. Eric Santner, "Response," *JCRT (Journal of Cultural and Religious Theory)* 12, no. 1 (2012): 44–52 (quotation from 44), accessed December 22, 2014, http://www.jcrt.org/archives/12.1/.

5. See Eric Santner, *On Creaturely Life* (Chicago: University of Chicago Press, 2006), 76–83 for this discussion.

6. Santner, *Psychotheology*, 30. Here and elsewhere, Santner is of course drawing on Giorgio Agamben, especially *Homo Sacer: Sovereign Power and Bare Life*, trans. David Heller-Roazen (Stanford, CA: Stanford University Press, 1998).

7. See Santner, *Psychotheology*, 19, where Santner compared the "undeadening" and "disturbing surplus animation" that troubled Franz Rosenzweig to the king's " 'second body' posited by theorists of sovereignty," and Santner, *On Creaturely Life*, 29 (drawing on the work of Julia Lupton) and 81–82 (discussing Walter Benjamin).

8. Ernst Kantorowicz, *The King's Two Bodies: A Study in Mediaeval Political Theology* (Princeton, NJ: Princeton University Press, 1997), 46. Kantorowicz's study was first published in 1957.

9. Eric Santner, *The Royal Remains: The People's Two Bodies and the Endgames of Sovereignty* (Chicago: University of Chicago Press, 2012), 50–51.

10. For Kantorowicz's reading of Richard II's devolution from divine kingship to naked "flesh ... exposed to contempt and derision," and his larger argument that *Richard II* is "the tragedy of the King's Two Bodies," see chap. 2 of *The King's Two Bodies* (24–41, quotation from 37). For Santner's discussion of Kantorowicz's treatment of Shakespeare's play, see *The Royal Remains*, 44–50.

11. My choice of Wordsworth has to do not only with this first line from one of his *Lyrical Ballads* ("Goody Blake and Harry Gill") but also more generally—and significantly—because his poetry is so deeply attuned to what his major autobiographical poem, *The Prelude*, called "the ghostliness of things" (*1850 Prelude*, 6.428, quoted from *The Prelude, 1799, 1805, 1850*, ed. Jonathan Wordsworth, M. H. Abrams, and Stephen Gill [New York: W. W. Norton, 1979]). David Simpson has forcefully argued that Wordsworth's oeuvre at large grasps profoundly the logic of the commodity form and

represents its spectrality. See Simpson, *Wordsworth, Commodification, and Social Concern* (Cambridge: Cambridge University Press, 2009). Although in very different texts and rather different terms, this is a logic and topic that Santner explores in these lectures, especially the second.

12. See, for example, *The Royal Remains*, 28.

13. In Santner's argument, the new materialism is represented by Jane Bennett's *Vibrant Matter: A Political Ecology of Things* (Durham, NC: Duke University Press, 2009). For a wider sample of the movement's various practitioners and positions, see Diana Coole and Samantha Frost, eds., *New Materialisms: Ontology, Agency, and Politics* (Durham, NC: Duke University Press, 2010).

14. "Internal alterity" is Santner's phrase in *Psychotheology*, 9.

15. See Santner's "Preface," (29). Since "subject-matter" and "flesh" are both part of the same, larger complex concept, they sometimes appear in apposition to each other in the lectures. Their precise relationship, to my mind, emerges most clearly in Santner's discussion of Jacques-Louis David's *The Death of Marat*, an analysis that he initiated in *The Royal Remains* and continues in these lectures; here the flesh is a *"medium in which* our precious subject-matter circulates and in which our fundamental social bonds are sealed" (30), my emphasis.

16. See, for example, *The Royal Remains*, 5, 29, 31.

17. Quotations are from Maurice Merleau-Ponty, *The Visible and the Invisible*, ed. Claude Lefort, trans. Alphonso Lingis (Evanston, IL: Northwestern University Press, 1968), 139, 141. For a new materialist appropriation of Merleau-Ponty on the flesh, see, for example, Diana Coole's "The Inertia of Matter and the Generativity of Flesh" in Coole and Frost, *New Materialisms*, 92–116. It is worth noting that when Santner first invoked the flesh in *The Royal Remains*, his Merleau-Ponty was mediated by Claude Lefort's use of the term in an essay, "The Permanence of the Theologico-Political?" Like Santner, Lefort maintains the entanglement of religious and political spheres. Discussing the "primal dimensionality of the social," Lefort argues that social division—like the division between the realms of the economic and the political, or the juridical and the religious— "can only be defined ... insofar as it represents a division within a single milieu, within one flesh." See *Democracy and Political Theory*, trans. David Macey (Minneapolis: University of Minnesota Press, 1988), 218.

18. On the distinction between *sarx* and *soma*, see James D. G. Dunn, *The Theology of Paul the Apostle* (Grand Rapids, MI: Wm. B. Eerdmans, 2006), 70–73. My thanks go to David Marno for this reference and for sharing his own fine discussion of these terms in his manuscript, "Holy Attention."

19. Here I have in mind in particular Santner's brilliant article, "History Beyond the Pleasure Principle: Some Thoughts on the Representation of Trauma," in *Probing the Limits of Representation: Nazism and the "Final Solution,"* ed. Saul Friedlander (Cambridge, MA: Harvard University Press, 1992), 143–54.

20. Karl Marx, *Capital, Volume One,* trans. Ben Fowkes (New York: Vintage Books, 1977), 131.

21. In *On Creaturely Life, Santner* anticipated the complementary relationship between *The Royal Remains* and *The Weight of All Flesh,* when he suggested that as "the divine charisma that had [once] stuck to the sovereign became disseminated throughout social space as an 'exciting' phantasmagorical presence," biopolitics and modern industrial capitalism and commodity production "emerge together in or, rather, as the field of this dissemination" (*On Creaturely Life,* 81–82).

22. Santner interestingly here returns to a paradox he grappled with in *On the Psychotheology of Everyday Life,* where he noted the ironic proximity between the uncanny animation or "undeadness" that Franz Rosenzweig identified during his own crisis of investiture (as an academic, a route he did not pursue) and the vitality that, for Rosenzweig, might respond to it: "There is ... often a thin line between the passions infusing our engagement in the world and our defenses against that engagement, between what is genuinely enlivening in the world and what is 'undeadening' in it" (*Psychotheology,* 19). His next sentence then compared the latter to the king's fantasmatic body. See note 7 of this introduction.

23. The dialectical image, as Benjamin describes it in N2a, 3 of *The Arcades Project,* is "that wherein what has been comes together in a flash with the now to form a constellation." This relation between "what-has-been to the now is dialectical: it is not progression," but "suddenly emergent." See Walter Benjamin, *The Arcades Project,* trans. Howard Eiland and Kevin McLaughlin, ed. Rolf Tiedemann (Cambridge, MA: Belknap Press, 1999), 462.

24. Jacques Derrida, *Specters of Marx: The State of the Debt, The Work of Mourning, and The New International* (New York: Routledge, 1994), 3 (emphasis in the original).

25. Santner, "Response," 49.

26. *Royal Remains,* xix–xx. Santner is discussing two of Benjamin's short pieces: "On the Mimetic Faculty" and "Doctrine of the Similar."

27. See, for example, the comments in Sigmund Freud, *The Standard Edition of the Complete Psychological Works of Sigmund Freud,* 24 vols., ed. and trans. James Strachey (London: Hogarth Press, 1953–74), 12:107, 12:112, 18:39, and elsewhere.

28. A recording of the seminar is available online at "The Tanner Lectures on Human Values at UC Berkeley," last accessed on January 3, 2015, http://tannerlectures.berkeley.edu/2013-2014/.

29. Julia Lupton and C. J. Gordon, introduction to *JCRT* 12, no. 1 (2012): 1.

30. Freud, "Remembering, Repeating, and Working Through," *Standard Edition*, 12:155 (emphasis in original).

The Weight of All Flesh: On the Subject-Matter of Political Economy

ERIC L. SANTNER

Preface

I

In my last book, I argued that the subject matter that Ernst Kantorowicz elaborated in his famous study of medieval and early-modern political theology, *The King's Two Bodies*, never disappeared from the life of the citizen-subjects of modern, constitutional states.[1] My claim was, rather, that the "stuff" of the king's glorious body—the virtually real supplement to his empirical, mortal body—was in some sense dispersed into new locations as a spectral materiality—I called it a *surplus of immanence*—that summoned on the scene new forms and practices of knowledge, power, and administration charged—or rather, *surcharged*—with coming to terms with and, indeed, cultivating these "royal remains" injected into the life of the People. To use Freud's locution for the pressure of the drives, these remains now insisted as an uncanny *Arbeitsanforderung*, or demand for work. This was, in other words, work in excess of any apparent teleological order, work that kept one busy beyond reason. Among these new forms I counted first and foremost the new modalities of statecraft analyzed by Michel Foucault under the heading of the disciplines and biopower. My claim, however, was that what these new forms of knowledge and control were at least in part "on to," the subject matter they were tracking without fully being able to conceptualize it, came into view in Freud's theory and practice as, precisely, *subject-matter:* a peculiar and often unnerving materiality, a seemingly formless or *informe* remainder of processes of subject-formation. I argued that psychoanalysis could itself be understood as the science of "royal remains" insisting—beyond reason—as a quasi-discursive and quasi-somatic pressure in the souls of modern citizen-subjects. The usual genealogy of Freud's new science—its neurological lineage—was thus to be supplemented by one addressing its emergence out of a displacement and redistribution of "emergency powers" previously concentrated in, *enjoyed* and *embodied* by, the sovereign person—in a word, by a political theological lineage. My further claim was that a variety of modernist aesthetic projects had found their own ways to elaborate and give provisional form to the *informe* surplus of immanence pushing against the skin of "modern man," to the inflammatory pressure emerging at a newly configured jointure of the somatic and the normative, a new symbolic knotting or suturing of *physis* and *nomos*, of man's being as animal and his being as locus of initiative in the space of reasons, commitments, responsibilities. In the following I would like to continue these investigations by extending them into a realm I had heretofore neglected—that of political economy. In a certain sense I will be repeating my previous argument, but now with a view to its relation and relevance to Marx's conception of the critique of political economy. This, then, is very much a *partial* repetition: one concerned with the "partial object" of political economy with respect to which no one ever remains fully impartial.

II

A crucial point of reference in *The Royal Remains* was provided by Jacques-Louis David's famous painting *The Death of Marat*, which I took to be an emblem of the troubled transition from the representational regime of the King's Two Bodies to that of the People's Two Bodies. My reading took its lead from T. J. Clark, who rather boldly proposed that one view the painting as the inaugural work of European visual modernism. For Clark, *Marat* enjoys this status insofar as its particular—and particularly intense—engagement with politics "tells us something about its [modernism's] coming to terms with the world's disenchantment in general."[2] The public service—we might say, liturgical labor—performed by earlier painters such as Velázquez was, according to Clark, "to transmute the political, to clean it of the dross of contingency, to raise it up to the realm of allegory"; David succeeds—and so becomes modern—precisely by failing to do any such thing, by articulating its impossibility, by allowing his painting to turn—and in some sense to keep turning—"on the impossibility of transcendence" (22). And all of that in the context of a new liturgy meant to consolidate the consistency of the People as uncontested bearer of the principle of sovereignty.[3] We might say that what David's painting puts on display is precisely the insistent *remainder* of such efforts at sublimation/allegorization, that it offers them as the new subject matter—and I would add, quasi-carnal *subject-matter*—of painting.

The simultaneously political and painterly form of the impossibility of transcendence or, as we might put it, the political and painterly form of a new surplus of immanence, appears as an abstract materiality that would seem to issue from Marat's mutilated body and fill the upper half of the painting. As Clark puts it, David's treatment of the body "seems to make Marat much the same substance—*the same abstract material*—as the empty space above him. The wound is as abstract as the flesh" (36; my emphasis). The flesh that can no longer be figured as the virtually real, glorious body of the king becomes the *abstract material* out of which the painting is largely made. The empty upper half of the painting stands in for a missing and, indeed, impossible representation of the People: "It embodies the concept's absence, so to speak. It happens upon representation as technique. It sets its seal on Marat's unsuitability for the work of incarnation" (47). The scumbled surface forming the upper half of the painting thus no longer functions as a simple absence but, rather, as a positive, even oppressive presence, "something abstract and unmotivated, which occupies a different conceptual space from the bodies below it. This produces,"

Clark continues, "a kind of representational deadlock, which is the true source of the *Marat's* continuing hold on us" (48). This is the "endless, meaningless objectivity produced by paint not quite finding its object, symbolic or otherwise, and therefore making do with its own procedures" (48). This is what Clark means when he speaks of painting "turning" on the impossibility of transcendence. That characterization brings to mind—well, to my mind—a short text by Kafka:

> Es wurde ihnen die Wahl gestellt Könige oder der Könige Kuriere zu werden. Nach der Art der Kinder wollten alle Kuriere sein. Deshalb gibt es lauter Kuriere, sie jagen durch die Welt und rufen, da es keine Könige gibt, einander selbst die sinnlos gewordenen Meldungen zu. Gerne würden sie ihrem elenden Leben ein Ende machen, aber sie wagen es nicht wegen des Diensteides.
>
> (They were given the choice to become kings or messengers. Just like children they all chose to be messengers. For this reason there are only messengers; they race through the world and, because there are no kings, they call out to one another proclamations that have become meaningless. They would happily put an end to their miserable life but because of their oath of office they don't dare.)[4]

We might say that a new form of *business*—of quasi-official busy-ness and busy-body- ness—comes itself to function as the work of incarnation, as the production site of the flesh of the People. For Clark, such agitated racing about is precisely what is *happening* in the upper half of David's painting, a spectral state of affairs—the messengers have outlived their purpose—that constitutes a kind of *shame* that will forever haunt modernism. (At some level Clark seems to be saying that *artists* would like to put an end to their miserable life, but because of their oath of office they don't dare.) We might even say that the abstract material out of which the upper half of the painting is made just is the ectoplasmic substance of this haunting: "In a sense ... I ... am saying that the upper half is a display of technique. But display is too neutral a word: for the point I am making, ultimately, is that technique in modernism is a kind of shame: something that asserts itself as the truth of picturing, but always against picturing's best and most desperate efforts" (48). In David, this shame emerges precisely at the point and in the space where " 'People' ought to appear" (48). What appears at the missing place of the new sovereign body is, rather, a kind of dreamwork made painterly flesh in the pure activity of painting; the empty upper half of the image forms not so much a vacancy as the site of an excess of pressure, a signifying stress that opens onto a vision of painting as *Triebschicksal*, as a vicissitude of the drive recalling the seemingly senseless running about—the uncannily busy bodies—of Kafka's messengers:

> And yet the single most extraordinary feature of the picture ... is its whole upper half being empty. Or rather (here is what is unprecedented), not being empty, exactly, not being a satisfactory representation of nothing or nothing much—of an absence in which whatever the subject is has become present—but something more like a representation of painting, of painting as pure activity. Painting as material, therefore. Aimless. In the end detached from any one representational task. Bodily. Generating (monotonous) orders out of itself, or maybe out of ingrained habit. A kind of automatic writing. (45)

Keeping Kafka's text in mind, we might characterize this writing as *traumamtliches Schreiben*, a neologism that brings together the meanings: dream, trauma, and *Amt*, or office. My argument in the following lectures will be that Marx's labor theory of value concerns precisely this dimension of the *traumamtlich* as the site at which a surplus of immanence—the royal remains left to the People—comes to be elaborated and managed as the real subject-matter of political economy. His theory concerns, that is, the flesh as a social substance *materially abstracted* from the busy body of labor, a substance he will famously refer to as *gespenstische Gegenständlichkeit*, the spectral objectivity/ materiality of Value. As will become clear, what is truly at issue in Marx's labor theory—the nature of this spectral stuff and its modes of production—spans the distinction between industrial and "office" work.

To return to *The Death of Marat*: that this inaugural moment of modernism is one that already pertains to political economy and to the "busy-ness" matters with which it is concerned is signaled in the painting by way of a small, easily overlooked detail. Clark dedicates considerable attention to the bits of paper visible in the painting, the most legible of which is Charlotte Corday's own letter of introduction and appeal to Marat's benevolence. More important for Clark is the barely legible scrap on the orange cart that would appear to be Marat's own last letter. Apropos of the words just out of sight in the letter and presumed to be *"de la patrie,"* Clark asks, "But is there a final phrase at all? Of course there looks to be something; but it is so scrappy and vestigial, an extra few words where there really is no room left for anything, that the reader continually double-takes, as if reluctant to accept that writing, of all things, can decline to this state of utter visual elusiveness. Surely if I look again—and look hard enough—the truth will out. For spatially, this is the picture's starting point. It is closeness incarnate" (40). Clark adds that these bits of painted writing "become the figure of the picture's whole imagining of the world and the new shape it is taking. . . . The boundaries between the discursive and the visual are giving way, under *some pressure the painter cannot quite put his finger on, though he gets close"* (42; my emphasis).

But as Clark has so persuasively argued, it is in the swirling, vertiginous void that fills the picture's upper half that this pressure finds its "proper" place—its *non-resting place*—in the visual field. The spectral materiality of the flesh torn from the body of the king finds its inaugural *modern* figuration in that dense, agitated, painterly writing on the wall. Clark is right, then, to see in the painting the opening on to a new aesthetic dimension and one that has a very precise historical index. What makes modernism modernism is that its basic materials are compelled to engage with and, as it were, model the dimension of the flesh inflamed by the representational deadlock situated at the transition from royal to popular sovereignty. What in historical experience can no longer be elevated—sublimated—by way of codified practices of picture making to the dignity of religious, moral, or political allegory, introduced into a realm of institutionally (and, ultimately, transcendentally) authorized meanings, now achieves its sublimity in a purely immanent fashion. The vicissitudes of this abstract materiality itself become the *subject-matter* of the arts: what art deals with, the formal and thematic subject matter of its aesthetic negotiations; but also where the subject is inscribed, where it is libidinally implicated and *at work* in the image.

Toward the very end of his chapter on the painting, Clark returns to the remaining bit of paper resting on the crate, an assignat for five *livres*. This piece of revolutionary currency first issued in 1790 as an emergency measure in response to the flight of gold and coin from the country would come to be guaranteed, at least in principle, by the value of confiscated properties of the Church and aristocracy. The currency lost most of its value in a matter of years, and by 1797 this experiment in financial engineering was finally declared to be a failure. (As Clark notes, the Terror, by intensifying the force and pace of expropriations, initially led to a temporary increase in the value of the currency.) This was the same year that the English Parliament passed a law releasing the Bank of England from the obligation to convert paper currency into coin upon demand.[5] For Clark, the presence of the assignat in the painting serves as a placeholder for a fundamental uncertainty that must have haunted the revolution as a whole and Jacobins like David in particular, one that concerned the "arbitrariness of the sign"—and so the possible lack of any ultimate reference—under which the revolution was staged: "To believe in oneself as ushering in Nature's kingdom, and to think there was no time to lose if it was to be secured against its enemies; and yet to know in one's heart of hearts that what was being built was just another form of artifice, was wayward and unpredictable as the rest. Another arbitrariness. Another law for the lion and the ox" (50). Clark suggests, in other words, that the question haunting the revolution and at some level symbolized by the fragile value of its currency concerned the ultimate source of legitimacy for the displacement and redistribution of the exceptional power and authority previously concentrated in the sovereign person.

What I will be exploring in the following pages is a more specific question signaled, in my view, by the presence of the assignat in this inaugural painting of modernism, namely that of the role of political economy in this displacement and redistribution. What the assignat indicates, in my reading, is that the *abstract material* that seems to flow from the body of Marat to the upper half of the painting darkly figures—in a nonfigural manner—what would ultimately provide the substance of value circulating through the new bourgeois order: the (surplus) value *materially abstracted* from the body of labor, the very "stuff" that would, in Marx's view, come to form the medium of the social bond in capitalist societies. What David's painting bears witness to is thus not only the passage from royal to popular sovereignty—and the impasses haunting the representation of the People for post-monarchical societies—but also from the political theology of sovereignty to the political economy of the wealth of nations. What is at issue in this peculiar effluence that comes to fill the upper half of David's painting is, I am arguing, a shift in the nature of the medium in which our precious subject-matter circulates and in which our fundamental social bonds are sealed. We will, in other words, be tracking in the domain of political economy what I have characterized as a surplus of immanence released into the social body by the ostensible "excarnation" of sovereignty. Marx, as I've noted, analyzed this surplus under the rather remarkable heading of *gespenstische Gegenständlichkeit*, or spectral materiality. It is, I will argue, only against this background that we can fully grasp the logic behind Jacques Derrida's decision to accompany his study of the spectral in Marx's work by a running commentary on *Hamlet*.

The editors of a volume of essays on the "Republican Body" have put the subject-matter at issue quite succinctly: "With democracy the concept of the nation replaced the monarch and sovereignty was dispersed from the king's body to all bodies. *Suddenly every body bore political weight....* With the old sartorial and behavioral codes gone, bodies were less legible, and a person's place in the nation was unclear."[6] My interest here is in the nature of the *matter* that accounts for the new political weight and value of every citizen and in political economy as a site in which this weight begins to be taken into account precisely by efforts to weigh it, reckon with it, subject it, as it were, to double-entry bookkeeping without ever really grasping the real nature of the "double" involved. My claim is that the fantasmatic substance once borne by the bearer of the royal office becomes a *traumamtlich* dimension of social life elaborated, above all, in economic activities and relations. The King's Two Bodies becomes, as it were, every body's busy-ness.

III

In a recent book-length essay on the unique temporal ubiquity of contemporary global capitalism with the telling title of 24/7, Jonathan Crary has argued that sleep represents the last fragile remnant of the human life-world not yet fully colonized by the mad rhythms of production and consumption, the site where our busy bodies can still, if only for ever briefer intervals and often only with the help of medication, withdraw from their "oath of office."[7] Building on Marx's reflections on the "natural barriers" to capital accumulation, Crary implicitly compares the "triumphal installation of a 24/7 world" (17) with an act of *decreation* whereby the most basic distinctions established by the act of creation—those between night and day and darkness and light—have been revoked. "More concretely," he writes, "it is like a state of emergency, when a bank of floodlights are suddenly switched on in the middle of the night, seemingly as a response to some extreme circumstances, but which never get turned off and become domesticated into a permanent condition. The planet becomes reimagined as a non-stop work site or an always open shopping mall of infinite choices, tasks, selections, and digressions" (17). A prerogative belonging to the sovereign—the decision on the state of emergency/exception—has, in a word, at some level bled into the chronic rhythms of economic life. What Crary is suggesting is that exposure to the exceptional force of law (that can in principle suspend its application), and exposure to the exigencies of an economic machine that now runs 24/7, enters into a zone of indistinction, to use Giorgio Agamben's favored formulation. To be caught in the glare of such floodlights that would seem to decrease night and day is, paradoxically, to be rendered ever more creaturely, ever more purely enjoined to the mere management of life, however infinite and entertaining the choices it might constitute.[8] To use Nietzsche's famous term, the life of "the last man" is, in all its blithe nihilism, an infinitely busy one.

Against this background, one might link the manic state of those creaturely messengers described in Kafka's short fragment to the moment in *The Castle* when the novel's protagonist, K., is shocked out of his cognac-induced somnolence by the sudden lighting of the courtyard where he had been resting under blankets in a sleigh, ostensibly waiting for the mysterious castle official Klamm: "At that—just as K. was engaged in taking a long sip—it became bright, the electric light came on, not only inside, on the stairs, in the passage, and in the corridor, but outside above the entrance. Footsteps could be heard descending the stairs, the bottle fell from K.'s hand, cognac spilled onto a fur, K. jumped from the sleigh."[9] We might say that both the messengers and K. are addressees of an imperious interpellation that no longer issues from this or that identifiable agent or official, but from a life-world that has itself come to resemble a kind of office that never goes dark. In this sense, "24/7" can be viewed as another formula for what I have characterized as the *traumamtlich* dimension of modern life.

Here one will recall that K.'s fundamental dilemma pertains to the question of whether he was truly "called" to be a land surveyor by the castle, whether he has a proper vocation there, a proper *Berufsarbeit*, to use the term favored by Max Weber in his account of the spirit of capitalism. In a certain sense, K. is demanding of the castle officials that they issue a proper *Arbeitsanforderung*, or demand for work. K.'s business at the castle would, at some level, seem to be to reanimate the old spirit of capitalism that calls one to a proper calling. What he encounters instead is a sort of constant chatter that provides no orientation, but only diffuse "excitations" (from *ex-citare*, "to call out" or "summon").[10]

This is quite literally the case in the episode early in the novel when K. tries to clarify the nature of his *Berufsarbeit* by calling the castle authorities from the telephone at the inn where he has spent the first night of his sojourn in the village at the foot of the castle hill. Overcoming the general suspicion among the patrons at the inn that his efforts would remain fruitless, K. picks up the phone. What he hears on the other end is something like the acoustic equivalent of the battery of floodlights in Crary's image of a state of exception that has become the norm in the unworlded world, the decreated creation, of 24/7:

> From the mouthpiece came a humming [*aus der Hörmuschel kam ein Summen*], the likes of which K. had never heard on the telephone before. It was as though the humming of countless childlike voices—but it wasn't humming either, it was singing, the singing of the most distant, of the most utterly distant, voices—as though a single, high-pitched yet utterly strong voice had emerged out of this humming in some quite impossible way and now drummed against one's ears as if demanding to penetrate more deeply

into something other than one's wretched hearing. K. listened [*horchte*] without telephoning, with his left arm propped on the telephone stand and he listened thus [*horchte so*]. (20)

What Crary ultimately wants to underline with that image of floodlights—and the essay as a whole might be viewed as an unpacking of this basic insight—is the belonging together of the logic of the security state, with its demand for constant vigilance and ubiquitous surveillance, and that of neoliberal political economy with its demand for constant production, consumption, communication, interconnectedness, inter-indebtedness, and profit-oriented self-management. The pressure of 24/7 vigilance informs, that is, not only the security apparatus of the state but its political economy as well. The blurring of the boundaries between corporate and state data mining—our most recent "extractive" industry supported, in turn, by the mining of rare-earth metals—would then be only one symptom of this convergence of political and economic tendencies in a ubiquitous pressure for productive wakefulness.[11] Sleep, as Crary argues, would thus indeed seem to represent something like a final frontier where the exigencies of a 24/7 world—a world at some level unworlded or, as I have put it, decreated—run up against the recalcitrance of human embodiment. The paradox of a 24/7 environment would thus seem to be that only in sleep do we inhabit a truly human world, one not fully adapted to, (de)created for, the inhuman rhythms of 24/7 routines of work, consumption, connectivity, and vigilance.

In his novels, Kafka's protagonists are everywhere falling asleep at precisely the wrong moment. In one of the final episodes of *The Castle*, for example, we find K. walking the corridors of the *Herrenhof*, the inn where castle officials stay when they have business in the village. He is still searching for ways to reach Klamm, if only by way of further intermediaries. He finally enters a room where he hopes, if only by chance, to find one of those intermediaries, Erlanger, "one of the first secretaries of Klamm" (239). He finds himself in "a small room, more than half of it occupied by a wide bed" (257). The bed's inhabitant, another secretary named Bürgel, welcomes K. and initiates him into various aspects of his life as a castle official, which, as Bürgel suggests, is the only life one has there since, as he puts it, "we don't acknowledge any distinction between ordinary time and work time. Such distinctions are alien to us" (262). All life is, in a word, official life, *amtliches Leben*—or more accurately, *traumamtliches Leben*, one in which the distinction between living and dreaming has been officially suspended, where the *Arbeitsanforderung* of one's office ramifies into the most intimate parts of one's life. All space thereby becomes a kind of office and a bed is a form of office furniture: "Oh, for anyone who could stretch out and sleep soundly, for any sound sleeper, this bed would be truly delicious. But even for someone like myself, who is always tired but cannot sleep, it does some good, I spend a large part of the day in it, dispatching all my correspondence and questioning the parties" (259). The rest of the chapter is for the most part taken up by Bürgel's vague and convoluted account of rare contingencies that might in principle allow "a party" to achieve his goals with castle authorities, goals normally impossible to achieve even with "a lifetime of grueling effort," as he puts it (261). The reader gets the very strong sense that Bürgel is effectively hypnotizing K., seducing him into somnolence, by way of a description of the possibilities of the sort of decisive and saving action that K. has been seeking all along, possibilities that are, however, effectively available only there, in the "here and now" of Brügel's own speech. K. is put to sleep by a discourse on the need for vigilance; he sleeps through the moment being described to him as his singular possibility of salvation. In Freudian terms, it is as if K. falls asleep at the precise point of a possible analytic breakthrough in the "here and now" of the transference. Kafka, ever the master of proliferating ambiguities, also hints that this "act" of falling asleep might itself be viewed as the true and heroic triumph K. has been pursuing all along. This and other such hints, however, get immediately taken up into the darker story of constantly—and somehow inevitably—missed chances.

In a 24/7 economy it is clear that one is "chronically" at risk of missing an opportunity, of failing to be vigilant, of failing to be in the know. Crary thus emphasizes the *fantasmatic* aspect of life lived under the pressure of its demands:

> Now there are numerous pressures for individuals to reimagine and refigure themselves as being of the same consistency and values as the dematerialized commodities and social connections in which they are immersed so extensively. Reification has proceeded to the point where the individual has to invent a self-understanding that optimizes or facilitates their participation in digital milieus and speeds. Paradoxically, this means impersonating the inert and the inanimate. ... Because one cannot literally enter any of the electronic mirages that constitute the interlocking marketplaces of global consumerism, one is obliged to construct *fantasmatic compatibilities* between the human and a realm of choices that is fundamentally unlivable. (99–100; my emphasis)

As Kantorowicz has argued, such fantasmatic compatibilities—at least with respect to wakefulness—were in the late Middle Ages and early modernity conceived as part and parcel of the office of the king. More precisely, they were seen as part of the charge of the king's virtually real double. The ideal of the *rex exsomnis*, the king who has no rest, added the dimension of perpetual vigilance to the other attributes sustained by the king's "second body," those of his ubiquity, his character of *lex animata*, and his infallibility.[12] One might thus view the 24/7 regime of neoliberal capitalism as a sort of popularization/democratization of the ideal of the *rex exsomnis* and its diffusion into the broader fabric of social life. Then, 24/7 would thus be another "name" for the displacement, or *Entstellung*, of the political theology of sovereignty by the political economy of the wealth of nations, of the metamorphosis of the King's Two Bodies into the People's Two Bodies.[13] We might say that at this point, the psychopathology of everyday (waking) life and the interpretation of dreams enter into a zone of indistinction.

Michel Foucault has for his part argued that the attribute of perpetual vigilance entered into our general conception of governmental power largely by way of the ideal of "pastoral" care developed in biblical and classical antiquity and was further elaborated in Christianity. As Foucault put it in the first of his Tanner Lectures delivered in 1979, "The Greek leader had naturally to make decisions in the interest of all; he would have been a bad leader had he preferred his personal interest. But his duty was a glorious one: even if in war he had to give up his life, such a sacrifice was offset by something extremely precious: immortality. He never lost. By way of contrast, shepherdly kindness is much closer to 'devotedness.' That's his constant concern. When they sleep, *he* keeps watch." With respect to the ideal of shepherdly vigilance, Foucault adds, "First, he acts, he works, he puts himself out, for those he nourishes and who are asleep. Second, he watches over them."[14]

In the second lecture, in which he takes up the modern elaborations of at least certain strands of pastoral power, Foucault addresses the institution of the police that was, in the seventeenth and eighteenth centuries, understood broadly as public policy or civil administration. Among the areas of concern of police administration we find a return of the dimension of glory—now under the heading of *splendor*—that he had first seen as standing outside the purview of the pastoral paradigm. Drawing on one of the first utopian programs for a fully policed state, Turguet de Mayenne's *Aristo-Democratic Monarchy*—a work that includes the first mention of the term "political economy"—Foucault divides the duties of the police into two categories: "First, the police has to do with everything providing the city with adornment, form, and splendor. Splendor denotes not only the beauty of a state ordered to perfection; but also its strength, its vigor." The second category, which Turguet brings under the heading of "communication," includes the charge of fostering "working and trading relations between men, as well as aid and mutual help." Summarizing his findings, Foucault suggests that the task of the police—their fundamental charge—was in effect to cultivate a sort of *surcharge*, or *surplus of life*, on behalf of the state: "As a form of rational intervention wielding political power over men, the role of the police is to supply them with *a little extra life*; and by so doing, supply the state with a little extra strength."[15] The following reflections will attempt to gather these motifs into a coherent story about the fate of this surplus life, the vicissitudes of this splendid surcharge of animation that became the *subject-matter* of classical political economy and has become an ever more dominant dimension of contemporary capitalism. As we shall see, the story concerns historical dislocations and displacements in the sites, procedures, and fantasies in and through which social bonds are formed in the flesh of embodied subjects, flesh that at a certain moment in our history comes to be weighed in balances that ever more determine our individual and collective destinies.

During the final, proofreading stage of the preparation of this volume, I was alerted to Gil Anidjar's new work on the historical semantics of blood, an element and medium at times opposed to, at times figured as the very life and soul of, the virtually real dimension I address here under the heading of "flesh."[16] Reading Anidjar at this late date made me feel a bit like Shylock in the trial scene in *The Merchant of Venice*—a scene I will discuss in detail in Lecture 1—when Portia, in the guise of a young doctor of law, informs him that this bond allows him to cut a pound of flesh from Antonio's body, but that he must do so without spilling a drop of the latter's Christian blood. Anidjar's work compellingly insists on the insistence of blood in the story I have tried to tell here, a story about the transformation of social bonds and the fantasies that in large measure sustain them.[17] My own sense is that we are, in the end, both addressing the same dimension—the same *subject-matter*—of social bonds as they have been elaborated in the Christian West, but that where I focus on the aspect of *conge-lation,* Anidjar emphasizes the eternal recurrence, if I might put it that way, of *liquefaction.* We are, that is, addressing different *states* of the subject-matter at issue in the elaboration of social bonds in the early-modern and modern State, in the former within a political theology of sovereignty, in the latter within a political economy of wealth. As we shall see, Marx himself addresses these two aspects or states in his analysis of the commodity form (his example here is so-and-so-much fabricated linen): "Human labor-power in its fluid state, or human labor, creates value, but is not itself value. It becomes value in its coagulated state [*in geronnenem Zustand*], in objective [*gegenständlicher*] form. The value of the linen as a congealed mass of human labor [*als Gallerte menschlicher Arbeit*] can be expressed only as an 'objectivity' ['*Gegenständlichkeit*'], a thing which is materially different from the linen itself and yet common to the linen and all other commodities."[18] It is this objec-tivity or materiality that our very doings invoke or conjure that Marx characterizes as spectral, as *gespenstisch,* and it is above all this aspect, one that Marx, two paragraphs later, explicitly links to the *Leibesgestalt,* the fleshly form, of the sovereign, that is my concern in these pages.

I would like to conclude these preliminary remarks by citing a brief passage from Rainer Maria Rilke's 1910 novel, *The Notebooks of Malte Laurids Brigge,* a work I discussed in detail in the final chapter of *The Royal Remains.* As I argued there, Rilke's poetic anthropology of modernity tracks the royal remains into the fabric of everyday life—showing what can happen, that is, once the King's Two Bodies come to belong to every body, become every body's busy-ness. The novel's protagonist, a young and now impoverished Danish aristocrat wandering the streets of Paris and struggling to become a writer, visits, at one point, the psychiatric clinic at the Salpêtrière in the hopes of finding relief from agonizing anxieties he is unable to master on his own. While waiting to be seen by these new sorts of masters—in Foucault's terms, these biopolitical experts—the anxieties begin to take shape—to congeal—as the carnal pressure of a sort of second head pushing against the boundaries of the skin. It is a pressure that Malte first experienced in the steadily decaying manor houses—the *Herrenhäuser*—of his childhood, houses at one time linked, as the novel makes clear, to the Danish royal house. At the center of the experience is the registration of a demand—an *Arbeitsanforderung*—to sustain this uncanny carnality, this "extra life," with his own blood:

> And then . . . for the first time in many, many years, it was there again. What had filled me with my first, deep horror [*Entsetzen*], when I was a child and lay in bed with fever: the Big Thing [*das Große*]. . . . Now it was there. Now it was growing out of me like a tumor, like a second head, and was a part of me, although it certainly couldn't belong to me, because it was so big. It was there like a large dead animal which, while it was alive, used to be my hand or my arm. And my blood flowed through me and through it, as through one and the same body. And my heart had to beat harder to pump blood into the Big Thing: there was barely enough blood. And the blood entered the Big Thing unwillingly and came back sick and tainted. But the Big Thing swelled and grew over my face like a warm bluish boil, and grew over my mouth, and already my last eye was hidden by its shadow.[19]

As the novel as a whole makes clear, what Malte experiences here as *Entsetzen*, or horror, is linked to the historical *Ent-setzen*, or deposition of the king and more generally of the form of life organized, at a symbolic and imaginary level, by way of the political theology of sovereignty. The subject matter of Malte's *Entsetzen* is, to use a Lacanian locution, the appearance in the real of his *subject-matter*, a surplus of inflamed and agitated flesh with no proper socio-symbolic resting place. It was, as I will be arguing in the following pages, the genius of capitalism to keep this dimension from going to waste or, rather, to convert this waste product of political theology—these *Königsreste*—into the treasure of political economy, the fundamental substance of which Marx characterized as *gespenstische Gegenständlichkeit*. Under Marx's gaze, what Rilke still elaborated as a psycho-politico-theology of everyday life thereby comes into focus as a psycho-economico-theology of everyday life, a life whose uncanny surplus—whose subject-matter—becomes the subject matter of political economy.

Notes

1. Eric Santner, *The Royal Remains: The People's Two Bodies and the Endgames of Sovereignty* (Chicago: University of Chicago Press, 2011).

2. T. J. Clark, *Farewell to an Idea: Episodes from a History of Modernism* (New Haven, CT: Yale University Press, 1995), 15. Subsequent page references are made in the text. See chap. 4 of *The Royal Remains* for a more in-depth discussion of the painting.

3. Clark notes that as one of the museum section's important Jacobins, David very likely took part in producing the *Ordre de la Marche* for the highly stage-managed activities in the context of which his painting was presented to the public, activities that followed the execution of Marie Antoinette. See Clark, *Farewell to an Idea*, 15–55.

4. Franz Kafka, *Beim Bau der chinesischen Mauer und andere Schriften aus dem Nachlaß* (Frankfurt: Fischer, 1992), 235–36. Unless otherwise noted, translations are mine.

5. For a discussion of these two events in the context of the "spectral" history of financial instruments in modern capitalism, see Joseph Vogl, *The Specter of Capital*, trans. Joachim Redner and Robert Savage (Stanford, CA: Stanford University Press, 2015). Originally published as *Das Gespenst des Kapitals* (Zurich: Diaphanes, 2010).

6. Sara Melzer and Kathryn Norberg, eds., *From the Royal to the Republican Body: Incorporating the Political in Seventeenth- and Eighteenth-Century France* (Berkeley: University of California Press, 1998), 10–11 (my emphasis).

7. Jonathan Crary, *24/7* (London: Verso, 2013). Subsequent page references are made in the text. As Crary notes, his essay can be understood as a continuation and updating of Anson Rabinbach's groundbreaking study of the modern preoccupation with fatigue as a threat to both political and economic survival. See Anson Rabinbach, *The Human Motor: Energy, Fatigue, and the Origins of Modernity* (Berkeley: University of California Press, 1992).

8. For a fuller discussion of this paradox, see my *On Creaturely Life: Rilke, Benjamin, Sebald* (Chicago: University of Chicago Press, 2006).

9. Franz Kafka, *The Castle*, trans. Mark Harman (New York: Schocken, 1998), 103–104. Kafka's novel is a crucial point of reference for Crary as well.

10. Kafka thereby already provides us with a sense of the libidinal economy of what Luc Boltanski and Eve Chiapello have called the "new spirit of capitalism." See their *New Spirit of Capitalism*, trans. Gregory Elliot (London: Verso, 2007).

11. One is tempted to say that when, in the wake of the 9/11 disaster, New York City's Mayor Rudolf Giuliani appealed to the citizens of the city to go shopping as a sign of a return to normality, he was at some level reminding them of their duty or "oath of office" in a regime of 24/7 business, a duty linked, in turn, to the series of states of exception—suspensions of law in the name of security—invoked in the aftermath of the terrorist attacks.

12. Ernst Kantorowicz, *The King's Two Bodies: An Essay in Medieval Political Theology* (Princeton, NJ: Princeton University Press, 1957), 142–43n167, 496.

13. Alexei Penzin has made this argument in *Rex Exsomnis: Sleep and Subjectivity in Capitalist Modernity*, dOCUMENTA (13): 100 Notes—100 Thoughts, no. 97 (Osfildern: Hatje Cantz, 2012). I am grateful to Penzin for sharing material from his work in progress on a critical cultural history of sleep.

14. Michel Foucault, *Omnes et Singulatim: Towards a Criticism of "Political Reason,"* Tanner Lectures on Human Values, delivered at Stanford University, October 10, 16, 1979, http://foucault.info/documents/foucault.omnesetsingulatim.en.html, 229–30.

15. Foucault, "Omnes et Singulatim," 246.

16. See his *Blood: A Critique of Christianity* (New York: Columbia University Press, 2014). I am grateful to Marcia Klotz for alerting me to Anidjar's work.

17. As Anidjar phrases the fundamental question of his study, "Does blood 'itself' insist, then? And if so, what is the nature of this insistence?" (Anidjar, *Blood*, 22.)

18. Karl Marx, *Capital: A Critique of Political Economy, Volume 1*, trans. Ben Fowkes (New York: Vintage, 1977), 142. German text is taken from Karl Marx, *Das Kapital: Kritik der politischen Ökonomie, Erster Band* (Berlin: Karl Dietz Verlag, 2008), 65–66.

19. Rainer Maria Rilke, *The Notebooks of Malte Laurids Brigge*, trans. Stephen Mitchell (New York: Vintage, 1990), 61–62.

Lecture 1

As I've indicated in the preface, I am attempting to unpack the ambiguity embedded in the phrase, "the subject-matter of political economy." My claim is that what is generally studied under the heading of political economy—its subject matter in the conventional sense—demands a special sort of materialism, one attuned to the strange matter or materiality generated by the emergence and sustenance, under ever-changing historical circumstances, of human subjectivity. If political economy has a proper subject matter, it has to do with an improper "surplus of matter," a locus of pressure that drives the pursuit of the wealth of nations, that first turns the rational pursuit of ends into a drive. (In the following, when I want to emphasize this second meaning, I will use the hyphenated form: *subject-matter*. The topic or subject matter of this book is, one could say, the modern vicissitudes of subject-matter.) No doubt a great deal hangs on the nature of this impropriety, this state of being out of place, un-owned, and unclean, a cluster of meanings that bring to mind the famous definition of dirt as "matter in the wrong place." Freud, one will recall, cited that definition in an essay in which he showed "primitive accumulation" in the economic realm to be not so much incremental as excremental in nature, to be linked in a fundamental way to the dirty business of *waste*, the work of *waste management*, and the character traits that may be called for in response to its demands.[1]

Some years ago, Jacques Derrida addressed the "hauntological" dirt of political economy in his sprawling study, *Specters of Marx*.[2] The question that interests me here is one that Derrida repeatedly invokes—or to use his own favored term, *conjures*—without fully developing. It has to do with the guardian spirit of his study, *Hamlet*, and with the historical transformations that link the crisis of sovereignty staged in Shakespeare's play to Marx's elaboration of the spectral objectivity/materiality—Marx calls it *die gespenstische Gegenständlichkeit*—immanent and indeed vital to the commodity form. The nature of this "vitality," this "animation," is, in my view, what is ultimately at issue in the spectral analysis of capitalist modernity and what links this project to the larger field of contemporary thinking on the concept of life and of so-called *vibrant matter* more broadly. My hunch is that what is behind the contemporary efflorescence of new materialisms in the humanities is not only a new ethical sensitivity to the liveliness and agency of nonhuman animals, things, "actants," and environments. In my view, they have emerged in large measure under the pressure that Rainer Maria Rilke—in many ways the canonical poet of vibrant matter—characterized as the "vibration of money," the flows, fluxes, and intensities—the vibrancies—of capital in our everyday life.[3] The new materialisms attempt, however, to dispense with subject-matter, the materiality proper to human subjectivity. The modern and postmodern mutations of that subject-matter which function, as I see it, as a hidden object/cause, as the real *Anstoss*, of the new materialist turn, are my concern here.

To return to the frame of Derrida's study, *Hamlet*/Marx: What finally links the ghost of a violently deposed king to a central, if fantasmatic, feature of economic life under capitalism, to what we might call its *virtual real*? To relocate the question I first asked in my last book, *The Royal Remains*, I want to ask here what remains of the royal in that domain of activity in which, to use Adam Smith's famous formulation, we seem merely to actualize our basic human capacity to truck, barter, and exchange one thing for another. What allows for the apparent metamorphosis of at least some part or aspect of the king's deposed body—some *partial object* of political theological legitimacy—into the substance of value of commodities?[4]

At some level the question concerns the shift from one form of fetishism to another, from the fetishism of persons to that of objects of exchange. It is the question of a shift in the locus of the Thing that was with the king, to the (ever more imperious) realm of commodities that thereby come to promise "the real thing." In *Capital*, Marx makes only a few brief references to the earlier, ostensibly pre-modern mode of fetishism. In his initial presentation of the relative form of value in his analytical reconstruction of the commodity form, Marx writes, for example: "An individual, A, for instance, cannot be 'your majesty' to another individual, B, unless majesty in B's eyes assumes the fleshly form [*Leibesgestalt*] of A, and, moreover, changes facial features, hair and many other things, with every new 'father of his people.' " In a later passage, Marx cites Hegel's notion of a *Reflexionsbestimmung*, or determination of reflection, as the key to this sort of relational identity: "For instance, one man is king only because other men stand in the relation of subjects to him. They, on the other hand, imagine that they are subjects because he is king."[5]

The point is that the king acquires his royal flesh, comes to enjoy the second, glorious body that forms the subject matter—in both senses of the term—of Ernst Kantorowicz's magisterial study, *The King's Two Bodies*, by virtue of his place within a specific set of socio-symbolic relations sustained—or better, *entertained* (in German, *unterhalten*)—by way of the liturgical practices of courtly life beginning with those of anointment, consecration, and ritual acclamation. As Kantorowicz puts it, "the vision of the king as a *persona geminata* is ontological and, as *an effluence of a sacramental and liturgical action* performed at the altar, it is liturgical as well."[6] And as Slavoj Žižek has concisely written apropos of such "effluence," "What is at stake is . . . not simply the split between the empirical person of the king and his symbolic function. The point is rather that this symbolic function *redoubles his very body,* introducing a split between the visible, material, transient body and another, sublime body, a body made of a special, immaterial stuff."[7] What is crucial here is that a symbolic investiture establishes not simply the jointure of body and office—a new suturing, as it were, of the somatic and the normative—but generates in addition, at—or better, *as*—the locus of that suture, the pressure of a surplus carnality, of an additional bit of flesh, that can be—and historically has been—elaborated and figured as a kind of second, virtually real and, indeed, glorious body.[8] It is in this context that Žižek refers to Lacan's remarks apropos of Hamlet's inability to slay Claudius: "What stays Hamlet's arm? It's not fear—he has nothing but contempt for the guy—it's because he knows that *he must strike something other than what's there*."[9] The problem is, in a word, in finding the proper locus of the strike, the locus, that is, of a "special, immaterial stuff" (along with its mode of production). The problem becomes only exacerbated once the king no longer serves as the principal bearer of sovereignty. New topologies will be needed to orient new kinds of "strikes."

Marx's theory of the fetishism of the commodity and the labor theory of value on which it is based is a contribution to just such a new topology; they allow us, precisely, to approach and analyze this immaterial stuff in its new, thingly location. They concern, I am arguing, a kind of metamorphosis of the king's royal flesh into the spectral materiality of the product of human labor, into the substance of value qua congelation of abstract, homogeneous human labor. What Marx characterizes as the dual character of the labor embodied in commodities is, in a word, a two-body doctrine transferred from the political theology of sovereignty to the realm of political economy. The famous "metaphysical subtleties and theological niceties" [*metaphysische Spitzfindigkeit und theologische Mücken*] that Marx discovered in the realm of commodities once belonged, as Kantorowicz's study makes abundantly clear, to the realm of the king; they are aspects of what I have characterized as *royal remains*.[10] Marx's point is that these remains will remain a locus of unfreedom until we learn to work through them in their simultaneously ontological and liturgical dimensions or, as Derrida characterized the zone in which these two dimensions converge, in their "hauntological" aspect.

This is, in my view, what generates such difficulties for a Marxist theory and practice of revolution. Marx argues, in effect, that a revolutionary, too, *must strike something other than what's there.* It is this very difficulty that Walter Benjamin tried to adumbrate in his discussion of the *general strike,* in his famous essay on the "Critique of Violence," and that he would continue to elaborate as the properly messianic dimension of human action. This difficulty is no doubt behind so much of our recent preoccupation with messianism, the messianic, and "messianicity," to use the term Derrida introduces in his Marx book. And as the reference to Lacan also reminds us, this is the very field of action that Freud tried to open as the space of the psychoanalytic clinic. *Striking something other than what's there* would thus seem to be a task located at the intersection of political and libidinal economy, a zone that resonates with tensions vital to the messianic tradition of religious thought and action.

I will have more to say about Marx's contributions to the mapping of this zone in Lecture 2. The crucial signpost in that mapping is his notion of the fetishism of the commodity, our relation, that is, to its special, immaterial stuff. For now I would like to return to the historical question about the mutations and dislocations of that stuff, to what I have characterized as a metamorphosis of the subject-matter of political theology into that of political economy. We might think of it as a shift from the "sovereign form" to the "commodity form" of social mediation, of those processes, that is, through which people come to be bound to one another, to "subjectivize" their social ties within a historical form of life that thereby comes to matter for them.

II

The metamorphosis we are tracking is registered in its own peculiar way in Benjamin Franklin's famous advice to a young tradesman, counsel that became one of Max Weber's central proof-texts for his thesis about the Protestant origins of the "spirit of capitalism." It's worth noting that, in his famous study, Weber's argument had already blurred the boundary between spirit and specter. Weber's central claim was that an irrational kernel of cultic doctrine and practice, one condensed in the notion of the vocational call, or *Berufung* (along with the activity of laboring in a call, of *Berufsarbeit*), formed the impetus of the economic rationality of modern capitalism. Weber famously characterized the *manic frugality* of this rationality as a paradoxical mode of enjoyment, one he named "worldly asceticism." As Franklin puts it in a passage cited by Weber, "He that kills a breeding-sow, destroys her offspring to the thousandth generation. He that murders a crown, destroys all that it might have produced, even scores of pounds."[11] The strangeness of Franklin's formulation derives not only from its elevation (in the first metaphor) of a once decried perversity proper to chrematistics—the art of making money—to the highest virtue; it derives as well from the fact that the metaphor of the murdered crown owes its meaning to a prior displacement, murderous or not, of the *sovereign* of the realm by the *coin* of the realm, one prefigured by the imprint of the sovereign's own figure on coins. We can murder a crown in Franklin's sense—perform *economic regicide*—only if the political theology of sovereignty has already been largely absorbed by and translated into the terms of the political economy of the wealth of nations, only when the stuff of the king's "surplus body" has been transformed into that of surplus value, the product of a certain mode of human labor the glorious amplification of which Franklin enjoins the young tradesman to enjoy. My argument will be that such enjoyment constitutes the libidinal core of what I see as the *doxology of everyday life* in modern capitalist societies.

Aristotle provides the canonical account of the "fertility" of money as unnatural, as a perversion of nature, in his efforts in Book 1 of the *Politics* to clarify the boundary between the management of the household—economy proper—and the art of gaining wealth. The latter is presented as having no natural limit and thus as inherently *masslos*, without proper measure. Freud will, of course, make the same claim about human sexuality: it is inherently perverse, inherently in excess of teleological function (the reproduction of the family qua basic economic unit). Like the *clinamen* of the ancient atomists, human sexuality emerges on the basis of a constitutive swerve, in this case from a norm that is established only retroactively. In the terms Derrida uses in his discussion of Marx, Aristotle would seem to want to "exorcize" the perverse dimension of chrematistics from the *oikos*, a dimension that, Aristotle suggests, enters human life by way of coined money, an institution introduced in Greece only a few centuries earlier. (As with nearly all later standard economic theory, Aristotle assumes that money was introduced to resolve practical and logistical obstacles presented by the practice of barter; as David Graeber and others have suggested, such views might be characterized as "infantile economic theories" concerning the emergence of money and markets, theories on a par with what Freud analyzed under the heading of infantile sexual theories concerning the emergence of babies and the nature of the "exchanges" going on between parents.[12]) That questions of the vitality proper to human flourishing—in contrast to the perversely "vibrant matter" of money—are involved are clear from Aristotle's claim that those bent upon the accumulation of money without limit "are intent upon *living only*, and not upon *living well*," something exemplified in the life of our canonical misers from Plautus's Euclio to Molière's Harpagon to Balzac's Gobseck and Dickens's Scrooge.[13] What these misers all show, however, is that such "bare living" can have its own peculiar intensity and *jouissance,* and indeed one that brings it into uncanny proximity with a life of virtue, though one that would perhaps have been unrecognizable to Aristotle.[14] We might call it "compulsive fidelity to the *clinamen.*"

The boundary between human life and the perverse vitality of money qua symbolic medium of exchange takes center stage in Shakespeare's *The Merchant of Venice* in the guise of the pound of flesh around which the action of the play largely orbits. I'd like to dwell on the role that this famous "piece of the real" comes to play in the play or, perhaps better, on the *work* it performs in the play's narrative and dramatic economy. My hunch is that Derrida's appeal to *Hamlet* to draw out the spectral dimension at issue in Marx's thought becomes more compelling if supplemented—if fleshed out—by reflections on the *Merchant.* In order to grasp the stakes of Shakespeare's most famous tragedy—especially for modern readers—we need, I am suggesting, the resources of his most problematic comedy. (As a non-specialist, I find discussing Shakespeare always feels terribly presumptuous; it is hoped one will view this trespass less as tragic hubris and more as a bit of comedic *chuztpadik.*)

There can be little doubt that this work is deeply informed by the Pauline tradition concerning the notion of the flesh and the larger semantic field in which it figures, one articulated as a series of oppositions—not only flesh and spirit but also letter and spirit, literal and figural, particular and universal, law and love, and no doubt many more. As I've suggested, what ultimately drives the formation of this series of oppositions, along with the various individual and collective "dramas" associated with them, is the enigmatic jointure of the somatic and the normative that defines human life. What Paul, too, is struggling with in these oppositions is the difficulty of conceptualizing the substance of that jointure, this third element in excess of both the somatic and the normative that both links and leaks into the two domains as the uncanny cause of various inflammatory conditions. Whether such conditions are determined to be "autoimmune" or not will depend, in the end, on how one comes to understand this third element, and whether it needs to be cured, managed, quarantined, put to work, put into play. Freud, for his part, staked his own new science on the hypothesis that this element was the very subject-matter of human sexuality—what he called *libido*—and that our "sexuation" comprises the generic site of its turbulent and often traumatic emergence, of our (surplus) life in the flesh.[15] The shift from the political theology of sovereignty to the political economy of the wealth of nations is, I am arguing, a shift from one "epochal" mode of shaping our life in the flesh to another.

To begin, it's worth recalling that the first metaphor invoked by Franklin to illustrate the fecundity of capital is used by Shylock in his initial negotiation with Antonio. As a usurer, Shylock embodies the perversion of chrematistics in its purity, a perversion that is of course less visible in the practices of Antonio, the real merchant of the play's title. The fact that people often think that the title refers to Shylock is echoed in the first question asked by Portia (dressed as Balthazar, a young doctor of law) in the famous trial scene: "Which is the merchant here? and which the Jew?" (4.1.174).[16] According to Aristotle, however, they both belong together as those who pursue a spurious kind of wealth:

> There are two sorts of wealth-getting.... One is a part of household management, the other is retail trade: the former necessary and honorable, while that which consists in exchange is justly censured; for it is unnatural, and a mode by which men gain from one another. The most hated sort, and with the greatest reason, is usury, which makes a gain out of money itself, and not from the natural object of it. For money was intended to be used in exchange, but not to increase at interest. And this term interest [*tokos*, lit. "offspring"], which means the birth of money from money, is applied to the *breeding of money* because the offspring resembles the parent. Wherefore of all modes of getting wealth this is the most unnatural.[17]

It was W. H. Auden who first noted that Antonio would seem to be guilty of yet another perversion of nature and natural fecundity, namely homosexuality. And indeed, the various forms of lack that seem to lay at the bottom of his melancholy have encouraged at least one reader to see him not simply as a sinner or *pécheur*—one given over to the life of the flesh—but also as a new incarnation of the *roi-pêcheur*, the wounded Fisher King who can no longer fulfill his office as head of the Grail Society—who can perhaps reign but no longer govern—and so has become dependent on new forms of nourishment/enrichment that are material and unnatural rather than spiritual and supernatural.[18] As we shall see, for both Foucault and Agamben, that the king reigns without governing represents the culmination of the process whereby the political theology of sovereignty is absorbed into the political economy of the nation-state and the modes of management adapted to life in commodity-producing societies. In this context it's worth recalling Hans Jürgen Syberberg's stunning dramaturgical innovation in his film version of Wagner's *Parsifal*. There, the status of the *roi-pêcheur* as king who reigns but no longer governs—we might say, who is valid but no longer has any meaning, *der gilt, aber bedeutet nicht*—is externalized as a fleshy remnant of the "second body," as a free-floating bit of *gespenstische Gegenständlichkeit* (perhaps just about a pound's worth), now displayed on a pillow carried by the members of the Grail Society.[19] It is a disturbingly apt rendering of the epochal caesura between the no longer viable political theology of sovereignty and the not yet hegemonic political economy of the wealth of nations, a caesura in which the royal remains remain as yet unclaimed. Syberberg's staging emphasizes the aspect of a stalled sacrament, a Eucharist no longer able to establish the communion and community of a *corpus mysticum*.[20]

Shakespeare's play takes off, of course, from Bassanio's desire to dig out from the mountain of debt in "money and love" he admits to owing Antonio (1.1.131). The pursuit of the beautiful, virtuous, and wildly wealthy Portia is his way of doubling down on those debts, of staking everything on one last gamble. And indeed the entire play is organized around the seemingly inextricable knots tying money and *eros* together, knots tied, in turn, by a series of oaths, contracts, and covenants. Antonio agrees to finance the venture, but lacking liquidity he ends up turning to Shylock, thereby breaking with his custom of generally avoiding the giving or taking of interest on loans.[21]

In their initial encounter in the play, Shylock appears to justify the taking of "usance" by reference to Jacob's innovative pastoral intervention that caused Laban's "ewes" to birth the striped lambs that were by prior agreement to be his. When asked by Antonio whether this scriptural reference were "inserted to make interest good"—that is, whether his gold and silver were, in essence, so many ewes and rams—Shylock curtly replies: "I cannot tell, I make it breed as fast" (1.3.96). In an aside to Bassanio, Antonio characterizes Shylock's brief "midrash" as an example of *hermeneutic* usury, of squeezing out of Scripture a surplus sense that serves one's own advantage. Antonio repeats the metaphor after hearing Shylock's inventory of insults and curses that he, Antonio, had, over the years, heaped upon the Jew: "If thou wilt lend this money, lend it not/As to thy friends, for when did friendship take/A breed for barren metal of his friend?/But lend it rather to thine enemy,/Who, if he break, thou mayst with better face/Exact the penalty" (1.3.132–37). Here Antonio seems to be engaging in his own bit of biblical exegesis by alluding to the Deuteronomic stipulation that prohibited Jews from lending to their Jewish brethren. (This Old Testament passage is thought to be among the first documented *prohibitions* of usury in antiquity.)

After listing the insults he has had to endure, Shylock effectively turns the other cheek and offers to Antonio an interest-free loan. He does, of course, insist "in merry sport" (1.3.145) on the famous penalty: "let the forfeit/Be nominated for an equal pound/Of your fair flesh, to be cut off and taken/In what part of your body pleaseth me" (1.3.148–51). That Antonio accepts the offer as a sign that "there is much kindness in the Jew" (1.3.153) suggests that Shylock's offer to "take no doit/Of usance" (140–41) was read as a sign of quasi-Christian fellowship, as the extension of the narrow, "particularist" sphere of Jewish brotherhood into the universal one of the Church. At this point, a surplus of "usance"—we might say, of *jew-usance*, or Jewish enjoyment of usury—is seemingly replaced by a surplus of kindness, one that provisionally serves as a sign of being of the same kind. In the end, of course, all bets are off and this economy of kindness is undone in the most exorbitant ways in large measure, no doubt because of Shylock's own forced forfeiture of flesh, his daughter Jessica. Keeping with Portia's famous characterization of the quality of mercy, we might say that Shylock is, in the end, mercifully strained to choose Christian "kindness." As Mladen Dolar has argued, the final gift of mercy Shylock is compelled to accept—he is made an offer he can't refuse, as Don Corleone would have put it—introduces a new level and intensity of indebtedness. We might summarize Dolar's argument by saying that Portia's achievement in this context is to "portially" adjust the logic of the debt economy ostensibly represented by Shylock in the direction of its infinite *amourtization*.[22]

As I've noted, the figure of the "pound of flesh" is profoundly overdetermined in the play. We don't actually know until the quite late in the play what part of the body is involved in the penalty added to the contract "in merry sport." It's not unreasonable to assume that Shylock is invoking the rite of circumcision, that the penalty in question involves a demand that, so to speak, Antonio put some *foreskin* in the game. But not unlike the "anal object" in Freud's understanding, the figure of the pound of flesh quickly enters into a series of equivalences—consonant with but also exceeding the Pauline field of terms—that extend from money to child to foreskin to phallus to the literal and spiritual flesh of the heart, while the cutting of the flesh oscillates—"vibrates"—in meaning so as to suggest butchery, circumcision, castration, homicide, and the cruel rigor of the debtor-creditor relation and of contract law more generally. Indeed, the flesh and its cutting seem to mark the very site and action of the opening of the space of possibility of this series of equivalences and the "primary process" of their associative movement—that is, of the very splitting between and the various modes of jointure of the literal and figural, the concrete and the abstract, the material and the spiritual. These primary processes are also palpable in the play through the proliferation of punning, beginning with Antonio's offer to Bassanio, upon hearing of his friend's plan to get clear of debt, to share with him "my purse, my person, my extremest means" (1.1.138). The puns in the play function as sites where, as it were, the word becomes flesh and the flesh becomes word—sites where words themselves come to assume the status of "partial objects." The pound of flesh finally offers us the figure of a value that can be extracted—or perhaps better, *materially abstracted*—from a living body and weighed in the balance. What is weighed here is, however, no longer that which makes a king a king—the partial object of political theology—but something in or of the body that has been invested not with royal office but with economic value in a mercantile society.

There would seem to be little room for reflection about sovereignty in the play, little concern with the transformation of the King's Two Bodies into the People's Two Bodies, and the management of the latter by way of political-economic calculations. I would suggest, however, that just such a shift in the meaning of what is weighed in the balance is underlined by one of the biblical texts alluded to in the trial scene, the Book of Daniel. At different points in the scene, each party—first Shylock and then, for the other side, Gratiano—claims to see in Portia their own Daniel, their own learned and upright judge (*Daniel* means, in Hebrew, "God is my judge"). Portia, for her part, appears in the guise of a young doctor of laws whose name, Balthazar, evokes the name given to Daniel by his Babylonian masters, Beltheshazzar, as well as that of the king himself, Belshazzar. According to Daniel's interpretation of the writing on the wall of the king's vision, the sovereign has reached the end of his royal road: "This *is* the interpretation of the thing: MENE; God hath numbered thy kingdom, and hath finished it. TEKEL; Thou art weighed in the balances, and art found wanting. PERES; thy kingdom is divided, and given to the Medes and the Persians" (Dan. 6:26–28).

The biblical intertext inscribes into the trial proceedings a crisis of royal sovereignty, and therewith the beginnings of the metamorphosis of the subject-matter of political theology into that of political economy, of a partial object of political theological legitimacy—now found to be wanting—into what Marx would identify as the spectral materiality of the commodity, the value materially abstracted from the body of the worker and transferred, as so-and-so much special, immaterial stuff, as so much flesh, to the product of labor qua commodity. In the Shakespearean figure of the pound of flesh we glimpse, I am arguing, at what will be produced when the "Un-Nature" of chrematistics comes to be directly conjoined with the laboring body, when they form a single, wildly fecund matrix producing, of course, not just a pound of flesh but, as Franklin put it, "many scores of pounds." In *The Merchant of Venice*, a play written in the midst of England's transformation into a mercantile society, the way of all flesh long exemplified by the rise and fall of kings begins to be registered as the *weight of all flesh*, the rise and fall in the value of the substance of value.[23] As the play makes clear, such a transformation was imagined to be, at least on some level, linked to—we might say, haunted by—Jews, Judaism, Jewishness.

III

To return to Derrida, one will recall that he introduces the first chapter of his Marx book with a citation from Act 1 of *Hamlet*, in which the hero takes on the mandate of his father's ghost to set right what has been put out of joint by, precisely, the murder of a

Crown. Derrida, for his part, justifies the recourse to Shakespeare not only by noting Marx's own tendency to cite the poet but, above all, by underlining the famous opening line of *The Communist Manifesto*, "*Ein Gespenst geht um in Europa—das Gespenst des Kommunismus*": "As in *Hamlet*, the Prince of a rotten state, *everything begins by the apparition of a specter*" (4; my emphasis). Derrida quickly goes on to propose a *grand récit* of such apparitions, one exhibiting the sort of historicity without historicism that will allow him, later in the book, to posit a "messianicity" without messianism:

> Haunting is historical, to be sure, but it is not *dated*, it is never docilely given a date in the chain of presents, day after day, according to the instituted order of a calendar. Untimely, it does not come to, it does not happen to, it does not befall, one day, Europe, as if the latter, at a certain moment of its history, had begun to suffer from a certain evil, to let itself be *inhabited* in its inside, that is, haunted by a foreign guest. Not that that guest is any less a stranger for having always occupied the domesticity of Europe. But there was no inside, there was nothing inside before it. *The ghostly would displace itself like the movement of this history.* Haunting would mark the very existence of Europe. It would open the space and the relation to self of what is called by this name, at least since the Middle Ages. (4; my emphasis)

Paraphrasing somewhat, the claim here is that the European *economy*—its domesticity, its *oikos*—has always been troubled by an alien presence—something *unheimlich*—immanent to its very constitution. Against this background, one is tempted to replace the word *das Unheimliche* with *das Unökonomische*, "the Un-Economic." Both terms point to some excess, some surplus, in the household that both does and does not belong there, that is produced there but ought not to be there, a surplus that is not too much stuff, too many commodities but, rather, something more akin to a disturbing sort of remainder, to "matter in the wrong place."

It is, as Marx was to show, something that generates its share of confusion for the science of political economy. As I've noted, the anxiety pertaining to some excess in the *oikos* was already there in Aristotle's efforts to keep a certain improper and *un-natural* chrematistic stranger outside the household. What does management of the household—*oikonomia*, or economics—mean if it is *sur-charged* with managing spirits?

It is worth recalling that, in a remarkable essay on *Hamlet* from 1956, Carl Schmitt rehearses parts of his own earlier *grand récit* of the Eurocentric global order, of what he referred to there as the *Nomos der Erde*.[24] He proceeds by focusing on what he explicitly refers to as the *Mehrwert*, or surplus value, that in his view served to elevate Shakespeare's play from *Trauerspiel* to genuine tragedy, and indeed to transform it into a "living myth." Schmitt's search for the source of the sublime object of the play leads him along various paths of interpretation that need not detain us here. In the context of the present discussion, his crucial insight is that the surplus value circulating in *Hamlet* pertains not only to the turbulence generated for the figure of the sovereign by the religious strife of the period—turbulence that, in his view, came to be embodied in the person of James I. Equally important is the claim that at the core of this turbulence lay another, even greater challenge to the political theology of the sovereign: the emergence of England as a mercantile economy, or what Schmitt characterizes as England's "elemental appropriation of the sea [*dem elementaren Aufbruch zu der grossen Seenahme*]" (59):

> Measured in terms of the progress toward civilization that the ideal of continental statehood . . . signifies, Shakespeare's England still appears to be barbaric, that is, in a pre-state condition. However, measured in terms of the progress toward civilization that the Industrial Revolution . . . signifies, Elizabethan England appears to be involved in a phenomenal departure from a terrestrial to a maritime existence—a departure, which, in its outcome,

the Industrial Revolution, caused a much deeper and more fundamental revolution than those on the European continent and
which far exceeded the overcoming of the "barbaric Middle Ages"
that the continental state achieved. (65)[25]

What endows *Hamlet* with its surplus value is, in other words,
the fact that in it are registered historical currents that would culminate in economies organized around the production of surplus
value, and a world order in which the political theology of sovereignty will be more or less absorbed into the political economy of
nation-states (pushing, for their part, against the limits of their
internal and external juridical organizations). I am suggesting,
then, that *The Merchant of Venice* renders explicit what in *Hamlet*
is registered only as a sort of underlying dream-work summoned
forth—or as we might say, *excited*—by structural transformations
of the social order. It was Schmitt himself who argued apropos of
Hamlet that, "even the dreams that the dramatist weaves into his
play must be able to become the dreams of the spectators, with all
the condensations and displacements of recent events" (36). But as
Schmitt also argues, these "recent events" include the opening of
a *structural interregnum* that would not fully take shape in the
lifetime of the London audience of Shakespeare's play. *Merchant*
helps to identify the key historical forces at issue in this opening,
along with the semantic and symbolic transformations it brings in
its wake. As Ben Nelson has argued, these transformations ultimately push beyond the Pauline encoding of social relations still
operative in the play; they push, that is, from the universal brotherhood of Christian society toward the "universal Otherhood" that
characterizes the social relations of modern commercial societies.[26]
These are societies organized around the production, circulation,
and accumulation of the special, immaterial stuff once retained by
the sublime physiology of the king.

For Derrida as well as for me, what ultimately distinguishes the
spectral historicity of Europe from other histories of the "European

Spirit"—the Hegelian as well as the Schmittian one—comes down to the dimension that I have been calling the *flesh*:

> As soon as one no longer distinguishes spirit from specter, the former assumes a body, it incarnates itself as spirit, in the specter. . . . The specter is a paradoxical incorporation, the becoming-body, a certain phenomenal and carnal form of the spirit. It becomes, rather, some "thing" that remains difficult to name: neither soul nor body, and both one and the other. For it is *flesh and phenomenality* that give to the spirit its spectral apparition. (6; my emphasis)[27]

And as Derrida emphasizes, this "thing" that remains so difficult to name appears, in the context of *Hamlet,* and in medieval and early-modern sovereignty more generally, in—or perhaps better, with—*the body of the king*. It is, as I have been arguing, the very thing that leads to the strange doctrine explored by Ernst Kantorowicz in his *King's Two Bodies*. But as we have seen in our discussion of *Merchant*, once the political theology of sovereignty begins to give way to new paradigms of governmentality, to use Foucault's term, the flesh comes to be managed at new sites and in new ways; it comes to count—to be counted and weighed—as the subject-matter of political economy.

IV

At this point I'd like to make a few further remarks about what distinguishes the matter or materiality I am attempting to track, in the transition from the "sovereign form" to the "commodity form" of social mediation, from what seems to be at issue in the new materialisms that have appeared over the last years under different names. I am thinking here less in terms of right or wrong and more in terms of a difference in subject matter, insofar as these new materialisms are intent on dispensing, precisely, with

"subject-matter," the spectral materiality proper to human subjectivity, one with its distinctive *"flesh and phenomenality."*

Jane Bennett, for example, presents the notion of flesh according
to the perspective of what she calls "vital materiality" this way:

> Vital materiality better captures an "alien" quality of our own
> flesh, and in so doing reminds humans of the very *radical* charac-
> ter of the (fractious) kinship between the human and the nonhu-
> man. My "own" body is material, and yet this vital materiality is
> not fully or exclusively human. My flesh is populated and consti-
> tuted by different swarms of foreigners. The crook of my elbow,
> for example, is "a special ecosystem, a bountiful home to no fewer
> than six tribes of bacteria" [Nicholas Wade]. . . . The *its* outnum-
> ber the *mes*. In a world of vibrant matter, it is not enough to say
> that we are "embodied." We are, rather, *an array of bodies,* many
> different kinds of them in a nested set of microbiomes.[28]

The moral and political wager of this approach is that an awareness
of such diverse tribes and populations of "its" and "mes"—a kind
of multiculturalism at the cellular, or even molecular, level—will
inhibit us from producing and consuming "in the same violent
and reckless ways" that has characterized modern industrial and
postindustrial societies heretofore. As Bennett puts it, being mind-
ful "that the human is not exclusively human, that we are made
up of its," will contribute to the formation of "the newish self that
needs to emerge, the self of a new self-interest" (113). A curious
encounter: Adam Smith meets Gilles Deleuze.

The vital materiality that interests me here is one that is, as
Freud put it, composed not of multiple single or multicellular "its"
but, rather, something he called "It" precisely because it remains so
difficult to name (recall Derrida's remarks on the "thing" with the
king that remains so difficult to name: "neither soul nor body, and
both one and the other"). To put it simply, the "intensities" that
occupied—or better, *preoccupied*—the crook of the elbow, among
other body parts, of Freud's hysterics were not caused by tribes of

bacteria but, rather, by a complex disorder of the "tribe" to which these hysterics belonged, a disorder that in one way or another—and psychoanalysis is the effort to understand those ways—congealed as the uncanny cause of their desire, the "un-economic" dimension of their libidinal economy.

Bennett's reading of Kafka's famous story about the creature named "Odradek" (the title of the story is "Die Sorge des Hausvaters"[29]) offers an example of what can get lost in the homogenization of alterity performed in the name of multiplicity and hetereogeneity, something that is stated almost explicitly at the conclusion of her reading of the text: "Odradek exposes this continuity of watery life and rocks; he/it brings to the fore the becoming of things" (8). For Bennett, Odradek is Kafka's name for self-organizing matter, for spontaneous structural generation in the interstices between inorganic and organic vitality: "Wooden yet lively, verbal yet vegetal, alive yet inert, Odradek is ontologically multiple. He/it is a vital materiality and exhibits what Gilles Deleuze has described as the persistent 'hint of the animate in plants, and of the vegetable in animals'" (8). I've already discussed this text in detail in the first "volume" of my study of the afterlife of political theology, so I won't go into great detail here.[30] But it's crucial to underline what gets lost if one ignores that afterlife—its specific forms of "vital materiality"—with respect to a text written in the midst of the breakup of the Austro-Hungarian Empire into a "swarm" of independent, and at times tribally conceived, nation-states (the text was published in 1919).

As many scholars have noted, the word "Odradek," which Kafka's narrator suggests might have Germanic and/or Slavic roots, seems to signify, on the basis of family resemblances to words from these and other linguistic "households," a figure of radical rootlessness and non-belonging—*Od-radix, Od-adresa*. The meanings scholars have adduced for this word, that as the narrator indicates may not have a meaning at all, include: deserter from one's kind; apostate; degenerate; a small creature whose business is to dissuade; a creature that dwells outside of any kind, rank, series, order, class, line, or use; a creature beyond discourse or *Rede;* waste or dirt—*Unrat.* So, once again, it's "matter in the wrong place." All this suggests, I think, that Odradek's *ontological* statelessness—this is what Bennett emphasizes—cannot be separated from the sense of *political* statelessness evoked by the linguistic and historical overdetermination of its name (if it even is a proper name). It was precisely through the breakup of the Austro-Hungarian Empire that the state of statelessness came to be, as Hannah Arendt argued, the political symptom par excellence of modern Europe. And it was the particular "tribe" to which Kafka, along with Freud and Shylock, belonged—a tribe associated, of course, with a peculiar hybrid language of Germanic and Slavic—that came to embody a kind of foreignness having no natural fit within any state. This was a tribe whose members could never be fully "naturalized," absorbed without remainder—and indeed, thought by many of its own members to be, at its core, *passionately detached* from any historical nation-state. One might think of it as a tribe whose very form of life in some sense *mattered in the wrong place.*[31] It is, then, not so much a "newish self" forged on the basis of a vital materiality and new sense of self-interest that Kafka's text helps us to envision but, rather, the uncanny dimension of the "Jewish self" that he himself no doubt experienced as profoundly linked to a series of other dilemmas. Perhaps the most important of these was the dilemma of a writerly existence, an existence lived in passionate detachment from other social bonds and one apparently incompatible with being a *Hausvater,* the head of a household, or *oikos.* We might say that Odradek is, among other things, a figure of *Un-economic* man par excellence, a paradoxical "busy-body" serving no apparent use and yet not ever quite going to waste.

In the short fragment already cited in this book's preface, Kafka linked the "busy-ness" of such bodies, their form of life, to that of manic bureaucrats whose official duties and writings, whose "office work," has been cut loose from its erstwhile source of purpose and legitimation:

> They were given the choice to become kings or messengers. Just like children they all chose to be messengers. For this reason there are only messengers; they race through the world and, because there are no kings, they call out to one another proclamations that have become meaningless. They would happily put an end to their miserable life but because of their oath of office they don't dare.[32]

Against this background, and remembering Kafka's own "office writings" as an insurance official busy with issues of workmen's compensation—compensation for the damaged flesh of laboring bodies—Kafka's own literary writings become legible as the very paradigm of what I have referred to as *traumamtliche Schriften*—the traumatic dream protocols of officious busy bodies. It is a genre that is, I am suggesting, especially attuned to the subject-matter of political economy. My hunch is that it is above all by assuming our responsibility for *this* subject-matter, and for the ways in which we serve to sustain its current configurations, that we can begin to become truly responsive to the multiple forms of vibrant matter that border on and move through the human.

V

I'd like to return once more to Shylock and the nature of the "Jewish labor" to which he is assigned, and that takes place with reference to him, in the economy of *The Merchant of Venice*. In his magisterial study of "Anti-Judaism"—not so much *in* as *as* the Western tradition—David Nirenberg argues that the figure of the Jew in the West is essentially the figure—or perhaps better, the occasion—of a certain kind of work. This is the work that societies are in some way or another compelled to engage in to make sense of the world in the face of fundamental impasses and antagonisms generated by the logic of their own social organization. We might call this heavy lifting the *work of the real,* work no doubt correlated to the sense that the Jews, excluded from participation in most occupations and forms of labor, don't do *real work.* For Nirenberg, the Jews are not so much the subject or agent of the work at issue as its *Anstoss,* its uncanny cause and object.

"Why," Nirenberg asks, "did so many diverse cultures—even many cultures with no Jews living among them—think so much about Judaism? *What work* did thinking about Judaism do for them in their efforts to make sense of their world?"[33] Nirenberg uses Marx's disturbing reflections on the "Jewish Question" to point the direction for his own efforts to answer these questions:

> Marx's fundamental insight ... was that the "Jewish Question" is as much about the basic tools and concepts through which individuals in society relate to the world and to each other, as it is about the presence of "real" Judaism and living Jews in that society. He understood that some of these basic tools—such as money and property—were thought of in Christian culture as "Jewish," and that these tools therefore could potentially produce the "Jewishness" of those who used them, whether those users were Jewish or not. "Judaism," then, is not only the religion of specific people with specific beliefs, but also a category, a set of ideas and attributes with which non-Jews can make sense of and criticize their world. Nor is "anti-Judaism" simply an attitude toward Jews and their religion, but a way of critically engaging the world. (3)

For Marx, then, the critique of political economy was inseparable from an engagement with the "Jewish Question," one that, as Nirenberg underlines, must inevitably fall short if it simply puts fears and habits of thought about Jews, Judaism, and Jewishness "to a *new kind of work*: that of planning a world without private property or wage labor" (4; my emphasis).

Nirenberg's own project proposes to show how, from ancient Egypt to the present day, "different peoples put old ideas about

Judaism *to new kinds of work* in thinking about the world; to show how this work engaged the past and transformed it; and to ask how that work reshaped the possibilities for thought in the future" (5; my emphasis). As Nirenberg tells it, Western anti-Judaism is ultimately the story of the transmission of the demands of this peculiar sort of labor, of a fundamental, even foundational, *Arbeitsanforderung*, to use the word Freud favored in his efforts to characterize the nature of the drives. The story comes very close to repeating Derrida's brief sketch of European history as a compulsively repeated series of displacements of a spectral substance that no amount of conjuration, necromancy, and exorcism manages to fully elaborate and master. The specters of Marx have, for Nirenberg, too, a long history, but it is one that cannot be separated from the history of anti-Judaism in the West. And as is well known, at least since the time of Paul's canonical formulations, at the heart of that history is the preoccupation with the matter of the flesh in its divergence—its *clinamen*—from and threat to the spirit. Not surprisingly, then, Nirenberg also turns to Shakespeare—in this case not to *Hamlet* and the spectral dimension of political theology but to *The Merchant of Venice*, where, as I've argued, the *haunting grounds* of the King's Two Bodies begins to yield to those of the marketplace.

Once again, what is at issue is the nature of the "Jewish labor" performed within the economy of the play that, for Nirenberg, is ultimately that of working out a response to the fundamental question made urgent by the rise of a mercantile economy: "How can a society built on 'Jewish' foundations of commerce, contract, property, and law consider itself Christian?" (274). What is at issue is, thus, a kind of meta-work or *pre-occupation*—work done to facilitate a set of responses to a new organization of work, to the emergence of new relations of production. In psychoanalytic terms, this would be work "beyond the pleasure principle," a form of work done in advance of the work governed by the pleasure and reality principles, work that in some sense helps to install and sustain those

principles. (As Lacan might say, though this work brings no pleasure, it is not without its own form of *jouissance*.) The play lays out
a field of signifiers—a network of facilitations, or *Bahnungen*, to
use Freud's word—along which a surplus or surcharge of semiotic
pressure, a *signifying stress* generated at least in part by these new
relations of production, can move and be discharged, a movement
that will culminate in a fateful charge against Shylock that threatens to bring the comedy to the edge of the tragic. Paradoxically, the
play pulls back from that edge by way of the cruel irony of placing
the Jewish usurer in the position of becoming, finally, a Christian
merchant of Venice.

As Nirenberg emphasizes—much as Schmitt did with respect to
Hamlet—the anxieties and confusions associated with the increasing importance of contractual relations in the emerging mercantile
economy of England helped to generate this pressure in the first
place, and to initiate its "Jewish" dream-work. But what are we
then to make of the fact that Shylock seems, at least with respect to
his loan to Antonio, to be singularly uninterested in profit, in the
amplification of his wealth? Why does he refuse the offer of receiving, in lieu of his bond, many times the sum of his principle? Why
the insistence on the pound of flesh, on having his bond?

To begin, one might say that, with respect to Antonio, this bit
of business is, for Shylock, both personal and historical. It was
never about the money; it concerned, rather, vengeance for the
injustice—we might say, the radical and brutal *unkindness*—that
Shylock and his kind have had to suffer, since time immemorial,
from the likes of Antonio and his kind; it's an injustice amplified by
the loss of his daughter to the fleshpots of the aristocratic Catholic
world (Shylock at times comes across as a puritan reformer, one
suspicious of music, masques, and other "Catholic" frivolities).
That Shylock proposes a pound of Antonio's *fair flesh* as penalty for
nonpayment of the loan suggests that what was at issue all along
here was *fairness*, and indeed of a kind that exceeds that of economic calculation, that of a "fair deal." Shylock seeks vengeance for

the fundamental unfairness of being posited as a being ontologically lacking in all the fair qualities, a lack that allows the Christian world to treat and refer to him—this happens repeatedly in the play—as a dog (historically, the beautiful Jewess is always the possible exception). It is, in other words, clear that up to now—up to the beginning of the action of the play—Shylock has figured for the community as representative embodiment of *jew-usance*, as what is perceived to be the perverse libidinal economy demanded by an emerging mercantile economy. Shylock is ultimately seen—is *classified*, we might say—not so much as belonging to a different cultural and religious kind but, rather, as a figure of the *unkind*, one who unsettles the logic of kinds; Kafka's name for such a figure was, as we have seen, Odradek, and this is in large measure because Shylock is seen as embodying what is fundamentally unsettling in the social transformations that the larger society is undergoing. There is certain self-reflexivity at work here. We might say that Shylock's rage pertains to *the way he is represented in the play*, to the role to which he is assigned in it as representative of the social disorder attending to the emergence of a mercantile economy, an economy in which the global merchant Antonio is really the key player, the truly representative figure. One can almost understand Shylock's wanting a piece of this guy. The self-reflexivity I have noted suggests that, at least to a certain extent, Shakespeare understood this.

But I want to suggest that Shylock's insistence on the (pound of) flesh—an insistence that clearly exceeds any sense of economic rationality—should also be understood as an insistence *of* the flesh, as the dimension in which social bonds are sealed. At the most basic level, the source of anxiety and confusion that haunts the play concerns the nature of social bonds—what it is that binds friends, couples, communities, confessions, nations, peoples together at a moment of profound social, political, and economic transformation. As Shylock seems to know, social bonds always involve the dimension of the flesh. We might say that they are, ultimately, written in and with the flesh, that "part" of us inflamed by the normative pressure of the bonds at issue. They always imply, that is, *a becoming-flesh of the given word*. Shylock's insistence on having his bond could be understood, then, as an explicit insistence on and of this truth—one otherwise dispersed in the play into a series of slighter transactions, most notably the final comedy of errors pertaining to the rings and the pledges they signify.[34] But the play also shows that when the nature of social bonds and the forms of normativity associated with them change—in this case, we are moving from political theological normativity to a space of meaning governed by the normative pressures of political economy—so do the locations, actors, and scenes of that writing, of the relevant *Aufschreibesystem*, to use Friedrich Kittler's term. This is the system of social inscription—Foucault would call it a *dispositif*; Agamben, perhaps with Kafka's "In the Penal Colony" in mind, a *machine*—through which a signifier comes to represent the subject for other signifiers, an operation that always leaves a remainder of inflamed flesh that, like Shylock himself, insists, in and through those signifiers, on getting a fair hearing or, at the very least—Beckett might say, *unnullable least*—on making its presence felt.[35]

VI

In her own reading of *Merchant*, Julia Lupton highlights, among other things, the tense transitional space between the two key "systems" at work in the play—the political theology of sovereignty and the political economy of an emerging commercial society that already prefigures, in her view, fundamental features of modern liberalism.[36] The tension between the two systems comes to a head in the trial scene in which, by means of a legal ploy, Portia/Balthazar shifts the juridical coordinates by which Shylock's petition is to be adjudicated, a ploy that Nirenberg, among others, has characterized as outjewing the Jew. One will recall that she initially acknowledges the force of Shylock's claim and does so in words that closely mirror his own earlier appeal to the sanctity of contract on which the commercial life of Venice depends: "There is no power in Venice/Can alter a decree established./'Twill be recorded for a precedent,/And many an error by the same example/Will rush into the state. It cannot be" (4.1.218–22). It is precisely at this point that Shylock first characterizes Portia/Balthazar as "A Daniel come to judgement!" (4.1.223).[37] Within moments, however, Portia/Balthazar comes up with her surprising and surprisingly literal reading of the contract—this is where she ostensibly outjews the Jew—according to which Shylock must not only extract *exactly* one pound of flesh but must do so without shedding a drop of blood: "This bond doth give thee here no jot of blood;/ The words expressly are 'a pound of flesh.'/Take then thy bond, take thou thy pound of flesh./But in the cutting it, if thou dost shed/One drop of Christian blood, thy lands and goods/Are by the laws of Venice confiscate/Unto the state of Venice" (4.1.306–312; it is Gratiano who now claims Portia/Balthazar as an upright judge and second Daniel). As Lupton points out, this novel—and rather questionable—legal argument marks a shift from commercial to criminal law, one that promises to give Shylock, as Portia/ Balthazar puts it, something like a surplus of justice: "justice more than thou desir'st" (4.1.316). This surplus marks a return of the political theology of sovereignty at the very point at which political economic reckoning was poised to win the day:

> Whereas Venetian civil law had protected the "commodity of strangers"—international commercial transactions—in the minimal public sphere constituted by the economic contract, criminal law in this instance shields the rights of citizens, over against the "aliens" in their midst. The open port of Venice now retreats into its interior islands, reasserting the lines dividing the citizen and the noncitizen. Finally, the power of judgment and mercy,

the sacral attribute of kings, is now forcibly taken from the civil litigant-turned-defendant and delivered to the Duke who shifts from being ... nominal figurehead ... to empowered monarch. (95–96)

In a word, the duke shifts from being a sovereign who reigns but does not govern to one who reigns in excess of governing.[38] I am thus tempted to say that what would appear to be merely a clever legal tactic on the part of Portia/Balthazar, her claim—that is, that Shylock is allowed to cut a pound of flesh but drop no "jot" of (Christian) blood—alludes to the *virtual reality* of the element at issue, to the flesh as the special, immaterial stuff that now goes into the composition of the king's body, now into the substance of value.

Standing before this resurgent sovereign, Shylock now acquires the attributes of creaturely life; he "suddenly stands before the law as mere life or bare life, the life of the creature over against the civic life incarnated by Antonio.... Shylock, reduced to a mere 'jot' and bare 'Iewe,' stands shorn of the multiple covenants, laws, and promises, the material and spiritual bequests, that had bound him *as alien* to the civic life and history of Venice through the city's corporate structure and political theology" (96). But as Lupton sees it, Shylock's status, if we might still call it that, as "unnullable least" is strictly correlative to his partial reintegration, one that comes by way of the duke's act of mercy, the benevolent aspect of the sovereign exception. Though he remains a "Jewish *iota* ... that both dots and blots—completes and decompletes—the Christian-civic synthesis embraced by his daughter," Shylock embodies, for Lupton, precisely the sort of "discontented contentment" that accompanies the "provisional and procedural inscription in the polity" that would be institutionalized in liberalism. For Lupton, such a mode of inscription is opposed to "a mystical or ecstatic union sealed by imaginary forms of national identification" (100). It is, thus, Shylock who thereby "emerges as the strongest forerunner of modern citizenship at the close of act 4" (100).

What is staged in Shylock's fate, according to Lupton, is the "death into citizenship" that will eventually be demanded of all members of liberal societies, a mortification that in some sense never ceases. For Lupton, the spectral presence of Shylock at the end of the play exercises its own sort of ethical force, functions as the embodiment of the regulative idea of modern liberalism:

> Shylock's legal and psychological condition at the end of the play demonstrates the extent to which naturalization in a diverse polity not only can but should remain structurally incomplete, maintaining memories of suspended modes of affiliation that never dissolve completely into a new identity. In my reading Shylock undergoes not so much a forced conversion as a nominal or procedural one; his reluctant consent is measured and limited, like the rule of law itself. It is worth asserting that however ambivalent we may feel about Shylock's conversion, there is *nothing tragic* in his destiny. (100–01)

As compelling as I find Lupton's reading, I am not, in the end, persuaded by her claim concerning liberal society's ostensible evacuation of the imaginary forms of identification proper to medieval and early-modern corporate societies, forms that depend, as Marx insisted, on the fetishism of persons grounded in the logic of determinations of reflection. Indeed, my argument is that modern liberal societies largely relocate and restage that dimension in a variety of other scenes and according to new sets of dramaturgical—or better, *liturgical*—practices. And this is, as I understand it, what Marx ultimately meant by proposing that the key to the critique of political economy lay in grasping the displacement of the fetishism of persons by the fetishism of the commodity. The practices and social relations through which the production, exchange, and consumption of commodities would come to be organized—the ostensible subject matter of classical political economy—become the site in which, precisely, new "mystical and ecstatic" unions are sealed. This is what Marx meant with his infamous remarks about the theological, mystical, necromantic, and animistic aspects of life under modern capitalism. In the next lecture I will try to say more about these liturgical practices that mediate the transition from the glorification/valorization of sovereigns—the modes of production of the king's sublime body—to the self-valorization of capital—that is, the shift to new forms of the production of glory, splendor, and valor.

In the end, the question will be what to make—or rather, *what liberal, civil society will make*—of the "unnullable least" that remains of Shylock along his path toward citizenship under the protection of what remains of sovereign power and authority. How much, we might ask, does Shylock's own creaturely flesh now weigh in the balance? Can it be evaluated, reckoned with? How will it be put to work? These are, I think, the questions that Marx will take on in his efforts to understand the secret of the commodity form, a form that required, in his view, the prior emancipation of workers from all traditional affiliations and bonds. What remains of Shylock is, I am suggesting, related to what will become for Marx the *gespenstische Gegenständlichkeit* that emerges at the threshold of the transition from the fetishism of persons—above all, of sovereigns and their sublime, virtually real bodies—to the fetishism of things, a transition marking the reconstitution and organization of the flesh of the social bond.

Notes

1. See Sigmund Freud, "Character and Anal Eroticism," in *The Standard Edition of the Complete Psychological Works of Sigmund Freud*, ed. James Strachey (London: Hogarth, 1981), 9: 169–75.

2. Jacques Derrida, *Specters of Marx: The State of the Debt, the Work of Mourning, and the New International*, trans. Peggy Kamuf (New York: Routledge, 1994). Subsequent page references are made in the text.

3. Rilke uses the formulation in a letter to Lou Andreas-Salomé from March 1, 1912. See *Rainer Maria Rilke / Lou Andreas-Salomé: Briefwechsel*, ed. Ernst Pfeiffer (Frankfurt: Insel, 1989), 266.

4. See my *The Royal Remains: The King's Two Bodies and the Endgames of Sovereignty* (Chicago: University of Chicago Press, 2011).

5. Karl Marx, *Capital: A Critique of Political Economy, Volume 1*, trans. Ben Fowkes (New York: Vintage, 1977), 143; 149 (translation modified). German text is taken from Karl Marx, *Das Kapital: Kritik der politischen Ökonomie, Erster Band* (Berlin: Karl Dietz Verlag, 2008).

6. Ernst Kantorowicz, *The King's Two Bodies: A Study in Medieval Political Theology* (Princeton, NJ: Princeton University Press, 1981), 59 (my emphasis).

7. Slavoj Žižek, *For They Know Not What They Do: Enjoyment as a Political Factor* (London: Verso, 1991), 255.

8. As I've suggested in the preface to these lectures, I understand this surplus carnality in relation to the "little extra life" that, as Foucault argued, is administered by the police—that guardian of the state's splendor—in early-modern societies. See once more, Michel Foucault, *Omnes et Singulatim: Towards a Criticism of "Political Reason,"* Tanner Lectures on Human Values, delivered at Stanford University, October 10, 16, 1979, http://foucault.info/documents/foucault.omnesetsingulatim.en.html, 229–30.

9. Cited in Žižek, *For They Know Not*, 256 (my emphasis). The citation is from Lacan's seminar, "Death and the Interpretation of Desire in *Hamlet*," from 1959. Žižek is above all interested in the mutation of the king's two bodies into what he refers to as "Lenin's two bodies"—that is, how the people comes to be conscripted in the liturgical production of the special stuff of the totalitarian leader and party who—thanks to the logic of determinations of reflection—can offer themselves as the incarnation of objective reason in history. "In so far as the stuff they are made of is ultimately their body, this body again undergoes a kind of transubstantiation; it changes into a bearer of another body within the transient material envelopment" (258).

10. See Marx, *Capital*, 163; *Kapital*, 85.

11. Cited in Max Weber, *The Protestant Ethic and the Spirit of Capitalism*, trans. Talcott Parsons (London: Routledge, 2001), 15.

12. See David Graeber, *Debt: The First 5,000 Years* (Brooklyn, NY: Melville House, 2011).

13. Aristotle, *Politics*, I, 9: 1257–58, trans. Benjamin Jowett, in Richard McKeon, ed., *The Basic Works of Aristotle* (New York: Random House, 1941), 1139.

14. Much of my thinking about avarice developed in the course of a team-taught seminar with Mladen Dolar on the topic at the University of

Chicago, autumn 2013. I am deeply grateful to Mladen and to the seminar participants for numerous insights regarding this strangely virtuous sin.

15. The Freudian view is already prefigured in Paul's conception of the flesh as an amplification of human sentience by what he calls, in Romans 7, "another law . . . which dwells in my members": "I do not understand my own actions. For I do not do what I want, but I do the very thing I hate. Now if I do what I do not want, I agree that the law is good. So then it is no longer I that do it, but sin which dwells within me. For I know that nothing good dwells within me, that is, in my flesh. I can will what is right, but I cannot do it. For I do not do the good I want but the evil I do not want is what I do. Now if I do what I do not want, it is no longer I that do it, but the sin which dwells within me. So I find it to be a law that when I want to do right, evil lies close at hand. For I delight in the law of God, in my inmost self, but I see in my members another law at war with the law of my mind and making me captive to the law of sin which dwells in my members." *The Writings of Saint Paul*, ed. Wayne A. Meeks (New York: W. W. Norton, 1972), 79–80.

16. Shakespeare, *The Merchant of Venice*. *The Riverside Shakespeare*, ed. G. Blakemore Evans (Boston: Houghton Mifflin, 1974). Subsequent line references are made in the text.

17. Aristotle, *Politics*, I, 10: 1255–70 (my emphasis).

18. See Marc Shell, *Money, Language, Thought: Literary and Philosophic Economies from the Medieval to the Modern Era* (Baltimore: Johns Hopkins University Press, 1982), 47. I am grateful to Mar Rosàs Tosas for pointing out the minimal diacritical difference between the two words.

19. The thought of validity without meaning, *Geltung ohne Bedeutung*, is elaborated by Gershom Scholem in his epistolary exchange with his friend, Walter Benjamin, on the meaning of revelation in the works and world of Franz Kafka. I will return to this exchange of letters at the conclusion of the next lecture.

20. The historical and conceptual complexity of this concept, so central to our understanding of the way in which human bodies enter into normative "corporations," is explored in detail in a work to which Kantorowicz noted his own considerable indebtedness, Henri Cardinal de Lubac, *Corpus Mysticum: The Eucharist and the Church in the Middle Ages*, trans. Gemma Simmonds, Richard Price, and Christopher Stephens (Notre Dame, IN: University of Notre Dame Press, 2006).

21. That Antonio initially uses the word "excess" rather than "interest" could perhaps allude to the 1571 definition of usury as interest beyond an acceptable rate, generally pegged at 10 percent. It should also be noted that

among the complaints lodged against usury was that it represented, so to speak, a first instance of a 24/7 economy: interest-bearing capital never sleeps.

22. In a recent essay on the play, Mladen Dolar has argued that, in the end, the Christian offer of mercy effectively outbids the ostensibly Jewish insistence on the letter of the law (in this case, contract law) by infinitizing the debt of the recipient of mercy. As Dolar writes, "the crux of the matter is that mercy, behind the cloak of its generosity ... hinges on a surplus and extortion. Justice is equivalence, the just punishment and reward ... according to the letter. Mercy is the surplus over the letter, over law and justice, not as coerced taking, but as voluntary giving. But the gift indebts, all the more since its terms are not specified, and if they were to be specified this would cease to be mercy. Hence it opens an unspecified debt, a debt with no limits, an infinite debt. One is never worthy of mercy and however much one gives in return, as a response, it is never enough, it can never measure up to the free gift which has no equivalent, not in what one possesses. Hence one has to give what one doesn't possess, which is the Lacanian definition of love—mercy demands its equivalent only in love. Mercy is a usurer which, by not demanding a circumscribed surplus [I am tempted to add *circumcised* surplus] opens an absolute debt. It demands not 'an equal pound of flesh,' but 'an equal pound of soul'— this is why Shylock is granted mercy only on condition that he gives up his creed and converts to Christianity, the religion of love." Mladen Dolar, "The Quality of Mercy Is Not Strained," unpublished manuscript. I am grateful to Dolar for sharing his text with me.

23. A more fully "fleshed out" reading of *Merchant* would, of course, have to take into account the other storyline in the play concerning life, love, and precious metals, namely that of the three caskets. Portia, who, in the guise of Balthazar, "legally" forces Shylock to choose Christian love and mercy over the ostensibly Jewish letter of the law of contract, was herself bound by the letter of an "old testament" with respect to her choice of a husband. According to Freud's reading of the motif of the three caskets, Bassanio's victorious choice of the lead casket—a choice that wins him not only love but also considerable amounts of silver and gold—itself masks a deeper truth concerning wishful disavowals of forced choices. See Sigmund Freud, "The Theme of the Three Caskets," in Strachey, *The Standard Edition*, 12: 289–302. What he characterizes as Bassanio's unpersuasive—and seemingly forced, *gezwungen*— "glorification of lead"—represents, for Freud, an acknowledgment of the ineluctability of death. We will return to the subject matter (both with and without hyphen) of glory and glorification in the second lecture.

24. Carl Schmitt, *Hamlet or Hecuba: The Intrusion of the Time into the Play*, trans. David Pan and Jennifer Rust (New York: Telos, 2009). Subsequent

page references are made in the text. Derrida strangely omits this work from his reflections on the hauntological nexus linking Shakespeare and Marx.

25. Against this background, figures such as the Earl of Essex and Walter Raleigh—two examples of what Schmitt sees as a new elite of *adventure capitalists*—might be seen as typologically related to the figure of Antonio in *Merchant*.

26. See Ben Nelson, *The Idea of Usury: From Tribal Brotherhood to Universal Otherhood* (Chicago: University of Chicago Press, 1969). *Hamlet* and *Merchant* are each in their own way caught up in the turbulence of this "conversion." In this context see also Dietrich Schwanitz, *Das Shylock-Syndrom: Oder Die Dramaturgie der Barberei* (Frankfurt: Eichborn, 1997).

27. Here Derrida seems to be endorsing what he elsewhere calls into question, namely the translation of the German word *Leib* as "flesh"—*chair*—or at the very least as the uncanny combination of flesh and phenomenality. See, for example, his *On Touching—Jean-Luc Nancy*, trans. Christine Irizarry (Stanford, CA: Stanford University Press, 2005). I will return to the question of adequacy of the terms *flesh, chair,* and *Leib* in the final section of this volume.

28. Jane Bennett, *Vibrant Matter: A Political Ecology of Things* (Durham, NC: Duke University Press, 2010), 112–13. Subsequent page references are made in the text.

29. Stanley Corngold translates the title as "The Worry of the Father of the Family" in his edition of *Kafka's Selected Stories* (New York: W. W. Norton, 2007), 72–73.

30. See my *The Royal Remains*, 83–86.

31. Franz Rosenzweig's account of Jewish singularity in *The Star of Redemption* more or less turns into positive—though uncanny—features the negative attributes that Richard Wagner attributes to Jews in his famous essay, *Judaism and Music*. I discuss these matters in my *On the Psychotheology of Everyday Life: Reflections on Freud and Rosenzweig* (Chicago: University of Chicago Press, 2001).

32. Franz Kafka, *Beim Bau der chinesischen Mauer und andere Schriften aus dem Nachlaß* (Frankfurt: Fischer, 1992), 235–36.

33. David Nirenberg, *Anti-Judaism: The Western Tradition* (New York: W. W. Norton, 2013), 2 (my emphasis). Subsequent page references are made in the text.

34. As Portia says to Gratiano, who admits to having given his ring to Balthazar's clerk, "You were to blame, I must be plain with you,/To part so slightly with your wive's first gift,/A thing stuck on with oaths upon your finger,/And so riveted with faith unto your flesh" (5.1.166–69). Gratiano, for his part, had just begrudgingly expressed his regret to Nerissa for breaking

his oath by means of further sworn testimony that links the "hoop of gold" to the flesh of the genitals and the heart: "By yonder moon I swear you do me wrong;/In faith, I gave it to the judge's clerk./Would he were gelt that had it, for my part,/Since you do take it, love, so much to heart" (5.1. 142–45).

35. See Samuel Beckett, *Worstward Ho*, in *Three Novels by Samuel Beckett* (New York: Grove Press, 1996), 106. Kittler borrowed the term *Aufschreibesystem* from the memoirs of Daniel Paul Schreber, a text on the basis of which Freud wrote one of his five case studies and to which Jacques Lacan dedicated a year-long seminar. My own study of the case, *My Own Private Germany: Daniel Paul Schreber's Secret History of Modernity* (Princeton, NJ: Princeton University Press, 1996), lays much of the groundwork for the current project. Its focus is Schreber's experience of investiture crisis, of the failure of the symbolic processes of social inscription that then return in delusions that literalize and concretize those processes as the operations of actual machinery in and on the body, operations that seem to transform Schreber into a creature of intensified flesh marked as both feminine and Jewish.

36. Julia Lupton, *Citizen-Saints: Shakespeare and Political Theology* (Chicago: University of Chicago Press, 2005). Subsequent page references are made in the text.

37. In his own earlier appeal to the binding force of contracts, Shylock rubs the duke's nose in the darker side of Venetian commercial society:

> What judgment shall I dread, doing no wrong?
> You have among you many a purchas'd slave,
> Which, like your asses and your dogs and mules,
> You use in abject and slavish parts
> Because you bought them. Shall I say to you
> 'Let them be free! Marry them to your heirs!
> Why sweat they under burthens? Let their beds
> Be made as soft as yours, and let their palates
> Be season'd with such viands'? You will answer
> 'The slaves are ours!' So do I answer you:
> The pound of flesh which I demand of him
> Is dearly bought, as mine, and I will have it.
> If you deny me, fie upon your law!
> There is no force in the decrees of Venice.
> I stand for judgment. Answer—shall I have it? (4.1.89–103)

38. Dolar offers a concise formulation of this excess: "Sovereignty is based on exception, the sovereign can suspend the law, and mercy is precisely the

exception to the law, it is beyond law, beyond the contract, the reciprocal bond, as a surplus depending on the caprice of the sovereign, who can freely grant it or not beyond any obligation. Mercy is the state of exception at its purest." Cited again from Dolar's unpublished manuscript, "The Quality of Mercy Is Not Strained."

Lecture 2

I

The shift from the fetishism of persons—above all that of the singularly representative person, the *Staatsperson* or sovereign—to that of things takes place in the context of a long process of secularization that ostensibly drains the shared institutions of the public sphere of transcendental resources of legitimation; it is a process that, so the story goes, disenchants the world more generally, and evacuates from all aspects of life the last vestiges of otherworldly, animating spirits, be they divine or demonic. The critical thrust of Marx's theory of the fetishism of the commodity has been to demonstrate just how wrong this story is. Max Weber, who introduced the concept of the disenchantment of the world, formulated his own critical skepticism on this matter with the concept of the *spirit*—indeed, we might say *specter*—of capitalism. For Weber, the Reformation contributed to the disenchantment of the world—think of the devaluation of priestly sacraments—at the price of injecting into it a proliferation of harassing voices that never cease to remind the faithful to keep busy: essentially, never to cease to economize, and all *for the greater glory of God*. As we shall see, Weber's argument will be that the Protestant Ethic effectively transforms work itself into a sort of obsessive-compulsive *doxology*, the liturgical praise or glorification of God.

It is, I would suggest, Marx's labor theory of value that first opens the horizon against which Weber's argument unfolds. For Marx, however, it is not that secular society remains secretly bound to transcendence but, rather, that our ostensibly disenchanted world vibrates with a *surplus of immanence* that profoundly informs our dealings in the world, makes us into "busy-bodies" trying to discharge an excess of demand—an excessive *Arbeitsanforderung*, to use Freud's locution for the pressure of the drives—that keeps us driven even when we are ostensibly "idling," keeps us *neg*-otiating even in the midst of *otium*. Recalling T. J. Clark's characterization of modernism as "turning on the impossibility of transcendence," we might say that moderns keep obsessively *turning* or *spinning* in one fashion or another, and do so ever more according to the rhythm of "24/7." This is what Marx means when he claims that although the commodity "appears at first sight an extremely obvious, trivial thing," if looked at in the right way it shows itself to be "a very strange thing, abounding in metaphysical subtleties and theological niceties (*ein sehr vertracktes Ding ... voll metaphysischer Spitzfindigkeit und theologischer Mucken*)."[1] But it is not so much *we* who continue to engage in metaphysics and theology but, rather, our *busy bodies*. For Marx, it is commodity, and so value-producing labor—rather than labor as such or a religiously inflected work ethic—that is fundamentally doxological. Both the Marxist critique of political economy and the Freudian engagement with libidinal economy are, although at rather different levels, ultimately in the business of intervening in precisely this *busy-ness*, this uncanny mode of stress. The Freudo-Marxist concept of stress I am developing here is no doubt continuous with other approaches to ideology and efforts to isolate its "sublime object."[2] I hope, though, that by focusing on the afterlife of political theology in secular modernity—essentially, its mutation into political economy—it will be possible to shed new light on these matters.

As I've already noted, this surplus of immanence "at work" in the commodity is of a radically different nature from the vibrant matter, actants, and assemblages of the new post-humanist materialisms. The "animation" at issue for Marx is something that is ultimately deadening—or rather, *undeadening*—for human beings, something that drives them while holding them in place, a condition Walter Benjamin once referred to as "petrified unrest," *erstarrte Unruhe*.[3] For the new materialists, by contrast, "vibrant matter" is the very promise of a new sense of aliveness for a "new-ish self." Marx's critical intervention aims at a deanimation of this undeadness while the new materialisms seek to open human life to the "agency" of nonhuman material assemblages. What both approaches share, of course, is the very question as to the nature of human flourishing and the sense of urgency of this question. The fundamental difference may just be that the Marxist project—along with that of psychoanalysis—operates within a Judeo-Christian tradition for which the *creatureliness* of human life (I will have more to say about this term) is inseparable from being subject to normative pressures of various kinds, the generic source of which is our life with language. Life lived under normative pressure is a life suffused with questions of responsibility, answerability, and obligation. Such questions would, in turn, seem to draw us inevitably into the orbit of the semantic field of *debt*, of what we owe to others, to society, and to ourselves. The new materialisms, for their part, take up more "animist" traditions and habits of thought that aim to disperse the normativity proper to human orders of meaning into self-perpetuating patterns of organized matter (we are back, perhaps, at the difference between the Jewish and the "newish"). It is no doubt for this reason that the figure that keeps emerging as a key point of contestation in these debates is Spinoza, the great Jewish thinker of self-perpetuating being or *conatus* grasped under the heading of an *Ethics*. But that is a story that takes us beyond the scope of the present inquiry. I would simply note that in his final book, *Moses and Monotheism*, Freud tried to give an account of what he took to be the obsessive-compulsive *conatus* of Judaism itself.[4]

II

Before we can say more about the mutation of fetishism in the transition from political theology to political economy, we need to get clear about the nature of the disavowal—of the "unknown knowns"—at work in the first form, the fetishism of persons. What is it that is both affirmed and denied in the fetishistic activity—above all in the liturgical labor that, so to speak, congeals in the virtual reality of the king's second, sublime body? It is not, I think, simply the knowledge that the sovereign is really, after all, just another mortal being and that his kingship is just a fiction or social construction; it is not, that is, the knowledge of the "trick" of the *Reflexionsbestimmung* noted by Marx—that is, that the king is a king because his subjects treat him as a king (and not because he is already king). Bringing together the political theological problematic of the state of exception and the psychoanalytic concept of the partial object, Slavoj Žižek offers a concise formulation of what, I think, is really at stake in the fantasmatic physiology of the royal personage:

> The emergence of this sublime body is . . . linked to the illegal violence that founds the reign of law: once the reign of law is established, it rotates in its vicious circle, "posits its presuppositions," by means of foreclosing its origins; yet for the synchronous order of law to function, *it must be supported by some "little piece of the real" which, within the space of law, holds the place of its founding / foreclosed violence*—the sublime body is precisely this "little piece of the real" which "stops up" and thus conceals the void of the law's vicious circle.[5]

For Žižek, the "little piece of the real"—what Lacan famously called the *objet a*—holds the place of the *anarchic* dimension of the space of juridico-political normativity. To put it in terms I have used in earlier work, what I am calling the "flesh"—the stuff out of which the sovereign's sublime body is composed—emerges out of the entanglement of the somatic and normative pressures that constitute creaturely life. By "creaturely" I do not simply mean nature, living things, sentient beings, or even what the religiously minded would think of as the entirety of the "vibrant matter" of God's creation—*deus sive natura*—but, rather, a dimension specific to human existence, albeit one that seems to push thinking in the direction of theology. It signifies a mode of *exposure* that distinguishes human beings from other kinds of life: not simply to the elements or to the fragility, vulnerability, and precariousness of our mortal, finite lives, but also to an ultimate *lack of foundation* for the historical forms of life in which human life unfolds. This is what Žižek means when he speaks of the law's rotation in a vicious circle; it is a rotation around a gap that opens at the jointure of the somatic and the normative, life and forms of life. This gap, this crucial *missing piece of the world* to which we are ultimately and intimately exposed as social beings of language, is one that we thus first *acquire* by way of our initiation—Heidegger would say *thrownness*—into these forms of life, not one already there in the bare fact of our biological being. We could say that the vulnerability of biological life becomes potentiated, amplified, by way of exposure to the radical contingency of the forms of life that constitute the space of meaning within which human life unfolds, and that it is only through such anarchic "potentiation" that we take on the flesh of creaturely life.

Creatureliness is thus a dimension not so much of biological as *ontological vulnerability*, a vulnerability that permeates human being as that whose essence it is to exist in forms of life that are, in turn, contingent, contested, susceptible to breakdown—in a word, *historical*.[6] The normative pressure that suffuses human life always includes an excess, a "too much" of pressure that indexes the contingency of the norms in question. We are not simply answerable to one another according to the relevant norms of our social being—that is, as recognized bearers of normative statuses; we are also always subject to surplus or supplementary "negotiations" that, to use Žižek's terms, orbit around the void of the law's vicious circle and concern the lack of any ultimate grounding or authorization of those normative statuses. It is these surplus negotiations that *give flesh* to a form of life, infuse the bindingness of its norms with a dimension of psychosomatic passion. To put it somewhat differently, what "covers" the dimension of risk proper to our ontological vulnerability is the subject-matter elaborated by individual and social fantasy as *formations of the flesh*. Our investiture with normative statuses—this is what Lacan meant by entering the "symbolic"—always involves a dimension of libidinal investment of the subject and by the subject. We never simply just have an entitlement or "office"; whether we like it or not, we *enjoy it*, and this enjoyment is the fleshy stuff that our fantasies are made of.

It would be more accurate to say that the gap at the jointure of the somatic and the normative is always multiple and layered. It concerns the lack of ultimate foundations of the normative order, its lack of anchorage in, its nondeducibility from, the great chain of being. But it also concerns the jointure itself: the *missing link* between the somatic and the normative, a sort of blind spot at the point at which the latter "emerges," as one now tends to put it, from the former. Finally, there is the gap immanent to biological life itself, the point at which, at least in human being, it reaches a limit that requires supplementation by cultural prosthetics. The overlapping of these multiple gaps provides the site of the fleshly surplus enjoyed by humans as distinct from other living things.[7]

The political theology of sovereignty implies, among other things, that the sovereign incarnates and so represents this vulnerability for his subjects, and thereby allows them in some sense to avoid the void. It is the "business" of the sovereign, that is, to *cover the void* in two fundamental senses: to veil it with his or her glorious body; but also, on the basis of that very glory, to stand surety for it as for a primordial debt. The royal flesh—and this is the essence of the fetishism of persons—marks a kind of wound or tear in the fabric of being by covering it in these two senses, which means that the royal virtues always, at some level, serve to sustain the virtual reality of the sublime, royal flesh. My concern continues to be the ways in which what had been, to a large extent, localizable in early modernity, invested within the sphere and "physiology" of the traditional master or sovereign, disperses into the texture of the social space at large—into the life of the People—and so into the very soul of the modern citizen-subject. Marx's theory of the fetishism of the commodity is, I am suggesting, above all a contribution to an understanding of that process of dispersion. For Marx it is, above all, political economy that, as it were, *inherits the royal remains*, the dispersed and now "popularized" flesh of the king's sublime body in its function as glorious guarantor covering the missing link at the "anthropogenetic" knotting of the somatic and the normative. Political economy circumscribes the domain in which the production process not only of the wealth of the nation but also of the People's Two Bodies is managed, kept in business/busy-ness. The theory of the fetishism of the commodity serves as a kind of warning not to lose sight of the *gespenstische Gegenständlichkeit* of the People's second, sublime body, the virtually real product of commodity-producing labor. The labor theory of value is, I am suggesting, ultimately a theory of the production of the spectral flesh of the sovereign People, a process that depends, we might say, on the exchange of a (decapitated) head for an invisible hand in ceaseless motion. This motion—the imperative of capital accumulation—is, I am arguing, the political economic version of what Žižek characterized as the law's vicious circle, its rotation around an anarchic kernel, a foreclosed origin. Another way of putting it would be to say that political economy converts the fundamental dynamic of the drive into a *debt drive*, a ceaseless effort to redeem or indemnify a lack at the origin of the normative order to which we are, so to speak, joined at the hip.[8]

III

We can think of the king's sublime body as the congelation of a certain kind of labor, as the substance of the "royal value" produced by that labor. The elaboration of this value takes place, above all, by way of the liturgical practices—*liturgy* (from *laos*, "people," and *ergon,* "work") just means "public work"—in and through which the sovereign is acclaimed and sustained as sovereign. Such practices performatively enact the *Reflexionsbestimmung* of sovereignty noted by Marx. By, as it were, *fleshing out* the conceptual operation of that determination of reflection this work produces a virtual real *that can take on a life of its own.* This is why insight into the conceptual operation—the structure of a determination of reflection—fails to produce the critical effects one might expect. This was, at bottom, Freud's insight with respect to the therapeutic effects of insight into the logic of an analysand's symptoms by way of interpretation and analytic construction; for the most part, these effects simply fail to materialize. They fail, that is, as interventions into the relevant materiality, the subject-matter at issue. The "business" of a neurosis—the specific mode of *busy-body-ness* that constitutes it—requires an intervention into the labor process itself along with the quasi-somatic, quasi-normative pressures informing it, something that Freud for good reason called *working through.*

Over the last decades there has been a resurgence of interest in the concept of liturgy; not so long ago, a special issue of the journal *Telos* even proposed the notion of a new "liturgical turn" in political and social theory.[9] A good deal of this new work has concerned itself with ways to reanimate liturgical practices heretofore relegated to the religious sphere, to find in liturgical traditions resources of resistance against the flatness of a secular life artificially pumped up by what are characterized as the pseudo-liturgies of capitalist modernity. Among the more recent contributions to this literature, Giorgio Agamben's *The Kingdom and the Glory: For a Theological Genealogy of Economy and Government,* stands out for a number of reasons. First, he avoids the simple and, I think, too facile opposition between ostensibly genuine and patently fake liturgical practices by focusing on a dimension that both attempt to cultivate, namely *glory.* He furthermore situates his investigation against the background of what he, like so many other contemporary thinkers, sees as the global, neoliberal absorption of political thought and action by forms of economic rationality and behavior. What Agamben develops under the heading of the "archaeology of glory" turns out to be a rich resource for the analysis of this development. Finally and more generally, the "liturgical turn" allows us to revisit various questions previously explored under the heading of ideology. Ideology is a concept that, I think, still remains too attached to the ideational, to thought and image, to the ways in which people make sense of the world, while the concept of liturgy focuses our attention on the practices in and through which they form and consolidate the value—and so, at some level, the valor, the glory, the splendor—of their social being.

The concern with the fate of politics in modernity is not new. Weber, Schmitt, Arendt, Adorno, even Heidegger argued that forms of the economic-technical administration and management of life were becoming hegemonic in the modern world, that *Homo economicus* was coming to fully displace or absorb *Homo politicus*. Some of the names of this hegemony—names signaling an ostensibly post-political age—are familiar: Arendt called it "the social"; Adorno spoke of "the administered world"; Heidegger used a nearly untranslatable word, *das Gestell* (sometimes translated as "Enframing"); more recently, Alain Badiou has coined the term "democratic materialism." Agamben, for his part, follows Michel Foucault's lead by framing his investigation as one pertaining to the forms of "governmentality" that ostensibly supplant the juridico-political field of sovereignty in modernity.

Foucault formulated this transformation in different ways, most notably as the displacement of sovereign forms of power by a series of institutions and practices that did not so much reign or rule juridical subjects as manage and administer the lives of individuals and populations. At least for a time, Foucault grouped these practices under two headings: the "anatomo-politics of the human body" and the "biopolitics of the population."[10] Regarding the former, Foucault speaks of a disciplinary physics of power that supplants what had once been thought of as the magical effects of the king's touch: "The *body of the king*, with *its strange material and physical presence*, with the force that he himself deploys or transmits to some few others, is at the opposite extreme of this new physics of power . . .: a physics of a relational and multiple power, which has its maximum intensity not in the person of the king, but in the bodies that can be individualized by these relations."[11] With respect to the biopolitical administration of populations, the body of the king figures equally as Foucault's key point of departure. In his lectures at the Collège de France in 1975–76, for example, he opens his account of the post-revolutionary "embourgeoisement" of the nation-state (and so the emergence of the defining sphere of modern political economy, civil or bourgeois society) with remarks that could have been taken from Kantorowicz's *The King's Two Bodies*. What makes a nation, he writes, is the fact that its members "all have a certain individual relationship—both juridical and physical—with the real, living, and bodily person of the king. It is the body of the king, in his *physical-juridical* relationship with each of his subjects, that creates the body of the nation."[12] It is precisely the dispersal and reorganization of this "physical-juridical relationship"—of this royally representative jointure of the somatic and the normative—that is of interest to Foucault.

What is crucial to keep in mind here—and I think that this is what Foucault often fails to do—is that this hyphenation of the physical and the juridical "secretes" a new element or dimension—that of the flesh.[13] Foucault is, in a word, touching here on what I have characterized as a metamorphosis of the King's Two Bodies into the People's Two Bodies, and the emergence of new forms of power adapted to the management of the latter, of what is *more* than the body in the bodies of its citizen-subjects. Foucault's investigations lead us to conclude that the threshold of modernity is marked by the "massification" of the physical-juridical flesh of the king, its dispersion into populations that for that very reason must be placed in the care of biopolitical administration. What this means is that whenever Foucault speaks about the object of biopolitics—man as species, populations—he is also, although never explicitly and perhaps never even intentionally, addressing the fate in modernity of the royal remains of political theology, the dimension of the flesh in its new, modern form: *masses of busy bodies*. Biopolitics is always mass politics in the sense of dealing with the massive presence of a sublime object—the virtual reality of a fleshy mass—now circulating in and agitating the life of the People, which means, in turn, that political economy, the domain that Foucault came to see as a central site of biopolitical administration, acquires a certain sacramental dimension, the aspect of a "mass." It is no surprise, then, that Marx would discover "metaphysical subtleties and theological niceties" in the midst of our life with commodities.

In another series of lectures concerned with the shift from classical sovereignty to biopolitical forms of administration—from *reigning* to *governing*—Foucault writes:

> When it became possible not only to introduce population into the field of economic theory, but also into economic practice, when it became possible to introduce into the analysis of wealth this new subject, this new *subject-object*, with its demographic aspects, but also with the aspect of the specific role of producers and consumers, owners and non-owners, those who create profit and those who take it, when the entry of this *subject-object*, of population, became possible within the analysis of wealth, with all its disruptive effects in the field of economic reflection and practice, then I think the result was *that one ceased analyzing wealth and a new domain of knowledge, political economy, was opened up*.[14]

Again, what Foucault is saying here is, I am suggesting, that the subject matter of political economy includes an *un-economic subject-matter*, the disruptive force of which derives, precisely, from its uncanny, spectral materiality, its status as *gespenstische Gegenständlichkeit*.

There is another passage in this same series of lectures that helps to clarify a crucial aspect of Foucault's engagement with the subject-matter of political economy or what he refers to as its "subject-object." Addressing the semantic history of the institution "police," Foucault recalls that beginning in the seventeenth century, it refers broadly "to the set of means by which the state's forces can be increased while preserving the state in good order" (313)—that is, to the array of matters we would today group under the heading of "public policy." He goes on to note the use, in various sources, of a "rather strange word for describing the object of the police," namely *splendor*: "What is splendor? It is both the visible beauty of the order and the brilliant, radiating manifestation of a force. Police therefore is in actual fact the *art of the state's splendor* as visible order and manifest force" (314; my emphasis). One might say that the fundamental charge—or better, *surcharge*—of police/policy and the science it would become—in German, *Polizeiwissenschaft*—was the protection and administration not so much of the *Herrschaft* of the state as its *Herrlichkeit*, not so much its rule as its glory. Police, public policy, and, finally, political economy, were charged, that is, with securing and managing the substance of the social bond in its newfound glory as—or rather, as an immanent surplus to—the wealth of nations.

IV

Before turning to Agamben, I'd like to mention very briefly the important work done by Joseph Vogl in addressing the historical shifts of concern here. In an essay on the modern desire for/of the state, "Staatsbegehren: Zur Epoche der Policey," Vogl for the most part cleaves closely to Foucault's conceptual frame in tracking the shift in German political discourse from the early-modern sovereign reign over juridical subjects to the modern governmental project of "policing" the lives of individuals and populations.[15] He borrows from Kantorowicz's work to characterize the split introduced into the populations of modern states as one between two bodies: a juridical one that remains within the discursive orbit of law and rights, and an ostensibly empirical one that becomes increasingly the subject matter of a political anthropology whose forms of knowledge emerge out of the administrative practices of *Policey*.

> Alongside questions of natural right and reason, alongside the representation and limitation of sovereign power and the abstract body of the State-Person [*Staatsperson*], there emerged a materiality and reality of the state that was put together from the directions of diverse forces and an aggregation of self-interested individuals; [this new materiality] could not simply be systematized by way of juridical principles and laws: over against the force of law and the sovereign personage there emerged a physics of the state's forces. (611–12)

This Foucauldian assessment is, I think, all perfectly right, up to a point. What is finally missed is, I think, a dimension that escapes the conceptual grasp of both juridical rationality and the new anthropology, of both law and "physics." It is the dimension that Foucault himself points to with the notion of *splendor*, namely something in the empirical body that is *more* than the body, a surplus that, though it emerges on the basis of a symbolic investiture, of an "official" inscription in a symbolic order, cannot be simply equated with the symbolic fiction of office, let alone with the empirical body of its incumbent. What this account misses is the impossible dimension of public policy and risk management, the demand to cover what I have characterized as the ontological vulnerability proper to creaturely life. What ultimately comes to cover that dimension of risk is, as we have seen, a special, immaterial stuff elaborated by individual and social fantasy as formations of the flesh. These formations are to a very large extent sustained by the liturgical dimension—the "public work"—enacted in what otherwise appears as the policing of empirical bodies and forces. The "public work" in the *Policey* aims, that is, at what is in the body that is *more* than the body. This dual aspect of "police work" will, I am arguing, find its crucial modern form in the dual aspect of labor articulated in Marx's labor theory of value.

Vogl, however, goes a long way to recuperate this loss by emphasizing the role played by aesthetic theory and practice—his main point of reference is Schiller—in, as it were, covering or filling "the gap between sovereign representation and empirical state body" (613), in securing the jointure of norms and living bodies at a moment of profound social reorganization. In Vogl's view, around 1800 *Policey* and aesthetics—along with an emergent political economy—ultimately join hands in trying to come to grips with the "abstract material" that, as we have seen with respect to David's *Death of Marat*, began to come into view as a quasi-autonomous dimension in the visual field of an incipient modernism. If, as Vogl suggests, Schiller's aesthetic theory and practice are born "aus dem Geist der Policey" (618), it is crucial to emphasize that what infuses—what *surcharges*—the *Geist* or spirit of police work with its particular passion is the spectral aspect of its object and the need to extract from it the splendor of the state. If there is indeed a form of empiricism at work here, it is a peculiar one: call it the empiricism of the flesh as the virtually real dimension—as the fundamental *subject-matter*—of public policy. This still basically Foucauldian account of the emergence of *Policey* corresponds, in the terms of Jacques Lacan's discourses, to a displacement of the "discourse of the Master" by that of the "discourse of the University."[16] In the discourse of the Master, the subject-matter of the social bond serves to sustain/entertain the Master in his sovereign glory and nourish the king's sublime metabolism—his two bodies; while in the discourse of the University, it becomes the "subject-object" of an administrative-managerial paradigm charged with optimizing its potential (one might recall, in this context, Malte Laurids Brigge's visit to the Salpêtrière). Over the course of the eighteenth and nineteenth centuries, *Policey* effectively yielded to the regime of political economy as the primary locus of the production of splendor.

V

Agamben's researches aim at providing what the subtitle of his study refers to as a "theological genealogy of economy and government."[17] Foucault rightly grasped that what characterized the modern period was the supplementation and partial supplanting of sovereignty by forms of what he called "governmentality," central to which was, as we have seen, political economy. What he failed to see, however, was just how deep the theological roots of the semantic field of *oikonomia* go:

> the fact that ... the Foucauldian genealogy of governmentality can be extended and moved back in time, right up to the point at which we are able to identify in God himself, through the elaboration of the Trinitarian paradigm, the origin of the notion of an economical government of men and the world, does not discredit his hypotheses, but rather confirms their historical core to the very extent to which it details and corrects their historico-chronological exposition. (111)

It is not first in the early-modern period that the sovereign begins to *reign* as the provider of general, universal, and simple laws, rather than *govern* in the pastoral sense of providing for the individual and special needs of the people—tasks assumed by new forms and agents of knowledge-power; this difference between what in the theological tradition is referred to as *general* and *special providence* is, Agamben claims, the very signature of the Christian dispensation from the start and forms the basis for what he refers to as the "bipolar machine" of power in the West. Among the terms of that bipolarity, whose constantly changing articulations he sees as constitutive of the history of politics in the West, Agamben lists Sovereignty/Administration-Management, Law/Order-Police, Constituent Power/Constituted Power, and Legitimacy/Legality.

Much of the book is dedicated to reconstructing (in at times overwhelming detail) efforts by the Church Fathers to elaborate the

Trinitarian paradigm of this machine, to guarantee conceptually the unity in difference of the Father qua transcendent substance or Being of God, on the one hand, and the Son understood as the *visible hand* of God's redemptive action in the world, on the other. The details of these efforts, along with those of the Monarchist, Arian, and various Gnostic challenges they were meant to overcome, need not detain us here.[18] They largely serve to prepare the reader for Agamben's most significant insight—namely that the pole of the machine associated with governing, managing, "economizing," has, as Foucault said of the police at the beginning of the seventeenth century, largely been dedicated to the cultivation of splendor, glory, *Herrlichkeit*.

Over the course of his "archaeology of glory," Agamben draws on the work of several twentieth-century scholars, all of whom to a greater or lesser extent home in on the intimate relation of liturgical doxologies—the ritual praise and glorification of God that constitutes so much of the cultic activity of the Church—and the acclamations that have historically accompanied the investiture of rulers, whether ancient emperors, Christian kings, or, closer to the historical experience of some of those same scholars, the German *Führer*. (As Agamben reminds us, Nazi Germany produced some of the most famous acclamations in the modern period, most notably *"Heil, Hitler"* and *"Ein Reich, Ein Volk, Ein Führer."*) Among them are Carl Schmitt, Erik Peterson, and Ernst Kantorowicz. What this archeology turns up is, as Agamben puts it, an archaic sphere in which religious and juridical action and speech become indistinguishable, a sphere he had explored up to this point with respect to the semantic field of the sacred. "If we now," he writes, "call 'glory' the uncertain zone in which acclamations, ceremonies, liturgies, and insignia operate, we will see a field of research open before us that is equally relevant and, at least in part, as yet unexplored" (188). This field is framed by two fundamental questions: first, Why does power—heavenly or earthly—need glory? and second, What are the historical modes and relations of the production, circulation, and consumption of glory?

Perhaps the most important source in Agamben's efforts to get this new field off the ground is Erik Peterson's 1935 book *The Book of Angels: Their Place and Meaning in the Liturgy*.[19] Peterson argues that the liturgy—the people's work—that makes up the holy Mass is best understood as the Church's striving to participate in the hymnic glorification of God—the doxologies—that, for Peterson, constitute the very being of the angels—or at least the ones that truly matter for the Mass (all angelologies articulate a complex division of labor that need not detain us here):

> Their authentic being is not grounded in their immobility but in their movement, which they manage with the beating of those wings that Isaiah first describes with an unmatched power of perception. To this beating of wings ... there corresponds a distinctive gushing forth in word, in call, in song, of the Holy, Holy, Holy. In other words, the authentic being of these angels is grounded in this overflow into word and song, in this phenomenon. (137–38)

It is for this reason that knowledge of God—*theology*—culminates in praise of God—that is, in liturgical doxology. "For of what use," he continues, "are all the virtues of the angels, if their praise of God, their most authentic life, that for which alone they exist, *that through which their innermost form of being is set to vibrating* [das, wodurch ihre innere Seinsform in Schwingungen gerät], is not attainable by human beings?" (138; my emphasis).[20] What Peterson above all emphasizes is the public and, so, fundamentally political character of the cultic activity—of the doxological labor—aimed at reproducing the frequencies that constitute the "vibrant matter" of angelic being.

Peterson will ultimately want to claim that the peculiar theopolitical dimension of the liturgy elevates the Church above all political theology by, precisely, appropriating the core political dimension of doxologies, their resemblance to acclamations of rulers. By taking part in a heavenly worship—one sustained by angelic doxologies—the earthly Church converts political theological acclamation—Peterson personally witnessed the new efflorescence of such acclamations in Nazi Germany—into theo-political glorification:

> Characteristic for this worship in heaven is the way in which political and religious symbolic expressions are thoroughly intermingled, which is shown most clearly in the resemblance of the doxologies to acclamations. That the heavenly worship described in Revelation has an original relationship to the political sphere is explained by the fact that the apostles left the earthly Jerusalem, which was both a political and a cultic center, in order to turn toward the heavenly Jerusalem, which is both a city and royal court, and yet also a temple and cult site. With this is connected the further point: that the Church's anthem transcends national anthems, as the Church's language transcends all other languages.... Finally, it is to be noted that this eschatological transcending has as its ultimate result the fact that the entire cosmos is incorporated into its praise. (116)[21]

Ernst Kantorowicz published his own study of ritual acclamations immediately after the war and some ten years before the publication of *The King's Two Bodies*. The study, *Laudes Regiae: A Study in Liturgical Acclamations and Medieval Ruler Worship*, focuses on the history of a particular acclamation—it begins with the phrase, *Christus vincit, Christus regnat, Christus imperat*—central to Carolingian political theology.[22] As Agamben's discussion of this earlier study strongly suggests, it could be seen as a first attempt to grasp the nature of the labor that would congeal into the sublime flesh of the king's royal physiology. This comes across, above all, in the treatment of the coronation of Charlemagne in Rome. Regarding this rite of royal investiture, Kantorowicz argues that the *laudes* are essentially constative utterances lacking in performative force *and yet somehow crucial*:

> The laudes acclamation, representing the recognition of the king's legitimacy, was an accessory manifestation, impressive by its

festal and solemn character, *but not indispensable;* for legally the liturgical acclaim *added no new element of material power* which the king had not already received earlier by his election and coronation. . . . By means of this chant, the Church professed and publically espoused the king in a solemn form. However, *the weight of this profession or espousal cannot be measured by legal standards.* (*Laudes,* 83; cited in Agamben, 191; my emphasis)

As I have been suggesting, the *weight* at issue is that of the flesh, this virtually real element that enters into the composition of the king's sublime body. The *laudes,* then, are king-creating powers of a special sort—those that, to paraphrase Marx once more, flesh out the *Reflexionsbestimmung* of the being of the king and thereby "cover" it, gloriously secure it, or, to use more recent economic terminology, *securitize* it. Kantorowicz seems to suggest that the vibrant matter of this flesh is ultimately composed of, or at least transferred to, the king by way of the sonorous mass of acclaiming voices: "The shouts of the Romans and the laudes, as they then followed one after the other without a break, seem to have formed one single tumultuous outburst of voices in which it is idle to seek the particular cry which was 'constitutive' and legally effective" (*Laudes,* 84; cited in Agamben, 192). We might say, then, that what Kantorowicz later elaborated under the heading of the King's Second Body is a *sublimate* of just such a sonorous mass, a *congelation of its vibrant doxological matter.*[23]

VI

Agamben's insight is that there is no political theology of sovereignty without a theological economy of glory, no constitution of *Herrschaft* without the doxological production of *Herrlichkeit*—no *Herrschaft* that is not, at some level, "entertained," *unterhalten,* by *Herrlichkeit.* Agamben argues, in effect, that what might at first

appear to be a superstructural feature of a ruling state apparatus
is, essentially, its *libidinal economic base*, one that produces and
shapes the glorious flesh of the social bond. It involves, as we have
seen, a mode of production organized according to the circular logic
of determinations of reflection. To put it in terms of what we might
characterize, by way of an allusion to Freud, as *the economic problem of Christianism*, we could say: We glorify God because he is
glorious; the glory that God's creatures owe to God and produce
through cultic praise is already an essential attribute of God; the
earth is full of the glory that the faithful must return to God by way
of doxologies. This work would thus appear to be a mode of God's
own self-glorification, a peculiar sort of divine auto-affection that
makes use of creaturely life as its instrument or tool. Paraphrasing
Karl Barth's efforts to capture the paradoxical logic of doxological
labor, Agamben writes, "The circularity of glory here attains its
ontological formulation: becoming free for the glorification of God
means to understand oneself as constituted, in one's very being,
by the glory with which we celebrate the glory that allows us to
celebrate it" (215). One begins to sense the obsessional pattern and
rhythm here, doxology's resemblance to what Freud characterized
as the self-amplifying dynamic of the superego (the key, for Freud,
to the economic problem of masochism). At least in the context of
an obsessional neurosis, the ego is, in some sense, under constant
pressure to live for the greater glory of the superego, to "fatten"
its status as *Über-ich*, which might indeed be better translated as
surplus-ego. Agamben summarizes the dynamic as an embedded
series of paradoxes:

> Glory is the exclusive property of God for eternity, and will
> remain eternally identical in him, such that nothing and no one
> can increase or diminish it; and yet, glory is glorification, which is
> to say, something that all creatures always incessantly owe to God
> and that he demands of them. From this paradox follows another
> one, which theology pretends to present as the resolution of the

former: glory, the hymn of praise that creatures owe to God, in reality derives from the very glory of God; it is nothing but the necessary response, almost the echo that the glory of God awakens in them. That is (and this is the third formulation of the paradox): everything that God accomplishes, the works of creation and the economy of redemption, he accomplishes only for his glory. However, for this, creatures owe him gratitude and glory. (216)

The superegoic dimension of the paradox of glory fully emerges in the motto of Ignatius Loyola, *Ad majorem Dei gloriam*, which Agamben reads as the driving force of Jesuit labor: "One thing that is clear is that he takes the paradox of glory to its extreme, since the human activity of glorification now consists in an impossible task: the continual increase of the glory of God that can in no way be increased. More precisely ... the impossibility of increasing the inner glory of God translates into an unlimited expansion of the activity of external glorification by men, particularly by the members of the Society of Jesus" (216).

Readers of Weber will recognize here the core argument of his study of the "spirit/specter of capitalism." As Weber shows, what we have been calling the paradox of glory converges with the logic of predestination in Calvinism, according to which not only the dispensation of grace but its withholding as well serve as manifestations of divine glory that, in turn, calls on us to respond with acts of thanksgiving and glorification. As Weber puts it, "All creation, including of course the fact, as it undoubtedly was for Calvin, that only a small proportion of men are chosen for eternal grace, *can have any meaning only as means to the glory and majesty of God*" (59–60; my emphasis). There is nothing that does not testify to the glory of God, and for that very reason we must dedicate our lives to the further glorification of God. For the reformers, a Christian life was dedicated to God's glory, to live and work *ad majorem Dei gloriam*. As Weber argues, work itself thereby becomes a form of what we might call *the doxology of everyday life*. It must be performed as liturgical practice, as a mode of production of glory. To use Peterson's terms, our work must ceaselessly resonate, as a response to a calling, with the vibrating being of the order of angels. It should be clear that the doxological dimension of labor at issue here exceeds what could be grasped at the level of the rational pursuit of self-interest. The official capitalist creed of private vice and public virtue, of the production of the public good by way of the pursuit of private self-interest, remains, we might say, at the level of a sort of ego-psychology that has dispensed with the dimension of the unconscious and the sort of work conducted there.

Against this background, Agamben's own philosophical and political project—and they would seem to be inseparable for him—emerges as a fundamentally *paradoxological* one. It consists of various attempts to strike at—or perhaps better, to induce a "general strike" in—the doxological apparatus, our *glory-producing labor*. Agamben sees that labor as the striving to capture in a separate sphere—religion, economics, politics, culture—a fundamental inoperativity, a sabbatical *otium*, marking the absence of a purpose and destination proper to human life. It is a matter of suspending our incessant *negotiations*, of unplugging from what keeps us in the business of being busy-bodies—of vibrating—in the sense I've been elaborating here. What is at stake in the doxologies and ceremonials that seem merely to accompany power is, he suggests, a fetishistic disavowal of *what does not work* in human life; they present so many manic attempts to capture, incorporate, inscribe in a separate sphere "the inoperativity that is central to human life." The "flesh wound" that can't be countenanced is not, as Freud would have it, at the place of the missing maternal phallus but, rather, of a missing task or *telos* proper to human life:

> The *oikonomia* of power places firmly at its heart, in the form of festival and glory, what appears to its eyes as the inoperativity of man and God, *which cannot be looked at*. Human life is inoperative and without purpose, but precisely this *argia* and this

absence of aim make the incomparable operativity [*operosità*] of the human species possible. Man has dedicated himself to production and labor [*lavoro*], because in his essence he is completely devoid of work [*opera*], because he is the Sabbatical animal par excellence. (245–46; my emphasis)[24]

What is here translated as "operativity" might better be rendered as *busy-ness* or even *busy-bodyness*, a neologism that also, I think, captures much of what Heidegger is after in his phenomenology of everyday *Dasein* and its existential mode of "falling," of living within a diffuse and generalized mode of *Geschäftigkeit*.

What I have been calling the flesh covers, for Agamben, what the tradition has thought under the heading of *zoe aionios*, or eternal life, which, he suggests, is "the name of this inoperative center of the human, of this political 'substance' of the Occident that the machine of the economy and of glory ceaselessly attempts to capture within itself" (251). Recalling Žižek's formulation concerning the reign of law, glory, we could say, is one of the names of the "substance" that, as he put it, " 'stops up' and thus conceals the law's vicious circle." What Žižek calls the "illegal violence that founds the reign of law" is for Agamben a manifestation of the struggle to capture "the inoperative center of the human." What Agamben is after with the notion of "inoperativity" is, I'm suggesting, much the same thing that Žižek—among other Lacanians—often attempts to name with formulations like "the big Other doesn't exist." For Agamben as well as for Žižek, what is at issue is the transferential dynamic at work in the *Reflexionsbestimmug* of the Other underlined by Marx. The subject *works* at sustaining/ entertaining the *Instanz* or agency—feeding it with the splendor of surplus value—that, in turn, entitles the subject to enjoy its entitlements, its being in the Other. Against this background, a properly Marxist view of class struggle and revolutionary action would ultimately involve some form of intervention in these transferential relations, transactions, negotiations. This brings us to what we earlier referred to as a certain messianic dimension of the Marxist tradition and the need to strike something other than what's there. It would seem to involve the call for a strike on the liturgical labor in and through which the transferential dynamic is enacted—labor that, as Weber powerfully argued, is itself always already a response to a call. This struggle of call and counter-call, doxology and paradoxology, will thus always be at least one aspect of what it means to engage in class struggle.

VII

Among the more confusing parts of Marx's labor theory of value are those where he refers to its core subject matter as abstract, undifferentiated, homogeneous human labor and appears to equate that with the purely physiological expenditure of energy, muscle, nerves, and so on, in the labor process.[25] The confusion runs the risks of losing sight of the relevant *subject-matter* in the so-conceived subject matter. Recall that Marx posits the notion of abstract labor on the basis of what he sees as the *real abstraction* operative in the circulation of commodities. In *The Wealth of Nations*, Adam Smith had himself already apologized for the "obscurity [that] may still appear to remain upon a subject *in its own nature extremely abstracted*."[26] As soon as commodities are exchanged in denominations of a general equivalent of value—so-and-so-much money—the specific, concrete labor that goes into them—tailoring rather than weaving—becomes in some sense a matter of indifference. Of significance, instead, is only the quantity of *value-producing* labor. Tailoring produces not only shirts but also, and more importantly, so-and-so-much value—value that appears, in turn, as the exchange value of those shirts. That value may be equal to that of so-and-so-much cotton, wheat, iron, or whatever other commodity. Homogeneous labor is the labor that has, as Marx likes to say, *congealed* as value rather than taken phenomenal *shape* as this or that particular commodity. It is the labor that produces the value of, precisely, *whatever commodity*, the labor that is thus at some level—the level that counts, that gets counted—commanded with utter indifference as to its specific nature.[27] It is not we who are indifferent when we command the labor of others by purchasing this or that commodity; it's our money that is indifferent and it is the money that does the talking here, issues the commands, speaks in imperatives, takes the other to (his or her) task.

What is produced in response to such commands— *Arbeitsanforderungen* structurally indifferent to the specific form of labor at issue—is precisely what Marx characterized as the spectral materiality of the commodity:

> Let us now look at the residue of the products of labor. There is nothing left of them in each case but the same spectral materiality [*gespenstische Gegenständlichkeit*]; they are merely congealed quantities of homogeneous human labor [*Gallerte unterschiedsloser menschlicher Arbeit*], i.e. of human labor-power expended without regard to the form of its expenditure.[28]

Marx's own language has led readers to conclude that what he means with such formulations is simply a certain amount of physiological effort or output of energy.[29] They have understood what Marx calls the "dual character of the labor embodied in commodities" (131) as referring to the specific shape and nature of a particular, concrete form of labor, on the one hand (tailoring, weaving, baking), and the purely physiological expenditure of tissue and energy—I'm tempted to call it an expenditure of "biopower"—on the other. Among the passages often cited to support this view we find the following:

> If we leave aside the determinate quality of productive activity, what remains is its quality of being an expenditure of human labor-power. Tailoring and weaving, although they are

qualitatively different productive activities, are both a productive expenditure of human brains, muscles, nerves, hands etc., and in this sense both human labor. Of course, human labor-power must itself have attained a certain level of development before it can be expended in this or that form. But the value of a commodity represents human labor pure and simple, the expenditure of human labor in general. (134)

The remarks that immediately follow this passage suggest, however, that the very perspective or gaze that makes the double character of labor appear in this apparently straightforward and natural way must itself be seen as the object of Marx's critique of political economy. What remains of productive labor once we abstract from its qualitative dimension is, precisely, an *abstract materiality* generated by the historical relations of production *to which this gaze belongs.* What appears to be physiological expenditure, pure and simple—so-and-so-much biopower—is, at a different level, the substance of the social bond at the point at which political economy assumes its hegemonic place in the (self)governmental machine. As Moishe Postone has put it, *"die Materie* in Marx's 'materialist' critique is ... social—the forms of social relations."[30] What is at issue is, in a word, not a pound of brains, muscles, nerves, hands, and so on but, rather, of *flesh.* In Foucauldian terms, we might say that what appears on the face of it as "biopower" in the sense of measurable physiological expenditure is part of a larger matrix of biopower or biopolitical operations that, as Marx puts it, go on behind the backs of those involved:

And just as, in civil society, a general or a banker plays a great part but man as such plays a very mean part, so, here too, the same is true of human labor. It is the expenditure of simple labor-power, i.e. of the labor-power possessed in his bodily organism by every ordinary man, on the average, without being developed in any special way. (135)

It is in his anticipation of questions concerning this notion of simple labor-power that Marx shows his hand:

> *Simple average labor*, it is true, varies in character in different countries and at different cultural epochs, but in a particular society it is given. More complex labor counts only as *intensified*, or rather *multiplied* simple labor, so that a smaller quantity of complex labor is considered equal to a larger quantity of simple labor. *Experience shows that this reduction is constantly being made* [my emphasis]. A commodity may be the outcome of the most complicated labor, but through its *value* it is *posited* as equal to [the verb is *gleichsetzen*] the product of simple labor, hence it represents only a specific quantity of simple labor. The various proportions in which different kinds of labor are reduced to simple labor as their unit of measurement are *established* [festgesetzt] *by a social process that goes on behind the backs of the producers.* (135; my emphasis)

As Postone summarizes these and similar remarks in *Capital*, "the appearance of labor's mediational character in capitalism as physiological labor is the fundamental core of the fetish of capitalism."[31] What disappears from view, what is disavowed in the fetishism of the commodity, is precisely the process of "reduction" that produces the *Gallerte*, the gelatinous mass in and through which our sociality is constituted as a kind of quasi-religious, quasi-secular mass in the liturgical service of the self-valorization of Value.

With the shift from the "sovereign form" to the "commodity form" of social mediation, labor becomes the new locus for the production of the flesh of the social bond. Commodity-producing labor is charged, that is, not only with the production of goods to satisfy the needs and wants of a rapidly expanding *bürgerliche Gesellschaft* or civil society; it is also *surcharged* with a task of social mediation that had earlier belonged to hierarchically arranged symbolic statuses or "estates" revolving, at least since the late Middle Ages and early modernity, around a central locus of sovereign power and authority.[32] For Marx, *value* is now the locus of this surcharge and the labor theory of value concerns itself with its production and circulation. We could add that however one might choose to cultivate (or deconstruct) one's ethnic, religious, sexual, or cultural identity, political economy continues to lay claim to the *vital subject-matter* around which our lives now revolve and with respect to which we are, for the most part, measured and governed. This is what is at issue in the shift from the fetishism of persons to the fetishism of things; the political theology of the King's Two Bodies yields to political economy as the domain surcharged with the management—the *oikonomia*—of the subject-matter, the flesh of the social bond.

It should thus come as no surprise that when he introduces the immanent dynamic of capital as the self-valorization of Value—the quasi-autonomous life of this *surcharge* of our vibrant and vital matter—Marx will resort to the original Trinitarian terms of economic theology:

> It [value] differentiates itself as original value from itself as surplus-value, just as God the Father differentiates himself from himself as God the Son, although both are of the same age and form, in fact one single person; for only by the surplus-value of £10 does the £100 originally advanced become capital, and as soon as this has happened, as soon as the son has been created and, through the son, the father, their difference vanishes again and both become one, £110. (256)

We might add, *ad majorem Dei gloriam.*

VIII

That value is related to valor, glory, radiance, splendor, and that its substance results from the "change of state" that bodily expenditure undergoes under the pressure of real abstraction or "reduction"—call it the *alchemy of capitalism*—has long been in plain sight in the choice of objects historically used to incarnate this substance in the sphere of exchange relations: precious metals and, above all, gold. Gold is where the flesh of abstract, homogeneous human labor is, so to speak, directly deposited; this substance extracted from the earth serves as the glorious garment in which the spectral materiality extracted/abstracted from laboring bodies shines forth as the very substance of splendor.[33]

What is "cast" in the role of the general equivalent of value must be, at some level, superfluous to human needs, must be something that one can do without. It must, in a word, embody the ambiguous virtues of *waste* in the sense of pure superfluity, of what exceeds the needs of the maintenance of life but serves, rather, to "entertain" it. It is no doubt for these reasons that psychoanalysis has so often posited a link between excrement and money. Something emerging from one's own body, something the child in some sense works at producing as its own precious substance, is cast by his caregivers as, precisely, *matter in the wrong place*, the sort of superfluity that demands to be quickly evacuated and made to disappear: our first experience of waste management. For Freud, Ferenczi, and others, the anal *jouissance* attached to evacuation—a *jouissance* that includes the complex negotiations with those caregivers concerning the value and meaning of these first gifts—comes to be sublimated as the positive sense of superfluity attached to what will be extracted from the bowels of the earth and cast into—or, rather, *as*—the light, the *lux*, of luxury.[34] This sublimity manifests itself in the aesthetic dimension of precious metals.

Citing passages from Marx's *Contribution to the Critique of Political Economy*, Jean-Joseph Goux, whose work on the homologies linking diverse forms of symbolic economies has deeply informed my own thinking on these matters, concisely summarizes the aesthetic features that, as it were, help *to make gold gold*—namely:

Those qualities "that make them the natural material of luxury, ornamentation, splendor, festive occasions, in short, the positive form of abundance and wealth. They [gold and silver] appear, in a way, as spontaneous light brought out from the underground world"; gold dazzles the eyes with its orange rays, or reflects "only the color of highest intensity, viz. red light." It is in these "values people take out on holidays," in these products representing "pure and simple superabundance," that what Marx elsewhere calls the world of "profane commodities" converges as if toward the universal form that gives them their value. In short, society "acclaims gold, its Holy Grail, as the glittering incarnation of its inmost vital principle."[35]

Some of the more famous lines in German literature concerning the status of gold in human life come, not surprisingly, from Goethe's *Faust*, a play preoccupied with the "impossible" jointure of the somatic and the normative, the sensuous and the spiritual, the demonic and the angelic. After finding a casket containing jewelry placed in her closet by Mephistopheles, Gretchen puts them on and admires herself in a mirror:

Were these fine ear-bobs mine alone!
They give one quite another air.
What use are simple looks and youth?
Oh, they are well and good in truth;
That's all folk mean, though—pretty, fair.
The praise you get is half good-natured fuss.
For gold contend,
On gold depend
All things and men. . . . Poor us![36]

The last lines read in the original: *"Nach Golde drängt,/Am Golde hängt/Doch alles. Ach wir Armen."* The verbs *drängen* and *hängen* convey the sense, missing from the translation, of an impersonal passion or drive that seizes on human life. And *"wir Armen"* can signify not only "poor us" but also "we poor folk." I say this because Gretchen's class status is underlined from her very first encounter with Faust, when he addresses her on the street as *schönes Fräulein*, as "fair young lady" (2605). Her response is: "I'm neither fair nor lady" (2607). In later conversations she emphasizes in considerable detail the harshness and hardships of her home life—in a word, just how much domestic labor she must do and the toll it has taken on her. The characterization of her room as a *"kleines reinliches Zimmer"* evokes not only a sense of Gretchen's *Reinheit*, or purity—this is what, for example, Kierkegaard emphasizes about her—but also of the work invested here in home economics, something conveyed in the translation with the pedestrian formulation, "a clean little room."

Furthermore, what is translated here as "What use are simple looks and youth," reads, in German, *"Was hilft euch Schönheit, junges Blut?"* The phrase *junges Blut* signifies much more than youth; it conveys the sense of *young flesh*.[37] And indeed, after his first encounter with Gretchen, Faust threatens to part from Mephistopheles if he fails to procure her for him. In Walter Arndt's translation: "Let me be plain, and hear me right,/Unless I have that sweet delight/Nestling in my embrace, tonight,/The selfsame midnight hour will part us" (2635–380). The original reads: *"Und das sag' ich ihm kurz und gut,/Wenn nicht das süße junge Blut/Heut' Nacht in meinen Armen ruht;/So sind wir um Mitternacht geschieden."* Faust is addressing Mephistopheles as a sort of pimp and indeed puts it almost explicitly so in his initial imperative, *"Hör, du mußt mir die Dirne schaffen!"* (2618), a command rendered in English as "Here, get me that young wench—for certain!" The tragic love story of Faust and Gretchen begins, thus, not only as a story of seduction but also as one of prostitution based on the equivalence of young flesh and gold. What is furthermore clear is that what must happen for this story to proceed is that Gretchen must be torn from the form of traditional, if difficult, life in which she is embedded. She must become "modern," and she does so by entering into the system of exchange relations—relations in which flesh is directly exchange-able with gold—on the "ground floor," as it were.

Against this background it makes good sense that Mephistopheles first presents himself to Faust by way of the famous lines that at some level capture the paradoxical logic of commercial economies as theorized by Adam Smith, more or less contemporaneously with the composition of the early drafts of the play. When Mephistopheles introduces himself as "Part of that force which would/Do ever evil, and does ever good" (*Ein Theil von jener Kraft,/Die stets das Böse will und stets das Gute schafft*; 1335–36), it is hard not to hear the resonances of Smith's famous characterization of the logic of the market whereby the greater good is produced precisely by way of what at the very least looks like an abandonment of Christian moral teachings:

> But man has almost constant occasion for the help of his brethren, and it is in vain for him to expect it from their benevolence only. He will be more likely to prevail if he can interest their self-love in his favor and shew them that it is for their own advantage to do for him what he requires of them.... It is not from the benevo-lence of the butcher, the brewer, or the baker, that we expect our dinner, but from their regard to their own interest. We address ourselves, not to their humanity but to their self-love.[38]

The logic of the "oldest profession," the exchange of gold for flesh, is, like Faust, rejuvenated—finds new blood—by way of the Mephistophelian dynamic placed at the heart of political economy, a dynamic that, in the second part of the play, is potentiated, taken to a new level, by way of Faust's introduction of paper money into the financially drained empire. Among the precedents for this Faustian feat of financial engineering were, as we have noted, the introduc-tion of paper currency—the *assignat*—by the revolutionary gov-ernment in France, the brief viability of which was sustained by an infusion of wealth—not so much *junges* as *altes Blut*—seized from Church and aristocracy under the bloody regime of the Terror.

IX

As I've been arguing, the inner movement of capital can be grasped as a form of the dynamic logic of doxology, the paradigm of which is, as Agamben has compellingly argued, the Trinitarian *oikonomia*. The labor theory of value is, in other words, a theory of the fundamentally doxological nature of capitalism. The English translation of one of Marx's key concepts is actually helpful in this context. Just before introducing the Trinitarian allegory of the transformation of money into capital, Marx lays out in more explicitly Hegelian terms the logic at work in the elaboration of the subject-matter of political economy, of what in political economy is *not only substance but also subject*. The passage, though well known, is worth quoting at length:

> The independent form, i.e. the monetary form, which the value of commodities assumes in simple circulation, does nothing but mediate the exchange of commodities, and it vanishes in the final result of the movement. [At this point, that is, value does not yet function as a medium of social relations.] On the other hand, in the circulation M-C-M both the money and the commodity function only as different modes of existence of value itself, the money as its general mode of existence, the commodity as its particular or, so to speak, disguised mode. It is constantly changing from one form into the other, without becoming lost in this movement; it thus becomes transformed into an automatic subject. If we pin down the specific forms of appearance assumed in turn by *self-valorizing value [der sich verwertende Wert]* in the course of its life, we reach the following elucidation: capital is money, capital is commodities. In truth, however, value is here the subject of a process which, while constantly assuming the form in turn of money and commodities, it changes its own magnitude, throws off surplus-value from itself considered as original value [*sich als Mehrwert von sich selbst als usprünglichem Wert abstößt*], and thus *valorizes itself* independently. For the movement in the

course of which it adds surplus-value is its own movement, *its valorization is therefore self-valorization [seine Verwertung also Selbstverwertung]*. By virtue of being value, it has acquired the occult ability to add value to itself. It brings forth living off-spring, or at least lays golden eggs.[39]

The word *valor* nicely brings out the semantic field we have been exploring: glory, splendor, hymnic praise, and so on. The paradoxes of glory elaborated by Agamben are the very ones that Marx lays out here with respect to value. Value-producing labor—this is what he characterizes as abstract homogeneous human labor—figures for Marx as the tool or instrumental cause of value's own self-valorization, just as the faithful, liturgically joining in the angelic doxologies, serve the process of God's self-glorification. This is what is ultimately meant by religious *service*, by *Gottesdienst*.[40] Marx's abbreviation for the self-valorization of value—M-C-M—could thus be understood as the basic doxological formula of capitalism, its underlying *Sancta, Sancta, Sancta*—one that, as Peterson argued with respect to angelic being, goes on 24/7. Once the political theology of sovereignty disperses into the political economy of the wealth of nations, the doxological acclamations that once congealed in the king's sublime body metamorphose into the less theatrical, but no less liturgical, productivity that congeals in the commodity as the substance of its value. We might say then that what eventually comes to be known as the "service economy" is there from the very beginning of modern capitalism insofar as the economy as a whole functions as (liturgical) service.

Against this background one can now better see what Hannah Arendt gets wrong about Marx's understanding of labor. In *The Human Condition*, she argues that Marx shares in a modern ten-dency to posit labor as the hegemonic form of the *vita activa* to the detriment of the work of fabrication or making, on the one hand, and, more importantly, the kinds of action that constitute the space of politics proper, on the other (action that must, in turn, be nourished by labor and sheltered by fabrication). She sees Marx's standpoint as one that more or less cedes the space of making and acting to that of what she calls "the social," a domain that emerges once the mode of activity proper to the *oikos* expands out and absorbs the activities that once fabricated the stage for and animated the public sphere. From a purely social viewpoint, which, she writes, "is the viewpoint of the whole modern age but which received its most coherent and greatest expression in Marx's work,"

> all laboring is "productive." ... The social viewpoint is identical ... with an interpretation that takes nothing into account but the life process of mankind, and within its frame of reference all things become objects of consumption. Within a completely "socialized mankind," whose sole purpose would be *the entertaining of the life process*—and this is the unfortunately quite unutopian ideal that guides Marx's theories ... all work would have become labor because all things would be understood, not in their worldly, objective quality, but as results of living labor power and the functions of the life process.[41]

For Arendt, what is, above all, lost in "socialized mankind" is what distinguishes, to use the Aristotelian terms cited earlier and that inform her thinking on these matters, *living well* from *mere living*. For Arendt, the emergence of "socialized mankind"— really another name for what Foucault grasped as the regime of biopolitics—signals the collapse of human life into the *conatus* ostensibly common to all "vibrant matter." The virtues that define what it means to live well are those exhibited, above all, on the stage of politics and that involve, though doubtlessly in a quite different sense than in Christianity, the dimensions of splendor, glory, greatness, radiance. Commenting on Pericles's Funeral Oration as reported by Thucydides, Arendt writes that there as in Homer "the innermost meaning of the acted deed and the spoken word is independent of victory and defeat.... Unlike human *behavior* ... *action* can be judged only by the criterion of *greatness* because it is in its nature to break through the commonly accepted and reach into the extraordinary" (205; my emphasis). Pericles (or Thucydides), "knew full well," she continues, "that he had broken with the normal standards for everyday behavior when he found the *glory* of Athens in having left behind 'everywhere everlasting remembrance of their good and their evil deeds.' The art of politics teaches men how to bring forth *what is great and radiant*." (206; my emphasis).[42] But as I have tried to show, Marx's fundamental point is that capitalism is a social formation organized precisely around splendor and glory; the labor theory of value is fundamentally a theory of the production of glory, of the liturgical dimension of labor performed in the service of the greater valor, glory, splendor, of Value.[43]

The conclusion to be drawn from all this is that the critique of political economy is always an engagement with the dimension of glory and the liturgical labor that we are all, at some level, called to perform as citizen-subjects of capitalist modernity. The critique of political economy is, in a word, always at some level *paradoxological*: a working through of the doxological dimension of work. The urgency of this critique has only intensified with the most recent developments of capitalist modernity into ever more radical versions of what Guy Debord called the "society of the spectacle." There, what Arendt characterizes as the "entertaining of the life process" actually becomes something like *entertainment* in the everyday sense of the word. In the society of the spectacle, the management of life is, so to speak, just another day in the entertainment business, or what Adorno called the "culture industry." This also turns out to be Agamben's position at the end of his own archeology of glory. Bringing together Debord's analysis and Carl Schmitt's view that what we now refer to as "public opinion" assumes the function of acclamations in modern democratic societies, Agamben writes:

> What is in question is nothing less than a new and unheard of concentration, multiplication, and dissemination of the function of glory as the center of the political system. What was once confined to the

spheres of liturgy and ceremonials has become concentrated in the
media and, at the same time, through them it spreads and penetrates
at each moment into every area of society, both public and private.
Contemporary democracy is a democracy that is entirely founded
upon glory, that is, on the efficacy of acclamation, multiplied and
disseminated by the media beyond all imagination. (256)[44]

One thinks here perhaps of such "news" organizations like Fox
News, where the production of *doxa qua opinion* is understood
as the production of a certain mode of ostensibly patriotic *doxa
qua glory* (in such contexts it also becomes clear that the deliv-
ery of news and information has become another branch of the
entertainment industry). The ancient Greek word for common
opinion or belief that first takes on religious meaning when used
in the Septuagint to translate *kavod*, the Hebrew word for "glory,"
retains its sacral aura in occult, though in intensified form at the
very point at which it seems to return to its purely "secular,"
everyday social meaning.

It is no doubt in this context that we should also situate contemporary discussions about the pros and cons of social media and
the effects of being constantly "wired," "plugged in," "on line."
We know by now that social media function by monetizing our
sociality, by, for example, converting our own everyday "acclamations"—our likes and dislikes—into commodities. Our participation in social media thus tends to blur the boundaries between
production and consumption (the phrase being "on line" suggests
participation in a virtual assembly or production line). Our consumption of the services provided by social media is so often free
because it is part of the production process of data commodities, the
raw materials of marketing strategies designed to display the splendor of commodities and calling us to further consumption (perhaps even of more social media). In and through our participation
in social media, our labor as medium of social relations becomes
so fully transparent that it in some sense disappears, ceases to be

identifiable as labor. At this point, life as a whole becomes business, busy-ness, the life of a busy-body whose flesh vibrates with bits of digital sociality.

X

I would like to conclude by turning—or in my case, returning—to the famous debate between Walter Benjamin and Gershom Scholem concerning the status of "revelation" in Kafka's writings, a debate that we can now see as one concerned with the paradoxes of glory and the status of Kafka's writings as exercises in paradoxological thinking.[45] The central point of contention between the two friends concerns the status of theological trace elements in Kafka's work. Scholem insists that Kafka's work is suffused with the radiance of revelation, but a revelation, as he puts it, "seen from the perspective in which it is returned to its own nothingness" (letter of July 17, 1934, p. 126). Scholem will later characterize this "nothingness of revelation" as "a state in which revelation appears to be without meaning, in which it still asserts itself, in which it has validity but no significance [*in dem sie gilt, aber nicht bedeutet*]," a revelation "reduced to the zero point of its own content, so to speak" (letter of September 20, 1934, p. 142).[46] These remarks are meant to counter his friend's claim, made in his now well-known essay on Kafka, concerning the status of *Studium*, of learning and study, in Kafka's writings: "The gate to justice is study. Yet Kafka doesn't dare attach to this study the promises which tradition has attached to the study of the Torah. His assistants are sextons who have lost their house of prayer; his students are pupils who have lost the Holy Writ [*Schrift*]."[47] For Scholem this represents, as he puts it to his friend, "one of the greatest mistakes you could have made." For Scholem it remains absolutely crucial that the pupils of whom his friend speaks "are not so much those who have lost the Scriptures but rather those students who cannot decipher it" (letter of July 7,

1934). In a further attempt to clarify his position, Benjamin writes, "you take the 'nothingness of revelation' as your point of departure, the salvific-historical perspective of the established proceedings of the trial. I take as my starting point the small, nonsensical hope, as well as the creatures for whom this hope is intended and yet who on the other hand are also the creatures in which this absurdity is mirrored" (letter of August 11, 1934). It is in this context, he continues, "that the problem of Scripture [*Schrift*] poses itself":

> Whether the pupils have lost it or whether they are unable to decipher it comes down to the same thing, because, without the key that belongs to it, the Scripture is not Scripture, but life. Life as it is lived in the village at the foot of the hill on which the castle is built. It is in the attempt to metamorphize life [*in dem Versuch der Verwandlung des Lebens*] into Scripture that I perceive the meaning of "reversal" [*Umkehr*], which so many of Kafka's parables endeavor to bring about.... Sancho Panza's existence is exemplary because it actually consists in rereading one's own existence—however buffoonish and quixotic.[48]

For Scholem, then, Kafka's works are suffused with a barely visible effluence or radiance—a radiance composed out of the validity-without-meaning, the *Geltung-ohne-Bedeutung*, of tradition. It is a light that continues to transmit, to bear the trace of the sacred—we might say, the bare life of the sacred—while for Benjamin the energy of this light has been fully absorbed, fully converted into the "vibrations" of the busy bodies—this strange order of angels—barely living at the foot of the Castle hill. This is, I would argue, the sort of "bare life" that Benjamin had, in an early fragment, characterized as life caught in the cult of "capitalism as religion."

In this highly abbreviated text, Benjamin proposes to radicalize Weber's thesis on the spirit of capitalism by arguing that modern capitalism was not only deeply informed in its beginnings by religious fervor, but had itself mutated into a fully fledged and all-absorbing religious form of life that, as he puts it, "serves to allay the same anxieties, torments, and disturbances to which the so-called religions offered answers."[49] Benjamin goes on to identify three basic aspects of what he refers to as "the religious structure of capitalism": "In the first place, capitalism is a purely cultic religion, perhaps the most extreme that ever existed. In capitalism, things have a meaning only in their relationship to the cult; capitalism has no specific body of dogma, no theology. It is from this point of view that utilitarianism acquires its religious overtones" (288). There is considerable room for disagreement here. Indeed, one could argue that the classical theories of the self-regulation of the market from Smith's "invisible hand" to contemporary mathematical modeling of market dynamics form precisely this body of dogma.[50]

The second feature Benjamin identifies is "the permanence of the cult." This concerns precisely what I have referred to as the *doxology of everyday life,* an organization of time that serves to eliminate the distinction between workday and holiday, workday and Sabbath: "Capitalism is the celebration of a cult *sans trêve et sans merci.* There are no 'weekdays.' There is no day that is not a feast day, in the terrible sense that all its sacred pomp is unfolded before us; each day commands the utter fealty of each worshiper" (288).[51]

Finally, and perhaps closest to the spirit of Kafka's universe, Benjamin identifies the third aspect of capitalism as religion in its tendency to universalize the condition of indebtedness and consciousness of guilt, to make it absolute and so without the possibility of absolution. "Capitalism," Benjamin writes, "is probably the first instance of a cult that creates guilt, not atonement [*der erste Fall eines nicht entsühnenden sondern verschuldenden Kultus*]. . . . A vast sense of guilt that is unable to find relief seizes on the cult, not to atone for this guilt but to make it universal" (288). What Benjamin anticipates here is the phenomenon of *sovereign debt,* by which I mean not simply the debt owed by nation-states but also the *sovereignty of debt* over human life and its possibilities more generally.

Against this background, what Benjamin, in his letters to Scholem, refers to as *Umkehr*—or reversal—can, I think, be seen as pertaining to those modes of engagement with glory that I have called *paradoxological*. It involves an effort to reach into the doxological machine—the machine that sustains the religious structure of capitalism—and pull its plug, if even for a fleeting moment of Sabbatical inoperativity in which, perhaps, something new might be spelled out by, precisely, *spelling out the spell* cast by the doxology of everyday life. The repetition of such moments, their stringing together into a constellation, constitutes something on the order of what Freud called *working through*, a process that involves, as we have seen, an effort to strike something other than what's there. What Benjamin's preoccupation with Kafka in particular and literary language more generally suggests—Benjamin, one will recall, saw himself, above all, as a kind of literary critic—is that the "spelling" at issue here may ultimately fall within the purview of literature. A second field thus opens up next to the "archaeology of glory," the literary practice and theory of paradoxology. My hope is that my reflections here have helped to provide some provisional indications as to what the relevant sort of *fieldwork* might look like.

Notes

1. Karl Marx, *Capital: A Critique of Political Economy. Volume One*, trans. Ben Fowkes (New York: Vintage, 1977), 163. German from *Das Kapital: Kritik der politischen Ökonomie. Erster Band* (Berlin: Karl Dietz Verlag, 2008), 85.

2. My thinking on such matters continues to be inspired and informed by Slavoj Žižek's work on the mutations of ideology in modernity, though it has become ever more difficult to keep up with his writings.

3. Benjamin takes the phrase from a poem by Gottfried Keller. See my *On Creaturely Life: Rilke, Benjamin, Sebald* (Chicago: University of Chicago Press, 2006), 81, for a discussion of Benjamin's formulation.

4. I have discussed Freud's *Moses* at considerable length in "Freud's *Moses* and the Ethics of Nomotropic Desire," in Renata Salecl, ed., *Sexuation* (Durham, NC: Duke University Press, 2000), 57–105.

5. Slavoj Žižek, *For They Know Not What They Do: Enjoyment as a Political Factor* (London: Verso, 1991), 260.

6. Jonathan Lear has developed the notion of ontological vulnerability in *Radical Hope: Ethics in the Face of Cultural Devastation* (Harvard: Harvard University Press, 2006).

7. It makes sense that in his effort to capture the point at which dreams reach into a dark zone of illegibility—one that also marks the ultimate object-cause of dreams—Freud invokes the figure of the *navel* (of the dream), a bodily site that appears now as a hole, now as an uncanny excess of knotted flesh.

8. Pursuing a line of thought first laid out by Elaine Scarry in her *The Body in Pain* (New York: Oxford University Press, 1985), David Graeber has compellingly argued that the emergence of markets is always at some level grounded in violence, a violence that gets "covered" by the surplus value embodied by its victims, whether as flesh left on the ground in war or, more importantly, as the spectral materiality—a term he doesn't use himself—generated by enslavement, by *tearing* the vanquished from the fabric of their social being. The enslaved embody the ontological vulnerability of human life by converting it into a surplus of glory for the victor. Referencing the work of Orlando Paterson, Graeber describes the way in which the degradation of the vanquished gets converted into what he calls the *surplus dignity*—honor, magnificence, greatness, splendor—of the victor: "this ability to strip others of their dignity becomes, for the master, the foundation of his honor.... One might say: honor is surplus dignity. It is that heightened consciousness of power and its dangers that comes from having stripped away the power and dignity of others; or at the very least, from the knowledge that one is capable of doing so. At its simplest, honor is that *excess dignity* that must be defended with the knife or sword." Graeber underlines the fact that the use-value of the enslaved can be irrelevant in such politico-symbolic operations—i.e., that their value lies largely in their role in the production of glory, magnificence, *Herrlichkeit*, rather than in any purposeful project. They are, at some level, deployed as displays not of useful but, rather, of *wasted life*. See David Graeber, *Debt: The First 5,000 Years* (Brooklyn, NY: Melville House, 2011), 170.

9. Russell A. Berman and Paul Piccone, eds., "Toward a Liturgical Critique of Modernity," special issue, *Telos* 113 (Fall 1998).

10. Michel Foucault, *The History of Sexuality. Volume 1: An Introduction*, trans. Robert Hurley (New York: Vintage, 1990), 139.

11. Michel Foucault, *Discipline and Punish: The Birth of the Prison*, trans. Alan Sheridan (New York: Vintage, 1977), 208 (my emphasis).

12. Michel Foucault, *Society Must Be Defended: Lectures at the Collège de France, 1975-1976*, trans. David Macey (New York: Picador, 2003), 217 (my emphasis).

13. Recall, once more, Žižek's concise formulation cited in the first lecture: "What is at stake is . . . not simply the split between the empirical person of the king and his symbolic function. The point is rather that this symbolic function *redoubles his very body*, introducing a split between the visible, material, transient body and another, sublime body, a body made of a special, immaterial stuff." *For They Know Not*, 255.

14. Michel Foucault, *Security, Territory, Population: Lectures at the Collège de France, 1977-1978*, trans. Graham Burchell (New York: Palgrave, 2007), 76–77 (my emphasis). Subsequent page references are made in the text.

15. Joseph Vogl, "Staatsbegehren: Zur Epoche der Policey," in *Deutsche Vierteljahrsschrift für Literaturwissenschaft und Geistesgeschichte* 74 (2000): 600–26. Subsequent page references are made in the text.

16. These are Lacan's attempt to map the minimal structure of social bonds, the logic of the social mediation/circulation of subject-matter across historical change. Lacan presents his theory of discourses in *The Other Side of Psychoanalysis: The Seminar of Jacques Lacan. Seminar XVII*, trans. Russell Grigg (New York: W. W. Norton, 2007).

17. Giorgio Agamben, *The Kingdom and the Glory: For a Theological Genealogy of Economy and Government*, trans. Lorenzo Chiesa (Stanford: Stanford University Press, 2011). Subsequent page references are made in the text.

18. Agamben summarizes the task of the Church Fathers this way: "At the end of classical civilization, when the unity of the ancient cosmos is broken, and being and acting, ontology and praxis, seem to part ways irreversibly, we see a complex doctrine developing in Christian theology, one in which Judaic and pagan elements merge. Such a doctrine attempts to interpret—and, at the same time, recompose—this fracture through a managerial and non-epistemic paradigm: the *oikonomia*. According to this paradigm, the divine praxis, from creation to redemption, does not have a foundation in God's being, and differs from it to the extent that it realizes itself in a separate person, the *Logos*, or Son. However, this anarchic and unfounded praxis must be reconciled with the unity of the substance. Through the idea of a free and voluntary action—which associates creation with redemption—this paradigm had to overcome both the Gnostic antithesis between a God foreign to the world and a demiurge who is creator and Lord of the world, and the pagan identity of being and acting, which made the very idea of creation unconvincing. The challenge that Christian theology thus presents to Gnosis is to succeed in reconciling God's transcendence with the creation of the world, as well as his noninvolvement in it with the Stoic and Judaic idea of a God who takes care of the world and governs it providentially. In the face of this aporetic

task, the *oikonomia*—given its managerial and administrative root—offered a ductile tool, which presented itself, at the same time, as a *logos*, a rationality removed from any external constraint, and a praxis unanchored to any ontological necessity or preestablished norm" (Agamben, *The Kingdom and the Glory*, 65–66).

19. The *Book of Angels* appears in Erik Peterson, *Theological Tractates*, trans. Michael Hollerich (Stanford: Stanford University Press, 2011), 106–42. Subsequent references are made in the text. German text cited from the German translation of *The Kingdom and the Glory: Herrschaft und Herrlichkeit: Zur theologischen Genealogie von Ökonomie und Regierung*, trans. Andreas Hiepko (Frankfurt: Suhrkamp, 2010).

20. Throughout his study, Peterson takes pains to distinguish Christian from Jewish doxology. He notes, for example, "that the Christian liturgy was not satisfied just to repeat the simple expression of the prophet, according to which the seraphim 'cry and say': 'Holy, holy, holy is the Lord of Hosts'.... In contrast to Isaiah, the *eternal duration* of the cry of the 'Holy' is ... emphasized.... This stress on the *unceasing praise* of God by the angels is unknown in Judaism" (119, my emphasis). We might say that Peterson, a convert to Catholicism, emphasizes the Protestant work ethic of the angels. Or to recall our discussion of the "quality of mercy" in *The Merchant of Venice*, Christian doxology, as Peterson understands it, is the liturgical form of what I earlier characterized as a "Portia-lly" reformed debt economy, one that introduces into life the demands of its *infinite amourtization*.

21. Samuel Brody's fine dissertation on Martin Buber argues that the Jewish philosopher developed his own profoundly anarchic theo-political perspective, one that also took aim at the resurgence of political theology in fascist movements. See Brody, "This Pathless Hour: Messianism, Anarchism, Zionism, and Martin Buber's Theopolitics Reconsidered," PhD diss., University of Chicago, 2013.

22. Ernst Kantorowicz, *Laudes Regiae: A Study in Liturgical Acclamations and Medieval Ruler Worship* (Berkeley: University of California Press, 1946).

23. As I've noted, Kantorowicz himself experienced first hand the revival of this "archaic sphere" of doxological performativity. In the tumultuous mass politics of the early years of the Weimar Republic he belonged to the militant—and violent—far right wing of the political spectrum; as a Jew, he would be forced to flee a homeland whose maniacally anti-Semitic regime had put into operation a vast doxological machine to sustain the bonds of the *Volksgemeinschaft*, to synchronize the frequencies at which its members "vibrated." He himself thus brought a finely tuned ear to the revival of interest in the *laudes* among theologians and musicologists in the 1920s, as well

as for their appropriation in fascist liturgies of power. In my book, *Stranded Objects: Mourning, Memory, and Film in Postwar Germany* (Ithaca: Cornell University Press, 1990), I explore in detail Hans Jürgen Syberberg's often brilliant cinematic investigation into fascist doxology (and the place of cinema in it). The major critiques of Syberberg over the years could be summarized in the claim that his films succumbed to the spell they were spelling out, that they were insufficiently *para-doxological*. I will turn to this concept later.

24. In his Tanner Lectures on Human Values, Jonathan Lear argued that Aristotle's perverse achievement in his *Ethics* was, in effect, to establish just such a dimension of inoperativity in human life and to do so under the sign of happiness as the ostensible telos of human life. See his *Happiness, Death, and the Remainder of Life* (Cambridge, MA: Harvard University Press, 2000). "All the rest of animal nature," Lear writes, "is basically able to fulfill its nature unproblematically. There will be occasional mutants and occasions when the environment doesn't cooperate, but for the most part each species is able to flourish in its distinctive way. It is only humans who have a characteristic problem of failing to thrive. For humans, happiness *is* human flourishing, yet happiness by and large eludes them. Thus by injecting 'happiness' as the organizing goal of human teleology Aristotle manages to disrupt the teleological structure itself" (56).

25. The following section is deeply indebted to Moishe Postone's brilliant study, *Time, Labor, and Social Domination: A Reinterpretation of Marx's Critical Theory* (Cambridge: Cambridge University Press, 1993) and to numerous works by Slavoj Žižek.

26. Adam Smith, *The Wealth of Nations* (New York: Modern Library, 2000), 32 (my emphasis).

27. Smith characterizes the purchase of a commodity as a form of command that passes through the network of commodity producers; market economies are thus at some level decentralized "command economies": "After the division of labor has once thoroughly taken place, it is but a very small part of these [necessaries, conveniences, and amusements of human life] with which a man's own labor can supply him. The far greater part of them he must derive from the labor of other people, and he must be rich or poor according to the quantity of that labor *which he can command* or which he can afford to purchase. The value of any commodity, therefore, to the person who possesses it, and who means not to use or consume it himself, but to exchange it for other commodities, is equal to the quantity of labor which it *enables him to purchase or command*" (*Wealth of Nations*, 33, my emphasis).

28. Marx, *Capital*, 128 (translation modified); *Kapital*, 52. Subsequent page references for both editions are made in the text.

29. This is similar to what readers have at times thought with respect to Freud's understanding of libido, of the sexual "labor-power" that is, as Freud repeatedly emphasized, *perversely indifferent to its object*, only loosely "soldered" to it in the pursuit of its aim: more pleasure, pleasure in excess of any possible "use-value." Recent efforts to demonstrate the ways in which sex is beneficial to health should be seen, then, as attempts to "repurpose" sexuality, to demonstrate that it in no way swerves from teleological function—that it is in no way *wasteful*, that it is a materialism without *clinamen*.

30. Postone, *Time, Labor, and Social Domination*, 171.

31. Postone, *Time, Labor, and Social Domination*, 170.

32. Recall Foucault's formulation about the king as the *physical-juridical* quilting point of social mediation in the *ancien régime*. What makes a nation, he writes, is the fact that its members "all have a certain individual relationship—both juridical and physical—with the real, living, and bodily person of the king. It is the body of the king, in his physical-juridical relationship with each of his subjects, that creates the body of the nation." Foucault, *Society Must Be Defended*, 217.

33. As I've indicated in the preface, it would appear as if in contemporary "cognitive capitalism" *data mining* has become the dominant extractive industry, data the value directly extracted/abstracted from "cognitively" laboring bodies.

34. Aside from Freud's writings on anal eroticism, of particular interest is Sandor Ferenczi's "The Ontogenesis of the Interest in Money," in *The Psychoanalysis of Money*, ed. Ernest Borneman (New York: Urizon, 1976), 81–90. There Ferenczi suggests that feces undergo, under pedagogic pressure, a metamorphosis (by way of degrees of "dehydration") into mud, sand, pebbles, marbles, and, finally, gold.

35. Jean-Joseph Goux, *Symbolic Economies: After Marx and Freud*, trans. Jennifer Curtiss Gage (Ithaca, NY: Cornell University Press, 1990), 28. Georges Bataille's *The Accursed Share* is in its entirety a meditation on the laws of the "general economy" according to which living systems, whether organisms or societies, rid themselves of surplus energy that can serve no practical purpose, are of no use. If this "excess cannot be completely absorbed in its [a system's] growth, it must necessarily be lost without profit; it must be spent, willingly or not, *gloriously or catastrophically*." Bataille, *The Accursed Share: Volume 1*, trans. Robert Hurley (New York: Zone Books, 1991), 21.

36. Johann Wolfgang von Goethe, *Faust: A Tragedy*, trans. Walter Ardnt (New York: W. W. Norton, 2001), 76 (lines 2796–804). German text cited from *Johann Wolfgang Goethe: Faust-Dichtungen*, ed. Ulrich Gaier (Stuttgart: Reclam, 2010). In winter 2014 I sat in on a seminar on *Faust*

conducted by my colleague, David Wellbery. My views on the play have been strongly informed by the seminar discussions. This casket containing gold will, of course, turn out to have the mortal consequences that Freud linked to the base metal, lead, in his reading of the three caskets in *The Merchant of Venice*.

37. This would be a productive site for exploring alternative readings in the spirit of Gil Anidjar's *Blood: A Critique of Christianity* (New York: Columbia University Press, 2014).

38. Smith, *The Wealth of Nations*, 15. For a wonderfully lucid discussion of the Mephistophelian dimension of classical political economy, of its commitment to an "oikodicy," see Joseph Vogl, *The Specter of Capital* (Stanford, CA: Stanford University Press, 2015).

39. Marx, *Capital*, 255; *Kapital*, 168–69. For Marx, only in modern capitalism do Aristotle's anxious insights about chrematistics find their truth.

40. Agamben develops the concept of "instrumental cause" in the sequel to *The Kingdom and the Glory*, *Opus Dei: An Archaeology of Duty*, trans. Adam Kotsko (Stanford, CA: Stanford University Press, 2013). Agamben's key point of reference is Aquinas, for whom the priest functions as "instrumental cause of an act whose primary agent is Christ himself" (22).

41. Hannah Arendt, *The Human Condition* (Chicago: University of Chicago Press 1998), 89, my emphasis. Subsequent page references are made in the text.

42. Against this background one might say that for the Greeks, glory is linked to *immortality* sustained by literary and civic remembrance while in the Christian tradition it is linked to *eternity* sustained by faith embodied in cultic action. Arendt's concern with the fate of glory—and so of what is distinctive about the forms of action that constitute politics proper—is echoed in Alain Badiou's understanding of the "evental" opening of a "truth procedure" in the domain of the political. In *The Communist Hypothesis* (London: Verso, 2010), he writes: "The non-factual element in a truth is a function of its orientation, and this will be termed subjective. We will also say that the material 'body' of a truth, in so far as it is subjectively oriented, is an exceptional body. Making unabashed use of a religious metaphor, I will say that the body-of-truth, as concerns what cannot be reduced to facts within it, can be called *a glorious body*. With respect to this body, which is that of a new collective Subject in politics, of an organization composed of individual multiples, we will say that it shares in the creation of a political truth" (244–45, my emphasis).

43. As readers of *The Communist Manifesto* well know, large portions of that text read as quasi-hymnic, quasi-ironic praise—glorification—of the

accomplishments achieved under the regime of the self-valorization of Value, above all the destruction of much of what had heretofore been the object of doxological praise in European civilization.

44. Walter Benjamin's writings on nineteenth-century Paris including, above all, his unfinished *Arcades Project*, represent one of the landmark bodies of work in the field Agamben, no doubt deeply influenced by Benjamin, called the "archaeology of glory." Agamben's reflections on the doxological dimension of modern democratic societies are largely prefigured there. Writing, for example, about what he sees as the deep affinity between world exhibitions and Grandville's work, Benjamin writes, "World exhibitions glorify [*verklären*] the exchange value of the commodity. They create a framework in which its use value recedes into the background. They open a phantasmagoria in which a person enters in order to be distracted. The entertainment industry [*Vergnügungsindustrie*] makes this easier by elevating the person to the level of the commodity. He surrenders to its manipulation while enjoying his alienation from himself and others.—*The enthronement of the commodity, with its luster of distraction*, is the secret theme of Grandville's art. This is consistent with the split between utopian and cynical elements in his work. Its ingenuity in representing inanimate objects corresponds to what Marx calls the 'theological niceties' of the commodity." Walter Benjamin, *Paris, the Capital of the Nineteenth Century*, trans. Howard Eiland, in *Walter Benjamin: Selected Writings, Vol. 3: 1935-1938*, ed. Howard Eiland and Michael Jennings (Cambridge, MA: Harvard University Press, 2002), 37.

45. See Gershom Scholem, ed., *The Correspondence of Walter Benjamin and Gershom Scholem: 1932-1940*, trans. Gary Smith and André Lefevere (Cambridge, MA: Harvard University Press, 1992). The letters, along with other relevant texts, are collected in *Benjamin über Kafka: Texte, Briefzeugnisse, Aufzeichnungen*, ed. Hermann Schweppenhäuser (Frankfurt: Suhrkamp, 1981). If my preoccupation with this debate has the quality of a repetition compulsion—I refer to it in several books—it is, I think, because the stakes of the debate concern the dimension of human experience that Freud located beyond the pleasure principle and that seems to involve the demand for repetition.

46. As I've suggested earlier, we might hear this formulation as standing in relation to the figure of the king who reigns but no longer governs.

47. Walter Benjamin, "Franz Kafka: On the Tenth Anniversary of his Death," trans. Harry Zohn, in *Walter Benjamin: Selected Writings. Volume 2: 1927-1934*, ed. Michael Jennings, Howard Eiland, and Gary Smith (Cambridge, MA: Harvard University Press, 1999), 815.

48. The village in question is, of course, the setting of Kafka's novel *The Castle*. I would argue that in Robert Walser's novel, *Jakob von Gunten*, the Institute Benjamenta belongs to the same universe as this village and that Jakob counts among those creatures in whom, precisely on the basis of his uncannily "vibrant" being, the absurdity of the hope mentioned by Benjamin is mirrored. And indeed, at the end of the novel Jakob becomes a kind of Sancho Panzo to Herr Benjamenta's Quixote.

49. Walter Benjamin, "Capitalism as Religion," trans. Rodney Livingstone, in *Walter Benjamin: Selected Writings, Vol. 1: 1913-1926*, ed. Marcus Bullock and Michael Jennings (Cambridge, MA: Harvard University Press, 1996), 288. Subsequent page references are made in the text. The German text is found in Walter Benjamin, *Gesammelte Schriften. Band VI: Fragmente vermischten Inhalts*, ed. Rolf Tiedemann and Hermann Sheppenhäuser (Frankfurt: Suhrkamp, 1986), 100–103.

50. See once more Joseph Vogl's *The Specter of Capital* for his compelling reading of the various forms of "oikodicy" that inform political economic doctrine. One could add to this Luc Boltanski and Eve Chiapello's *The New Spirit of Capitalism*, trans. Gregory Elliot (London: Verso, 2007). There the authors analyze, among other things, the quasi-theological literature on *management* that informs this new spirit.

51. What is rendered here as "utter fealty" is, in the original, [*die*] *äußerste Anspannung des Verehrenden*. The word *Anspannung* conveys the sense of stress, tension states, and, perhaps, the condition of *undeadness* that Benjamin referred to as *erstarrte Unruhe*, or petrified unrest.

Comments

Charged: Debt, Power, and the Politics of the Flesh in Shakespeare's *Merchant*, Melville's *Moby-Dick*, and Eric Santner's *The Weight of All Flesh*

BONNIE HONIG[1]

[A]s for me, I am tormented with an everlasting itch for things remote.

—Melville's Ishmael in *Moby-Dick*

[W]ith a crucifixion in his face; in all the nameless regal overbearing dignity of some mighty woe.

—Melville (describing Ahab), *Moby-Dick*

Cursed be that mortal interindebtedness which will not do away with ledgers. I would be free as air; and I'm down in the whole world's books.

—Melville's Ahab in *Moby-Dick*

Moby-Dick inhabits this novel at once as the most material and the most abstract of bodies, at once as the bulkiest, heaviest, largest of all living beings and as a "phantom," a vision, and a fleeting mental image.

—Cesare Casarino, *Modernity at Sea*

"The matter of electric money does not matter," says Marc Shell in *Money, Language and Thought*, published over thirty years ago.[2] Shell describes the fall from the sort of money whose matter secured its value (gold) to one whose value is derived more from its inscription (coinage) to, later, a more neutral vehicle of the value of inscription (paper money), and then to various mechanisms of standing for value "in increasingly abstract ways" (electronic fund transfers) (1). Shell says: "With the advent of electronic fund transfers the link between inscription and substance was broken. The matter of electric money does not matter" (1).

But we might get a charge out of it anyway. The electric is by now the digital, and what it fingers, if Eric Santner is correct, is less a vitality—the vital electric—than a kind of deathlessness in which the flesh, always alive with nerve endings and host to all sorts of living things (such as bacteria, infection, parasites), is now beyond alive: animated, sensitive, and sensitized to the solicitations and inhabitations of the market and its fetishized objects, goods, desirings, and concepts.[3] In this sequel to the book *The Royal Remains*, Eric Santner's *The Weight of all Flesh* asks what remains or what becomes of a prior political theology of sovereignty, and he finds what I think should be called a theo-political economy, the source of a vital, vibrant materiality, not a "not matter" at all.[4]

If, as Shell hazards, the matter of *money* does not matter now, Santner suggests that is because, instead, our own materiality *does* matter and has, indeed, become the matter of the market and of the world it organizes out of the remains of past political theologies and current new fetishisms. Where Shell sees a shift from the "absolute adequation between intellectual inscription [the king's mark] and real substance to the complete dissociation of them" (2), a move that tracks in parallel the move from barter to trade that, for many critics of money's polymorphous perversities, is the original Fall from (referential) Grace, Santner sees not a fall nor an increasing abstraction, but a series of redistributions and occupations that have landed us in a theo-political economy in which our charges are charged.[5] The purchases that permeate the contemporary economy come with an electricity of their own. We get a charge out of them, even as we charge them to our accounts. The coin of the realm becomes the realm of the coin, in which money is not seen but always heard: "money talks" (a metaphor given new life by the Supreme Court decisions in *McCutcheon* and *Citizens United*). Less an object than a form of subjectification, money even inhabits us in language, thought, and metaphor according to Shell and, if Santner is right, it gets under our skin, too.[6]

Hence the focus on "flesh," a term that in Santner's work calls attention to both the "ultimately enigmatic jointure" and the embodied experience of normative and somatic pressure. For Santner, that jointure of the somatic and the normative "defines human life" (50). Though it is difficult to conceptualize "the substance of that jointure," he says, "this third element in excess of both the somatic and the normative that both links and leaks into the two domains [is] the uncanny cause of various inflammatory conditions" (50). These inflammations of the flesh may perhaps be "autoimmune," Santner comments. Whatever they are, they are what "drives" the most famous "dramas" of the flesh, including Shakespeare's *The Merchant of Venice* and all of our own dramas, as well.[7]

Santner's lectures are rich and range across psychoanalysis, Judaic studies, literary theory, German, continental philosophy, and more. Any reply must be selective. I attend here to how "flesh" works on Santner's account, focusing in particular on the first of his lectures (my assigned task), and I develop some thoughts regarding how *else* it might work, or how else it might be enlisted to work in the context of democratic theory.[8]

Santner intimates there is a politics in the transfer that he tracks from "sovereign of the realm" to "the coin of the realm" (48). But the problematics of politics—and specifically those of a democratic politics—are not Santner's express topic. His main aim is to give a psychoanalytic account of the flesh, and this generates a series of suggestive, innovative readings, including Shakespeare's *Merchant of Venice* (in Lecture 1) and Kafka's *The Castle* (in the Preface). *Merchant*, we could argue, normally is taken to offer an *ethics of the flesh*—in which we experience the universality of vulnerability

("If you prick us do we not bleed?").[9] One merit of Santner's reading of the play is precisely that it moves beyond that to address the flesh psychoanalytically. But could we move still further? Or in more directions, still? Is there a distinctive way to think about flesh not just ethically or psychoanalytically but also politically or democratically? Might there be a democratic theory of the flesh that is not reducible to the ethical or the psychoanalytic accounts (though still in communication with them, as it were)? Might the busy-ness with which Santner says we respond to certain demands and enigmas take the form not just of inflammations but also of mobilizations, for example, and call therefore not just for the analytics and practices of psychoanalysis but also for the work of democratic theory, not just for destituent power but also for constituent power? Might we perhaps be moved thereby from a kind of "self"-absorption to what Jason Frank, in a reading of *Moby-Dick*, calls "democratic absorption"?[10]

Inspired by Santner's turn to "flesh," and in quest of some traction in relation to this gelatinous stuff, I turn to Herman Melville's *Moby-Dick*, which I read precisely as offering a democratic theory of the flesh or, perhaps better, some fleshly incitements to democratization. My account of Melville's politics of the flesh does not only extend but also counters elements of Santner's account. The clash between our positions becomes clearest when I juxtapose Melville's Ishmael (as I and two other democratic theorists read him) to Bartleby, the figure associated by Santner (in the live event of the lectures and in *The Royal Remains*) and by Agamben with the "inoperativity" that becomes so important to the argument of Santner's second lecture. More generally, what I find in Melville are not just "royal remains" (as Santner called them in his last book).[11] In place of, or in addition to, the dispersal of sovereignty *into* the flesh, Melville tells a story of the revolutionary dispersal of sovereignty *by way* of the flesh. Melville's *Moby-Dick* does depict sovereign reoccupations of the flesh, but it also explores and even incites the power of flesh to break the spells

CHARGED: DEBT, POWER, AND THE POLITICS OF THE FLESH · 135

of sovereignty, theological as well as economic, and to inaugurate in their wake new forms of collectivity.[12]

The Market Takes Exception, or Debt by the Pound (of Flesh)

Hamlet was Eric Santner's Shakespeare play of choice in *The Royal Remains*, but now he shifts to attend as well to *The Merchant of Venice* because of the debt around which the play turns, and the pound of flesh that secures it.[13] That pound of flesh is Antonio's flesh, promised to the Jewish moneylender, Shylock, in surety for the loan to Antonio, whose ship has not come in but whose real purpose is to float Bassanio's boat. (Lara Bovilsky points out that Antonio launders Shylock's Jewish money for Bassanio's Christian purpose.[14]) As Santner rightly notes, the pound of flesh represents many things: money, foreskin, phallus, circumcision, castration, homicide, contract, and more. Also, situated between the play's many constitutive oppositions (Christian and Jew, mercy and vengeance, abstraction and concreteness), the pound of flesh marks and unsettles all of them (as will whale flesh, in Melville, too).[15] Most important of all, says Santner, that pound of flesh "finally offers us the figure of a value that can be extracted ... *materially abstracted*—from a living body and weighed in the balance" (55).[16] What is weighed here is, however, no longer that which makes a king a king—that is, one of the king's two bodies, which is "the partial object of political theology"—but, rather, "something in or of the body that has been invested not with royal office but with economic value in a mercantile society" (55).

Thus, *The Merchant of Venice* is the beginning of "the metamorphosis of the King's Two Bodies into the People's Two Bodies" (89), from the political theology of sovereignty into "the political economy of the wealth of nations"(51).[17] More or less in keeping with Santner's reading, viewers and readers of the play encounter here not a King (the sovereign figure of political theology), though also not "the people," but, rather, a Duke, one with quite limited power (he can pardon, it seems, but he cannot decide[18]), and the debt in question is flesh itself. In short, we have here an emergent biopolitics of debt. Audiences today may be shocked, still, when Shylock practically whets his knife to carve his due out of Antonio's breast, but surely we should not be. This Renaissance play about the emergence of a new mercantile form of life presages what has since come to be the economy we know, a theo-political economy of the flesh in which cutting and debt bondage are not exactly unheard of, nor unrelated.[19]

The shift from political theology to political economy, from "the 'sovereign form' to the 'commodity form' of social mediation" (60, 106), is telegraphed in Santner's lecture by Weber's citation of a bromide by Benjamin Franklin that uncannily echoes the play on which so much rests here: "As Franklin puts it in a passage cited by Weber: 'He that kills a breeding-sow, destroys her offspring to the thousandth generation. He that murders a crown, destroys all that it might have produced, even scores of pounds'" (48). Santner notes the corollary between the first part of the Weber/Franklin bromide—the reproductive sow and Shakespeare's play—when Shylock cites the biblical story in which Jacob manages to get striped lambs to be born of plain ewes, thus enriching himself according to his contract with his scheming father-in-law, Laban. But we might also note the corollary between the second part of Franklin's bromide—the crown that might have produced scores of pounds—and the second part of Shylock's analogy.

Shylock reports Jacob's intervention in livestock reproduction to defend *usury*, the very practice in which, after all, crowns do beget scores of pounds (and ducats beget ducats).[20] For Franklin, killing a sow and murdering a coin do have something in common: both forfeit a certain moneyed futurity.[21] But Shylock's analogy, because it builds on the positive and not the negative case, posits a shared trait of regeneration, and here the analogy falters. There is a signal difference between Jacob's self-interested manipulation of livestock breeding and Shylock's money-lending. Both are unnatural forms of reproduction (Jacob has to intervene in the breeding to get the desired improbable outcome), but as Antonio points out to Shylock, it is not unnatural, as such, for *ewes* to reproduce (i.e., Jacob modifies, he does not alchemize); it is, or so it was thought, unnatural for *money* to reproduce.[22] Indeed, as Jacques le Goff points out, summing up the twelfth-century view, which lasted well after: "Money is infertile, yet the usurer wants it to produce offspring."[23] What was once the exception and the transgression has since become the norm, of course. Banks today advertise their interest rates or investment records with the promise that, as one of their clients, you can watch your money "grow."[24]

Shylock's analogy, in its context, may have been a stretch, but it seems to have anticipated, uncannily, Benjamin Franklin's bromide, which seems to follow the same (il)logic—or to harbor the same odd association—as Shylock's.[25] Also uncanny is the fact that Franklin sometimes wrote under the nom de plume "busybody," Marx's term, borrowed by Santner, to single out the forms of theo-economic subjectivity he wants to track here, in these lectures, and which he sees as symptomatizing the gap between the normative and the somatic.[26]

The pound of flesh in *Merchant* is, for Santner, a synecdoche for the new "busy bodies" of late capitalism that psychoanalysis is especially able to address and that "a variety of modernist aesthetic projects had found their own ways to elaborate" (24). (This privileging of modernist aesthetics will license as well my own turn to *Moby-Dick*, a novel whose self-conscious, inventive literariness may certainly be seen as an effort to manage what I will argue are the *politics* of the flesh.[27]) In *The Royal Remains*, Santner argued (as he puts it), "that psychoanalysis could itself be understood as the science of 'royal remains'" (23) and, indeed, this is consistent with his reading, as well, of the Schreber case in *My Own Private*

Germany. As he goes on to say: the "usual genealogy of Freud's new science—its neurological lineage—was thus to be supplemented by one addressing its emergence out of a displacement and redistribution of 'emergency powers' previously concentrated in, enjoyed and embodied, by the sovereign person" (24). When Santner takes a moment in these lectures to criticize the new materialists, he makes clear that, in his view, psychoanalysis has more to offer than Spinoza: "To put it simply, the 'intensities' that occupied—or better, preoccupied—the crook of the elbow, among other body parts, of Freud's hysterics were not caused by tribes of bacteria [to which Santner takes the new materialists to be pointing] but, rather, by a complex disorder of the 'tribe' to which these hysterics belonged, a disorder that in one way or another—and psychoanalysis is *the* effort [emphasis added] to understand those ways—congealed as the uncanny cause of their desire, the 'un-economic' dimension of their libidinal economy" (61–62).

It is hard to dispute the usefulness of psychoanalysis, especially when reading Santner, who puts it to such good use. But political theory may have its own contributions to make to such an analysis. And *Merchant,* while instructive about the transfer from political theology to political economy may—perhaps because of its turn to law—call our attention only to theology and economy and obscure a key, albeit missing third term: the democratic. If we are in quest of that third term, we will need to turn from Shakespeare to what I have come to think of as the American *Merchant*: Melville's *Moby-Dick.* First, however, I turn to consider Santner's rejection of that alternative account of the flesh we have just seen him criticizing here.

Human-Animal Interlude

In his first lecture, Santner distinguishes his own interest in the "flesh" as the matter of theo-political economy from those new materialisms that also focus on the flesh as matter, albeit not in relation to human subjectivity but, rather, as an alien thing—one that, in Jane Bennett's words quoted by Santner, "reminds humans of the very *radical* character of the (fractious) kinship between the human and the nonhuman" (61). For Bennett, the benefit of talking about the flesh is not that it is a way in to understand new circuitries of subjectivity, or the manner of human electrification but, rather, that it is a way *out*. The vital materiality of the body, she says, is "not exclusively human." Our flesh is host to "an array of bodies," and if we attend to the fact "that we are made up of its" and not just me's, then perhaps a "newish self" might eventually emerge, "the self of a new self-interest."

Santner moves too quickly past Bennett, I think. They are close in many ways; this is clear already in Lecture 1, but even more so in Lecture 2. Both reject the idea that the secular world is disenchanted (Santner says it is *"ostensibly* disenchanted" [80, my emphasis]). Both look for sites of hidden enchantment. Both find them in certain overlooked vibrations that both might well call, as Santner does, "a surplus of immanence." Both favor interrupting contemporary economic imperatives that instrumentalize and alienate the human. Both approach human flesh as an alien thing. In Bennett it is host to vibrant worlds nonhuman; the bacteria that live on us should knock us off our human pedestal. True, Santner treats flesh as more spectral than vibrant (to borrow Diego Rossello's useful distinction[28]). (Santner calls it "ectoplasm" in *The Royal Remains* [100].) And he wants to preserve the human exception that Bennett wants to undo. Perhaps for this reason he, unlike Bennett, is drawn back into the disenchantment thesis he seems to want to reject, and drawn more to the spectral than to the vibrant.

This becomes clear when he allies the vibrancy he tracks with the undeadnesses of a world catapulted into perpetual motion by the need to cover over the void left yawningly open by the removal from the ontological and political scene of the King of political theology. "It is the 'business' of the sovereign," Santner will say in his second lecture, reprising the theme of *The Royal Remains*, "to cover the void in two fundamental senses: to veil it with his or her glorious body" and "stand surety for it as a primordial debt" (85). With no King and only a Duke in *The Merchant of Venice*, this task of standing surety falls to Antonio, who is both not up to the task (he lacks the glory) and too much up to it: he is too eager to be rendered precarious, not in order to pay the debt or cover it over, exactly, but (if Harry Berger Jr. is right) to put Bassanio in *his* debt, to keep him close while pretending to give him freely away to the bride who will be Bassanio's ship, come in.

The primordial debt, a figure of lack, is both too Lacanian and too Ahabian for Bennett, who calls on us to attend to the fullness, not the fulsomeness, of the world. In Santner, though, we are marked by that lack and by the fetish for that missing king who once veiled it, the one with the two bodies. Our fetish for the King is transformed, Santner now argues, into the fetishism of things, which Marx himself diagnoses as filling a metaphysical need. Even if not disenchanted, exactly, this post-political theological world—this new theo-political economy—is exposed in new ways. Instead of the liturgical support of the king's two bodies, we are now enmeshed liturgically, laboriously—"24/7," we might say—in a biopolitical administrative governance aimed at covering over the disenchanting loss of the meaning-securing sovereign.[29] This new governance turns now to the task of making us live.[30]

But if we return to the critique of human exceptionalism, lost when Santner moved us so quickly past Bennett, we might find something else worth attending to, something *between* the persons and things to which Santner confines our attention, something else that may also be contributing to the vibrations of the flesh—something between the somatic and the normative, the bacterial and the historical/economic.[31] That something is the flesh of the animal. It is the stuff of sacrifice, hunt, food, lubrication, and illumination, and it plays a central role in *Moby-Dick*, that other most famous drama of the flesh with which I want to put all of this into conversation.[32]

Melville's depiction of busy human and animal bodies in *Moby-Dick* offers some suggestive illustrations of the *agon* between political theology and political economy, but also something more important still, given Santner's own quest to chart the workings of the flesh. Moving past the insistence of psychoanalysis on the human exception and its confinement of our attention to the human realm, we may attend with Melville to the tons of flesh—gelatinous and liquefied, commodified and worshipped, revered and hated—that are the stuff of the whale at the center of *Moby-Dick*. The wager of my reply is this: were psychoanalysis to be put into tense, perhaps even agonistic partnership with the new materialisms that Santner hastens past (in the form of Jane Bennett's work on the flesh), as well as with other forms of democratic theorizing, it might be better positioned to make the kinds of worthy interventions Santner here seeks to make, and to take us beyond them to reflect on flesh not just as the new *mise en scène* of old hierarchies and distinctions but also, potentially, as the site of their liquefaction and the inauguration of alternatives to them.

If our concern is "the weight of all flesh," there are grounds to include animal flesh, and this one animal's in particular, he being the weightiest of all. Like Shakespeare's *Merchant*, Melville's *Moby-Dick* is a text about flesh—what it means, how it is valued, and how its meaning and value undergo vexed alteration in the metaphysically evacuated or attenuated context of an emergent mercantile economy that upends traditional ideals, norms, and habits.[33] The flesh in *Moby-Dick* is more whale than human and so, turning to it will take us away from the "landscape" Santner enlists psychoanalysis to negotiate and to the sea that we will also need to navigate if we are to explore the angst that drives the drama.[34] For onboard ship, all that is solid really does give way, though not to air: "There you stand, a hundred feet above the silent decks ...

while beneath you and between your legs, as it were, swim the hugest monsters of the sea."[35]

In Melville's novel, many of Santner's concerns are in play, but the concepts and categories to which Santner is drawn are elaborated differently. For example, Melville, too, pits the political theological (or what is left of it, in the form of the one-legged Captain Ahab) against the political economic (in the form of the mercantile and not so adventurous Starbuck). But Melville offers a third option that we might call democratic (which, contra Santner, is neither political theological nor political economic, but a third analytically distinct thing, though in practice always imbricated with the other two). Melville, too, is interested in the gap between the somatic and the normative (to use Santner's terms for what Melville might call the quest for meaning in an uncooperative or indifferent but still somehow enchanted world). And finally, flesh in *Moby-Dick* is everywhere, thematized as the stuff of heaven and death, matter and money, the key to both meaning and finitude. Recall Santner's claim that flesh comes to figure as the uncanny "substance of that jointure," something *"in excess of both the somatic and the normative* that both links and leaks into the two domains as the uncanny cause of various inflammatory conditions" (50, my emphasis). Melville's third democratic register, partaking of theology and economy but reducible to neither, appears in its most salient forms in the context of two distinct democratic moments or gestures, and both times the key to those democratic moments in the novel is flesh: animal flesh.

One final note before turning to the whale. One other reason to turn to *Moby-Dick* in the context of these lectures is to seek out Melvillean resources with which to combat much of left theory's love for Melville's "Bartleby, the Scrivener." We may note that Rancière, too, joins the ranks of left admirers of the Bartleby position. As Davide Panagia points out, in *Aisthesis*, Rancière canvasses dance, photography, sculpture, and other media that "are shown to spark the *'farniente* of reverie' (xv)—a critical term, it turns out, for Rancière's aesthetics of politics. The *farniente* (literally 'do-nothing') is the mode of acting of the 'no-part,' that odd form of political subjectivity that is the actant of Rancière's emancipatory politics. The no-part do no-thing: neither they nor their labors can count."[36] The fleshless Bartleby is the figure for the inoperativity that Agamben, Santner, and many others (for various reasons not all consistent with each other) see as a source of resistance, alternativity, or negativity.[37] If the problem to which Santner wants to alert us is that of the always *busy body*, then Bartleby's *un*busied body might well seem to provide a perfect counter. But there may be a reason to take the risk of busy-ness rather than try to avoid it, or try to rework rather than abandon it. Or, better still, we may want to do both those things: interrupt *and* re-orient the busy bodies of late capitalism.[38] To do so, democratic theory has reason to prefer Ishmael, the protagonist of *Moby-Dick*, who is so different from Bartleby: life-loving, good natured, good-willed, happy to work with others, though—like Bartleby, and this is key—Ishmael is also keenly sensitive to the soul-destroying properties of office work.[39]

The Human Takes Exception: Debt by the Ton (of Flesh)

Moby-Dick and *Merchant of Venice* are both texts about the changing meanings of flesh in the metaphysically evacuated or attenuated context of an emergent mercantile economy. Like *Merchant*, *Moby-Dick* is about a man who has been wronged and seeks satisfaction by exacting flesh from his opponent. The two texts both explore the experience of the loss of faith and the fury that may result. (Ahab is a blasphemer and Shylock goes from protesting that he cannot eat at a Christian table to doing just that.) Both texts oppose their central, wronged characters (Ahab and Shylock) with counterparts who get a charge out of them (Ishmael and Antonio). Melville's Ishmael and Shakespeare's Antonio both suffer from some form of ennui, listing in the doldrums of desire (-lessness). Both of these counterparts respond to their melancholy by putting themselves in danger. Though their modes of self-endangerment differ, both involve putting themselves in proximity to a vengeful man whose quest for satisfaction of a wrong vibrates through the lives and bodies of those around him.

Antonio says at the beginning of *Merchant*: "In sooth, I know not why I am so sad: /It wearies me; you say it wearies you;/But how I caught it, found it, or came by it: /What stuff 'tis made of, whereof it is born,/I am to learn;/And such a want-wit sadness makes of me,/That I have much ado to know myself" (1.1.1–7). Antonio will soon return to life, by exposing himself through the bond of debt to the tender mercies (or not) of the Jew, Shylock, the money-lender. In so doing, Antonio also creates a bond of debt between himself and the younger Bassanio, whom he loves.

Ishmael, Melville's narrator, will also find comfort in the arms of a man (who is more enigmatic and less self-seeking), but Ishmael finds his way to Queequeg because he, Ishmael, has a different, perhaps more American (less philosophical, more pragmatic) way of responding to melancholy than does Antonio: "Whenever I find myself growing grim about the mouth; whenever it is a damp drizzly November in my soul; whenever I find myself involuntarily pausing before coffin warehouses, and bringing up the rear of every funeral I meet ... then I count it high time to get to sea as soon as I can. *This is my substitute for pistol and ball*" (1; my emphasis). Waiting for his ships to come in, Antonio experiences a certain sadness, which he relieves by upping the ante so that he, and not just his ships, is at risk.[40] Ishmael gets on a ship, risking himself in order to relieve not ennui but, rather, the itch that is the symptom of confinement by land-based labor.

The flesh that is the enigmatic juncture between somatic and normative is different, though, in these two texts. In *Merchant*, it is

Antonio's own human flesh that is on the line, while in *Moby-Dick*, though Ishmael risks his life (and enjoys fleshly pleasures with the men of the *Pequod*), it is for the most part the flesh of the whale that is on the line: as white as Portia's flesh is pale (as Bassanio remarks), the whale's flesh is heavier and bears a greater weight, a teeming excess of signification, as many critics have remarked (as evidenced, for example, by chapter 42: "The Whiteness of the Whale," whose very long list ends with: "of all these things the Albino whale was the symbol. Wonder ye then at the fiery hunt?"[41]).

I focus here on three sites of the workings of the flesh in *Moby-Dick*, and these three, in particular, because the first two are arguably corollaries of the two regimes or epistemes in contention or in sequence in Santner's lectures: political theology (Ahab's view of whale flesh) and political economy (Starbuck's view of whale flesh).[42] But Melville offers a third (Ishmael's view of whale flesh), and gives us reason to call it "democratic." Santner knows flesh means many things (he offers a long list regarding *The Merchant of Venice*). But when he tracks its transformation from political theology to political economy, and restricts himself to the human "subject matter" of political economy, he avoids (some of) the *politics* of the flesh. One possibility is that out of the tensions between the political theological and the political economic, or in some sort of indebted agonistic relation to them, that third fleshly option might emerge: the democratic, which presses people up against each other, sometimes uncomfortably, sometime with joy in being together with others acting in concert, often jostled with and by the world of animality which has been leashed to our politics through the great figure of Leviathan since Job and, later, Hobbes (as Melville knows: he refers to both).

That the flesh of an animal might work the (dis)connection between the somatic and the normative makes sense because what we lose with the passing of political theology (*if* Santner is correct that it has passed and left only "remains," a point I contest later) is the practice of sacrifice, in which disturbing confrontations with the void (contingency, meaninglessness) are managed through the transitional ritual (a liturgical practice) of animal sacrifice: flesh burning. When Ahab chases the whale, without measure, he resurrects this extinct (and perhaps extinguished[43]) practice, hoping to find or make *meaning* rather than *money* out of the flesh of the whale.[44] Ahab has lost his pound(s) of flesh and seeks restitution—his bond—in the tons he blames for his injury.[45] Moby-Dick bit off Ahab's leg in a symbolic castration that binds these two creatures together in a kind of pact, like a circumcision. Ahab, that is, is the figure of lack. The bite has left Ahab maimed and desperate not only for vengeance but also for the sort of world in which injury can be repaid and an injured man can be made again whole. His is a political theological world, one in which a man can pile "upon the whale's white hump the sum of all the general rage felt by his whole race from Adam down" (267). Ahab's prosthesis is made of whalebone and so this figure of human sovereignty, captain of the ship and existentially enraged, is, like Kantorowicz's sovereigns, also (in a way) possessed of two bodies. (Ahab is also a *roi-pêcheur*, also in Derrida's terms, a figure of prosthetic sovereignty; also in Bennett's terms, his prosthesis is the "it" in the "I"—i.e., Ahab, too, *teems* with meaning.)

The brutely enigmatic quality of the whale, its legible illegibility (its forehead is said to be wrinkled with hieroglyphics: "I but put that brow before you. Read it if you can" [503]) both enables Ahab to imprint what he likes on it and drives Ahab mad since, as Dreyfus and Kelly put it, "the whale is a mystery so full of meaning that it verges on meaninglessness, so replete with interpretations that in the end they all seem to cancel out."[46] (However, the whale's whiteness may also be the whiteness of white supremacy, as Toni Morrison brilliantly suggests in *her* Tanner Lectures of 1988, casting Ahab as an antislavery zealot, like John Brown, out to topple the regime of white power. As noted, the whale's flesh teems with signification.[47]) Either way, the flesh of the whale stands at the juncture between the somatic and the normative (the very juncture at which Melville may himself have stood when he wrote to Hawthorne after finishing *Moby-Dick*: "I have written a wicked book [normative], and feel [somatic] spotless as a lamb."[48]

For Starbuck, Ahab's opposite, political theology has long since given way to political economy. The whale is only a commodity, flesh to be sold at market, and the sea voyage nothing more than a commercial venture.[49] Ahab's quest for vengeance is madness. Not only is it mad in its endangerment of ship and crew, it is also madness in that it makes no sense, and worse, it is blasphemous: "Vengeance on a dumb brute!" cried Starbuck, "that simply smote thee from blindest instinct! Madness! To be enraged with a dumb thing, Captain Ahab, seems blasphemous" (236). Starbuck does not mind the chase—"I am game for his crooked jaw"—nor the risks—"and for the jaws of Death too, Captain Ahab" (236). Though only "if it fairly comes in the way of the business we follow; but I came here to hunt whales, not my commander's vengeance. How many barrels will thy vengeance yield thee, even if thou gettest it, Captain Ahab? it will not fetch thee much in our Nantucket market" (236).

You cannot put a price on vengeance, Starbuck rightly says. To Ahab that makes it priceless. To Starbuck that makes it worthless. Unlike the rest of the crew, Starbuck is unmoved by Ahab's speeches, and unmotivated by the gold doubloon, nailed by Ahab just a few pages earlier to the mast to invigorate the ship's crewmembers to strive to be the first to sight the elusive white whale. That now *murdered coin* is a fetish that does not speak to Starbuck. He likes his coins the way he likes his blood: in circulation. So Ahab will appeal to him differently: "come closer Starbuck; thou requirest a little lower layer" (236).

At that lower layer, Ahab instructs Starbuck that all is not what it seems:

All visible objects, man, are but as pasteboard masks. But in each event—in the living act, the undoubted deed—there, some unknown but still reasoning thing puts forth the moldings of its features from behind the unreasoning mask. If man will strike, strike through the mask! How can the prisoner reach outside [to the Real] except by thrusting through the wall? To me, the white whale is that wall, shoved near to me.... He tasks me; he heaps me.... That inscrutable thing is chiefly what I hate; and be the white whale agent, or be the white whale principal, I will wreak that hate upon him. Talk not to me of blasphemy, man; I'd strike the sun if it insulted me. For could the sun do that, then I could do the other." (236)

The question is begged though, since the point of disagreement between Ahab and Starbuck is precisely whether the sun *can* insult a man—that is to say, whether Moby-Dick is capable of *wronging* Ahab, or whether the whale merely dumbly, instinctively bit him. From Starbuck's perspective, Ahab is surely like Sophocles's Ajax, who misfires (he is blinded, misdirected by the gods) when he murderously butchers animals in vengeance. If animal deaths can slake vengeance, it is through rituals of sacrifice, not murderous butchery. And if murderous butchery is what is called for—as in war or vengeance—then animals are the wrong objects to kill.[50]

More fundamentally, Ahab's response to Starbuck is that the whale is the occasion but not the goal. The goal in piercing through the whale is to see what is on the other side, to confront the divinity or lack thereof that makes (non)sense of the world of man and nature. Ahab wants to pierce through to the yawning open void that the King's two bodies once covered over with pasteboard masks and practiced liturgy. Starbuck is still unconvinced; he is not a metaphysical man, and so Ahab moves again to a different register, less fleshly and less philosophical, to prudence and glory. Referring to himself in the third person (never a good sign with Ahab), he points out that the crew are "one and all with Ahab, in this matter of the whale," warns that Starbuck cannot alone "[s]tand up amid the general hurricane," and appeals to Starbuck, "the best lance out of all Nantucket," to "not hang back" when the rest of the crew have signed on to the hunt and "every foremast-hand has clutched a whetstone" (237). Starbuck does not so much consent as acquiesce, with muttered reservations that will prove prophetic.[51]

Melville's drama of the flesh has one other site at which the flesh is thematized. Here, too, the flesh operates as an enigmatic source of passion and social adhesion, but it articulates or occasions a different form of sociality. The first site was political-theological: Ahab's monomania of the flesh into which the crew enlisted with enthusiasm (albeit supplemented by the lure of the gold doubloon). The second was political-economic: Starbuck's market perspective (albeit informed by religion—Starbuck accuses Ahab of blasphemy—and supplemented by Ishmael's warning that whale flesh costs not just money but also lives). We may note that this distinction is analytic. We may find in Benjamin, cited by Santner, a particularly apt (to Melville) post-Weberian reason to think of these two as always already co-implicated, because capitalism is said by Benjamin to be "probably the first instance of a cult that creates guilt, not atonement" (Benjamin, 288, cited in Santner's second lecture, 119). In this sense, Ahab may look more like what he surely also is: a creature of capitalism and not just a remainder of a prior political theology overcome by political economy.

Santner says that Benjamin here is pointing to "the *sovereignty of debt* over human life and its possibilities more generally" (119). And this invites us to ask: How else might we think of that debt? What might its other possibilities be? There is a third site of the flesh in Melville that may provide an answer. We may call it democratic, and it surfaces in a few key places.

First, in chapter 94, "A Squeeze of the Hand," the men of the crew are assigned the task of liquefying by hand the globules that remain in a whale's melted flesh (not Moby-Dick's; it is a different whale). Ishmael describes the scene:

> [W]ith several others, I sat down before a large Constantine's bath of it, I found it strangely concreted into lumps.... [A]s I bathed

my hands among those soft, gentle globules of infiltrated tis-
sues, wove almost within the hour; as they richly broke to my
fingers, and discharged all their opulence, like fully ripe grapes
their wine; as I snuffed up that uncontaminated aroma ... I for-
got all about our horrible oath [to hunt down Moby-Dick]; in that
inexpressible sperm, I washed my hands and my heart of it....
Squeeze! squeeze! squeeze! all the morning long; I squeezed that
sperm till I myself almost melted into it; I squeezed that sperm
till a strange sort of insanity came over me; and I found myself
unwittingly squeezing my co-laborers' hands in it, mistaking
their hands for the gentle globules. Such an abounding, affectionate, friendly, loving feeling did this avocation beget; that at last
I was continually squeezing their hands, and looking up into their
eyes sentimentally; as much as to say,- Oh! my dear fellow beings,
why should we longer cherish any social acerbities, or know the
slightest ill-humor or envy! Come; let us squeeze hands all round;
nay, let us all squeeze ourselves into each other; let us squeeze
ourselves universally into the very milk and sperm of kindness.
(600–601)[52]

In a reading attentive to the men, not the flesh (and usefully situated
in the context of nineteenth-century American politics, literature,
and tragedy), Jason Frank describes the scene as an "egalitarian
jouissance of collective undertaking ... which Melville portrays as
a kind of democratic absorption that resists incorporation into the
terrible logic of Ahab's quest."[53] In the end, Frank acknowledges,
the energies of this concerted action *will* be enlisted by Ahab for
his madness, rather than provide a democratic counter to his tyranny. But it is remarkable, nonetheless. For Frank, the "squeeze of
the hand" scene, we may say, is a "constituent moment" or a fugitive possibility, floated by Melville even though never entertained
entirely as its own autonomous alternative social arrangement.[54]

But we may go on to ask whether, contra Frank, the *jouissance* of the sperm squeezing scene, depends not just on the job at
hand, and not just on the men's proximity to each other, but also

(uncomfortably for the democratic view, perhaps) on the psychological proximity of the men in this scene to Ahab and the other flesh that haunts him, namely that of Moby-Dick. That is, might not these fleshpots borrow their boiling ardor from the very danger with which Frank wants to contrast them? If this "democratic absorption" truly "resists incorporation into the terrible logic of Ahab's quest," must that also necessarily mean that "democratic absorption" takes none of its charge from Ahab and his quest? The men who are transported by this work are not working on just any ship; they are on *Ahab's* ship, interpellated by his mad quest. They do their work not far from the mast to which he has nailed a murdered coin. If they are conscious in some way of their mortal interdebtedness, erotically or otherwise, that is surely because Ahab has brought to their consciousnesses a certain existential angst, debt, and terror. In his impossible quest to overcome his own demons, he has surely awakened theirs, charged them up. More to the point, he represents the very forfeit of futurity against which Benjamin Franklin's bromide warned: a willingness to let oneself go into a passion without regard for consequences. Surely the "squeeze of the hands" scene is informed or instructed by his example, charged up by his nearness, electrified by his passion?[55]

To all this we must also now add the flesh. Boiled, liquefied, globuled, the flesh is, like Jane Bennett's vibrant matter, desubjectified. Is it simply a social lubricant that overcomes "social acerbities," as Ishmael says?[56] Here, too, we may add to Frank's account, for the *jouissance* of the men is not accounted for just by the work they do together, nor even by (as I just argued) the fact that they work in Ahab's shadow. When Ishmael talks about its "uncontaminated" perfume, he recounts the experience of getting high on it, the feeling in which each individual man loses himself and finds others, and he lets us know that we are dealing here with something distinct, even if not as pure and uncontaminated as Ishmael thinks.[57] The whale flesh itself is not just the node of Ahab's bitter *ressentiment*, not just Starbuck's commodity for sale, and not just a conduit of democratic camaraderie. It is all of these, but also something more.

The *Pequod's* fleshpots (the term "fleshpot" matters: Moby-Dick—though not *this* whale whose boiled flesh the men squeeze—*is* referred to as Egyptian in chapter 79 and his hump is described as pyramidical, and to him is attributed a "pyramidical silence" [502]) are surely *charged*, electrified, by the aromatic, liminal flesh. The flesh is positioned between commodity and divinity, sale and worship, solid and liquid, tactile and aromatic, calculation and enthusiasm.[58] Moreover, sperm becomes placenta, the birthplace of something like (what Bennett calls) a "self-of a new self-interest," one that, as Hannah Arendt would point out, is "*inter-est*"—in between or among others.[59] In sum, where Bennett wants to recast human flesh as alien, vibrant matter, and Santner wants to enliven the flesh that is the spectral double of the human, my own move here has been to suggest that this animal's flesh does something related but analytically distinct: as it electrifies but also de-exceptionalizes the human, it becomes—or might become—the occasion of a new social relation.[60]

But the whale flesh, still charged by the theological and the economic, but not reducible to them, teaches still more, alerting us to some other, even more radical democratic lessons left to us by Melville. If Ahab longs for a lost political theology that still works, and Starbuck replaces it too readily with a deadening political economy that leaves workers vulnerable to—even hungry for—the incantations of the Ahabs of the world, the whaling does something else: it incites the men, and they incite us, to move in an altogether different direction. Their communal experience at the fleshpots imparts to them a certain insight, or opens them and us to it. The spermaceti whose globules the men squeeze comes not just from the body but also from the head of the sperm whale. Or better, with sperm whales, the head *is* the body and so the very whale that has long emblematized sovereignty itself as, precisely, singular head ruling over unruly body, the Leviathan that (very differently) from Job to Hobbes licenses the rule of god over man, ruler over subjects, *and* head over body, turns out to be a creature in which precisely this separation is not at all clear. The head *is* the bulk of the body, as Ishmael notes.[61]

How do we know this? Melville tells us! Tashtego falls into a whale's head when he is mining it for flesh, collecting spermaceti to be boiled for oil. He is rescued, but Ishmael muses: "Had Tashtego perished in that head, it had been a very precious perishing; smothered in the very whitest and daintiest of fragrant spermaceti; coffined, hearsed, and tombed in the secret inner chamber and sanctum sanctorum of the whale" (499). The head is the body—the site of flesh, oil, and of a certain mystery, because it is not immediately accessible to just anyone, no more than is "Plato's honey head" to which Melville immediately analogizes it (499). But which sort of head is *this*? Itself a pun for two different male body parts, it reminds us that it may be no accident, as it were, that when we unpack the head of leviathan it is not Reason that we find but sperm.[62]

In sum, Melville's leviathan, like that other one, makes the people possible. But it is a different people (the motley and audacious crew of the *Pequod*, not the obedient and more uniform *cives* of Hobbes[63]) and a different possibility (a sovereignty whose head *is* flesh and is therefore in no position merely to govern flesh or make it governable through incorporation under the head of reason). This possibility is one we can only begin to explore if we get inside the whale's head (or swim a mile in his flesh). Pictured as *whale* flesh, then, the move to the flesh does not just signal a transfer of sovereignty to the vibrating people, as Santner suggests. It dethrones the head's rule over the body and undoes that very distinction: either Hobbes's frontispiece image (featuring a giant ruling head over the body of the people, which turns into a rolling landscape at the groin) or the underpinning metaphor of Leviathan has to give way.

As Melville makes clear, the flesh exposes the fragility of sovereignty and its ambivalent dependence on the figure that is supposed to underwrite its power—Leviathan. Thus, the fact that the flesh that brings the men together belongs to the whale is most assuredly not incidental to the story but, rather, essential because the whale's anatomy is uniquely able to upend traditional figurations of sovereignty as a head that rules over the body of the people that it incorporates (into a body). As Melville makes clear, there is something uniquely important about the *whale* flesh that interpellates the crew into a charged circle and, having been so interpellated with them, we are uniquely able to see the impact of the flesh, whale flesh, on our own assumptions about sovereignty.[64]

Melville adds to the democratic stew when he has Ishmael make clear that the whale's topographic anatomy is known best not by scientists who study it or even by ship surgeons who witness it, but by whale hunters who engage with it. Against Linnaeus, he invokes "Simeon Macey and Charley Coffin, of Nantucket, both messmates of mine in a certain voyage" (194) and, later, "practical cetology," which Ishmael practices when he peruses two whale heads hanging off the sides of the *Pequod*. "Here, now, are two great whales, laying their heads together; let us join them, and lay together our own" (475). To study his subjects, all this practical cetologist has to do is cross the deck from one side to the other. And we learn something fundamentally important from this democratic source: the Leviathan that Hobbes relies upon to be all-seeing and powerfully surveillant? That "mortal god" that bridges the political and theological? When described by Ishmael from a whaler's perspective, leviathan turns out to be less than omnipotent.

Ishmael says that the whale's two eyes sit at such a distance from each other (where human ears are located, he says) that it is not possible for the whale to see what is straight ahead of him nor directly behind (476).[65] Consequently, ordinary whaling men in small boats can surround a whale and force it into a "helpless perplexity of volition" (478).[66] In the context of democratic theory, and given Hobbes's promotion of willing as central to theorizing freedom and sovereignty, such a description of the regal beast of sovereignty as easily paralyzed into volitional perplexity by a few whaling men working together sounds almost like an invitation, an incitation, an incantation.[67] High on the perfume of whale flesh, acting in concert, informed by the experiential knowledge of one of their own, and possessed of knight-like spearmen from the world over, the men can do anything, it seems.[68] So it does seem. In Melville's story, however, this capacity is never clean; it is always complicated by the fact that the men's ability to do anything together is stoked by Ahab's quest for vengeance and Starbuck's quest for profit. That is, the democratic lesson to be found here, and it *is* here, is impure: the men who can drive a whale into helplessness are themselves charged for the task by other men who lead, inspire, threaten, berate, and frighten them, as well as by remembered sensorial pleasures of the flesh and, perhaps, the anticipation of future ones.[69]

In any case, somewhere between political theology and political economy, Melville tracks or points to this third thing, perhaps generated by their clash and therefore somewhat obscured by Santner's sequencing (sometimes conceptual, sometimes historical) of theology and economy: this resistance to both, which is exhausted by neither, is thematized by Melville and personified by Ishmael, and it is what I have been calling the "democratic." In sum, if in Kantorowicz the King has two bodies with which to cover the worrying gap left by the evacuations or attenuations of metaphysics, in Melville the king is shown to have always had a third body: the supplement of whale (flesh) that both secures and attenuates the sovereignty that Hobbes meant only to re-secure with the figure of Leviathan. That third body, the oft-invoked Leviathan from Job to Hobbes and more, is sovereignty's supplement. (Perhaps this explains further why Ahab feels he must pierce this whale's body to penetrate the masks that block his vision: it is the King's third body, supplement to the political theological and the political economic.) And Melville, having established that supplementarity, goes on to work with that supplement to show that it is the source of the undoing of the very sovereign form and figure on which both theology and economy depend. (Such is the nature of the supplement, as Jacques Derrida suggests.) Here the material whale subverts the fetish of the whale as the sign of a certain political order. This material whale calls our attention not to a Hobbesian slavish multitude but to democratic men who work together to overpower the creature and force into a "helpless perplexity of volition" a creature that represents Hobbes's account of sovereign will and its power. In the mismatch between symbolic and material flesh, exposed by Melville, a democratic gap opens and an excess of agency appears.[70]

In the end, however, Melville leaves us with questions Santner commits us to posing (indeed, he implicitly posed some of these at the Tanner Lectures seminar on the last day). Is the third democratic register identified here merely the site of another set of things that busy bodies busy themselves with? Or is it something else altogether? Is it finally only absorbable into the very economies it seeks to upend? Is it even dependent upon them? Does it have inaugural powers of interruption? From the perspective of possible interruption, it is possible to say a few things by way of conclusion with the aim of pointing to the possibility of busy bodies busying themselves to undo or rework the demand to be a (certain kind of) busy body. One key thing is that the sort of debt that drives Ahab to demand repayment is replaced at the fleshpots with a different kind of inter-indebtedness. Busying ourselves with the latter alters the meaning, or it *might* alter the meaning, of being a busy body, and it might also alter our experience of the sort of existential debt that drives Ahab mad.

The Cult(ivation) of Debt and the Inoperative Sabbath, or: Ishmael versus Bartleby

Melville's *Moby-Dick* takes us full circle, while also perhaps breaking us out of some of the circles in which Santner here inscribes, or by which he circumscribes, us.[71] The action in concert in the "squeeze of the hands" scene Ishmael all but calls heavenly. It could be Santner's "grace-event." Regardless, it points to a much-needed third fleshly option between a political theology of Ahabian enthusiasm/*ressentiment* and the political economy of Starbuck's calculative market (even as we know the market runs on enthusiasm and tyranny is often more calculating than passionate). The men working at the fleshpots of the *Pequod* are busy bodies. Busying themselves with each other's bodies and with that of the whale, they seem to inaugurate also new political possibilities that are, however, never entirely free of the alternatives from which I have distinguished them here.

Recalling Benjamin's Franklin's bromide, we may note that the crew has killed a sow (the whale whose flesh they work to liquefy) and worked in the shadow of a murdered coin (the doubloon nailed to the mast), and so they may be said to be released for *jouissant* absorption precisely by the very forfeit of futurity that Benjamin Franklin could not countenance and that underwrites Ahab's terrifying quest. That *is* what is terrifying about it! And this is what the men learn from Ahab—his lesson to them is to give up on futurity.[72] Enchanted by the animals whose company they keep at sea (sometimes they merely watch, sometimes they hunt, sometimes they flee), the crew experiences its human investiture differently and perhaps more contingently than other people do. And this, too, may release them for a possible democratic future. (The idea of human investiture is Santner's, of course, and it highlights the fragility of the human that he has done so much to [psycho-] analyze.[73])

As I suggested, with Melville and with and against Hobbes, this third and lowest layer of the flesh may point to a generative, if impure, democratic possibility.[74] It is personified by Ishmael (and the crew), and offers a counter to Melville's other much-celebrated protagonist, Bartleby, the one who dies at work, by contrast with Ishmael, who works to die (which is only to say Ishmael seeks out the sort of work that makes him feel alive whenever a cold November settles on his soul). This, by contrast with the onshore Bartlebys Ishmael leaves behind when he joins up with the *Pequod*: "Posted like silent sentinels all around the town, stand thousands upon thousands of mortal men fixed in ocean reveries … all landsmen; of week days pent up in lath and plaster—tied to counters, nailed to benches, clinched to desks" (2).

For Agamben, on whom Santner will draw in the next lecture, and for Santner himself, Bartleby represents an admirable refusal, a work stoppage that can be allied with the Jewish Sabbath, an unplugging from the system and the culture of debt (Benjamin) that feeds on our flesh.[75] Agamben, cited by Santner, says: Man "is the Sabbatical animal par excellence" (245–46, in Santner, 102). Ishmael and the crew, enjoyers of the flesh, unplug, too (they leave the land where life grows dull and deadening). But they board ship hoping to plug *in* to something else, in quest of a future that eludes the more ectoplasmic, soon-to-be starved Bartleby.[76] Ishmael and the crew are more diverse, unruly, international, and connected than the groups of people who live and work on shore. In the end, Ahab hijacks or arguably fulfills their (suicidal) democratic potential. But he does not completely obscure it. We spend too much time in the men's company and under their tutelage to miss the fact that they show us a way out of the ontology of landed sovereignty. Hobbes's frontispiece, it will be recalled, represents the sovereign as a big headed, peopled body, corporeally cascading into rolling hills, where his genitalia ought to be. There is no water in view. Opening the sovereign figure's head to our view, the *Pequod*'s crew shows us the flesh that might alter our possibilities and invites us to leave behind the land surveyed by the sovereign. True, Ahab's crew is in the end nailed, like the doubloon, to the mast. But, still, they have their moments!

Democratic agency depends, however, not just on working our way out of the problem of sovereignty but also working our way back into it, perhaps even squeezing hands as we work our way through the lumps and globules that never entirely melt away.

Thus it is important that the alternative to the Sabbath of inoperativity, to which Agamben turns and which Santner, too, will invoke in Lecture 2, is also a kind of Sabbath, but this alternative is Sabbath *power*, not powerlessness; constituent, not "destituent," and it stems from the very same sources on which Agamben (partly) draws.[77] Thus even if it is true that Man "is the Sabbatical animal par excellence" (and such essentialism calls for critique), there is room to debate what it means to be a Sabbath animal. It cannot mean simply destituency, which is what Agamben seems to have in mind, because although it is true that Sabbath comes every week, it is also noteworthy that we speak of *"making"* Sabbath.[78] The preparations busy us, and this busy-ness is part of the very idea of Sabbath, not a prelude to it. In addition to the weekly Sabbath, moreover, the idea of the Sabbath includes land and debt sabbaticals. These *may* be understood as passive unpluggings. But they are not just that. They *may* be seen as momentary withdrawals from the economic order, but that is a misconstrual. They are active redistributions of goods and resources and their role or aspiration was once to redress or undo the accretion of inequality over time.[79]

Some activists have recently been inspired by these ideas. For example, Strike Debt's Rolling Jubilee project, a project of debt forgiveness, builds on the legacy of the Biblical Jubilee, also known as the Sabbath of Sabbaths. The biblical practice releases slaves and debts at a regular time ("And ye shall hallow the fiftieth year, and proclaim liberty throughout *all* the land unto all the inhabitants thereof: it shall be a jubilee unto you; and ye shall return every man unto his possession, and yet shall return every man unto his family" [Lev. 25:10]). Drawing on that practice, the Rolling Jubilee project buys debt randomly and cheaply, and forgives it.[80] In biblical times, debt forgiveness would have postulated a sabbatical infrastructure, but now, in our own time, an even more agentic, inaugural sort of Sabbath-power is required. It is important, though, that the Jubilee does not just forgive debt; it does still more. It makes debt into something other than a punitive and calculative institution. It postulates not just calculable citizens but also the sort of people sometimes willing to be positioned around fleshpots, squeezing hands, getting high on perfume. The Jubilee transforms debt into a collective practice and a communal responsibility.[81] It reverses and undoes the conversion of debt from public scandal to private shame, and in this sense it is not unconnected with the recent "public feelings" projects of Berlant, Cvetkovich, and others.

Sabbath-power postulates *both* destituent and constituent forms of power, both Bartleby and Ishmael. As Richard Dienst puts it in *The Bonds of Debt*, the way forward—what he calls "a radical politics of indebtedness"—may require combining two utopian attitudes that "might at first appear opposed or contradictory."[82] These are an acceptance of the fact that "human productivity itself requires indebtedness as a kind of irreducible technical prosthesis," and this is well pursued through practices like microcredit. The second, "associated with Jubilee . . . insists that people must always be able to refuse the obligations built into their circumstances. . . . [C]ancelling debts or going bankrupt is always somehow liberating. Not just once, but over and over" (183–84). Feed the beast; starve the beast. Key here is the idea that practices of debt and debt forgiveness position debt as a bond (as Shylock says) and not just as guilt (Benjamin).

Strike Debt's Rolling Jubilee project replaces the debt sanctuaries and refuges that once slackened sovereignty. In England, at Whitefriars, the Mint, and elsewhere, there were sanctuaries into which no bailiffs were allowed and which protected the lives (and sometimes also the assets) of those imperiled by debt and otherwise fated to live as bare life in debtors' prisons.[83] In our own time, these sanctuaries no longer exist.[84] But debt imprisonment does.[85]

In conclusion, following Santner's route from political theology to political economy as a biopolitics of debt, I want to add another step: a counter–politics of debt democratization that we could call, in political theological terms—*Sabbath-power*. This draws on the counter-narrative of political theology I developed in *Emergency*

Politics, where political theology does not only underwrite absolute sovereignty. It is not (as it sometimes seems to be in Santner's Kantorowiczian treatments) so univocal; it also works to solicit alternative sovereignties that are *potentially* more democratic.[86] This alternative political theology focuses less on the ruptures of divine miracle (as Schmitt does) and more on miracle's dependence on popular receptivity and subscription (as Franz Rosenzweig does). Against Shylock and Ahab (but also against Antonio), those extractors of pounds of flesh, and against Bartleby, the anti-flesh antihero who extracts his own flesh, democratic theory does well to embrace the history of resistance, the roads not taken and those forcibly foreclosed, which point beyond the covenant of the flesh (circumcision, bond, and debt). Among these could be the biblical Korach, who argues with Moses in the desert against his consolidation of "sovereignty" in his own person and against the increased privacy of his relationship with god, and Ishmael, the first one, the biblical infant left to starve in the desert as a castaway, but who lives because God sends water to rescue him from the dryness of the land. It is worth noting that the *Pequod* is full of such "renegades and castaways."

If I, and others, turn to the myriad legacies of Sabbath practice as a resource now, it may well be because, with political theology's passing or attenuation (*if* we accept Santner's premise), we lose not just the magic of the sovereign and not just his void-covering bodies, material and symbolic, somatic and normative, though we live with their remains. We also lose the sanctuaries and refuges that vented sovereignty when it was more fleshed out. To take up their work, it is necessary for us, we busy bodies, to poke our noses into other people's businesses. Randomly buying and forgiving debt is just one example of such work, which requires more agency than Bartleby can muster. Such actions may even excite the flesh of those who engage in them (hence Hannah Arendt's insistence on the often-thrilling pleasure of action in concert). The risk is that such actions are simply and merely ventings and that these support rather than undermine the sovereignty system they oppose. Concerns like this are what make Bartlebys out of potential Ishmaels. They often stem from the desire to know in advance that our actions will be really revolutionary in their impact, and not just remediative. But this we *cannot* know. They also assume sovereignty is elsewhere, and is something we oppose. But it might be here and it might be ours.

Psychoanalysis is Santner's preferred way to understand much of what we need to busy ourselves with. But in its attention to the individual and collective fantasies that provide subjects with the means to negotiate their sense of self and place, it risks neglecting the also important task of generating new fantasies or choosing the best ones for democratic futures. Ishmael understood the power of a good story to charge us up. So do Strike Debt and the new materialists. They know that to be re-charged for new forms of life requires unplugging from our old patterns of discernment, consumption, and indebtedness, *and* plugging into new ones: a new metabolization. Jonathan Lear, whom Santner often cites, sees psychoanalysis as itself opening "possibilities for new possibilities," but if psychoanalysis is to deliver on this, it may actually depend on certain supplements, like that of literature, as Eric Santner knows and does, and on democratic theory, and even on the new materialism, whose relentless horizontality might actually take some pressure off the human, rather than adding to it.[87] That said, what we risk missing with that move are the unconscious and enigmatic registers of human existence, those royal remains and human (dis) investitures that Eric Santner has made it his unique business (he is a busy body, too!) to track.[88] And for this, we are all in his debt.

Notes

1. This reply to Santner, about mortal interdebtedness, owes quite a lot to George Shulman, who has been teaching *Moby-Dick* for years, and whose

course on the novel inspired and guided mine. Thanks to the fabulous undergraduates who read *Moby-Dick* with me in my first class at Brown University, "Democracy Among the Ruins." For comments on an earlier draft of this essay I am grateful to Diego Rossello, Anna Bialek, Jane Bennett, Miriam Leonard, James Martel, Jason Frank, and George Shulman. Thanks to Paul Gutierrez for preparing the manuscript for publication, to Kevis Goodman for her incredible generosity as editor, and to Eric Santner for providing rich material with which to engage and argue.

2. Marc Shell, *Money, Language, and Thought: Literary and Philosophic Economies from the Medieval to the Modern Era* (Baltimore: Johns Hopkins University Press, 1993), 1. Subsequent page references are made in the text. Shell's book is about "money talk" (4). Some authors, he says, like those of *Faust* and *The Merchant of Venice*, try to account self-critically for "the money of the mind informing their own thought" (1). This is what I take Santner to be doing in these lectures, but from a different, psychoanalytic perspective.

3. With the Comaroffs, we might call this "Zombie flesh," but they connect it to specifics of *millennial* capitalism. Jean Comaroff and John Comaroff, "Alien-Nation: Zombies, Immigrants, and Millennial Capitalism," *South Atlantic Quarterly* 101 (2002): 779–805. They concern themselves with figurations of living deadness as symptoms of new market formations, specifically neoliberalization. Noting the appearance of stories of zombies in South Africa, they link new forms of "zombification," not to the dispersal of a politically theologized sovereignty, but to the failures of secular sovereignty. The state has, for them, abandoned its responsibility for governance under neoliberalism: "the concern with zombies in the northerly reaches of the country, while in many ways a novel confection, replays enduring images of alienated production. . . . Much like the story of labor itself, which, in an abstract sense, is still subject to the familiar "laws" of capitalism, yet, as concrete reality, has been substantially altered by the reorganization of the world economy as we know it" (798). They note, in particular, that the "much vaunted Reconstruction and Development Plan (RDP), designed to root out endemic poverty, has thus far had minimal impact" and that "its broad reformist objectives, which harked back to the age of the welfare state, soon hardened into GEAR, the government's Growth, Employment and Reconstruction strategy, which privileges development understood in terms of privatization, wage flexibility, and massive public service cutbacks" (791). Zombie stories and witchcraft accusations emanate from the rural north, so the authors note that "[l]ittle of the positive effects of these policies, or of recent post-Fordist expansion in domains like tourism, finds its way into the arid rural landscapes of the North or the Northwest Provinces" (791).

4. In these lectures, Santner tends to talk about a metamorphosis or transfer from political theology to political economy, but I take the argument of *The Royal Remains* and also much of what is said here to command, rather, an understanding of the post-political theology economy as always already a theo-political economy. Certainly Marx points us in this direction, too, when he talks about money as a "god" (in the *Economic and Philosophical Manuscripts* of 1844) and Benjamin, too, when he casts capitalism as a cult of guilt-inducing debt.

5. For a critique of this idea of abstraction from barter to money, offering historical evidence to the contrary, see Richard Seaford, *Money and the Early Greek Mind: Homer, Philosophy, Tragedy* (Cambridge: Cambridge University Press, 2004).

6. In "Milton and Usury," David Hawkes argues that money was always already a symbolic system, that its materiality did not anchor its symbolization powers but, rather, was a product of them, or both: "the abstract, imaginary nature of today's credit-money has interesting implications for literary critics," showing how "the financial and the semiotic do not occupy discrete areas of experience, or even separable spheres within the psyche. People are relearning what they once took for granted: that money is a system of signs, and that it is susceptible to the same ethical and aesthetic critiques as other systems of signs. Perhaps a facility in deploying the reproductive powers of money is connected to the skill of using the semantic power of language? Perhaps the distinction between money and language is artificial?" Hawkes, "Milton and Usury," *English Literary Renaissance* 41 (2013): 503–504. Santner would add, I think, that all systems of signs sign their signatures on and through the flesh of the subjects who are also the material and immaterial matter of all systems of signs. For Santner, focusing on the flesh as a semiotic system means also turning to psychoanalysis as a critical tool.

7. This focus on the flesh distinguishes Santner's argument from others exploring the same themes. Samuel Weber, for example, also looks at "the widespread appeal of the American model of . . . 'theological economy'" and conjectures: "If as Benjamin suggested, Capitalism is itself a Religion and not just the result of one; if qua religion its strength lies in the fact that it responds to questions and problems that previously only organized religions effectively addressed; and if moreover the religion that capitalism is follows in the wake of Christianity by developing the sense of universal culpabilization and indebtedness to include the deity itself, which today conceals itself behind individualist avatars, such as the 'star' and the 'state'—it is because the idea of inexpiable guilt and debt produce a 'cult'—an organized and repetitive practice—of consumption that allows credit and debt to appear as the

constituents of saving grace." Samuel Weber, "Money Is Time: Thoughts on Credit and Crisis" (manuscript on file with author, previously posted at http://www.complit.u-szeged.hu/images/weber_-_money_is_time.pdf), 12. Weber says he is "following the suggestive fragment of Walter Benjamin on 'Capitalism as Religion' . . . in which Benjamin argued that through its internal structure capitalism is not merely promoted by Protestantism but is the heir to Christianity as such" (1). Santner treats this essay by Benjamin in Lecture 2. Weber also works in detail with the passage from Benjamin Franklin, to which Santner alludes here. For another very useful take on capitalism and religion, see William Connolly, *Capitalism and Christianity: American Style* (Durham, NC: Duke University Press, 2008).

    8. We could also contextualize it within Santner's larger body of work. As Diego Rossello puts it in a review essay on Santner's work, Santner moves from a "spectral materialism" in *On Creaturely Life* to a "fleshy, vital materialism" in *The Royal Remains*. Rossello, "The Creature and the Sovereign: On Eric Santner's New Science of the Flesh," review of *On Creaturely Life: Benjamin, Rilke, Sebald* and *The Royal Remains: The People's Two Bodies and the Endgames of Sovereignty* by Eric L. Santner, *Political Theory* 42 (December 2014): 740. "Against liberal readers of Kantorowicz," Rossello argues, Santner's *The Royal Remains* treats the king's second body not "as mere fictional, symbolic trappings that cover the mortal, natural body of the monarch," but as the "'spectral yet visceral dimension of the flesh' (92), no longer incarnated in the monarch" and now materialized, "real and available, as an oppressive dark matter or 'ectoplasmatic substance' (93) that will eventually be reincarnated in the citizens of a democracy" (742). In Rossello's terms, we might say that in *The Weight of All Flesh*, the flesh is now both spectral and vibrant. Whether that is a sustainable position is a separate question.

    9. William Shakespeare, *The Merchant of Venice*, *The Riverside Shakespeare*, ed. G. Blakemore Evans (Boston: Houghton Mifflin, 1974), 3.1.66. Hereafter, lines are cited in the text.

    10. Jason Frank, "Pathologies of Freedom in Melville's America," in *Radical Future Pasts: Untimely Political Theory*, ed. Romand Coles, Mark Reinhardt, and George Shulman (Lexington: University Press of Kentucky, 2014), 452.

    11. Santner, *The Royal Remains: The People's Two Bodies and the Endgames of Sovereignty* (Chicago: University of Chicago Press, 2011).

    12. This brings me closer to Jane Bennett than Santner wants to be, I think. My position is not hers, but we both see the flesh, as we differently read it, as unsteadying sovereignty.

    13. The two plays are not that far apart for Santner, who says in his first lecture, "*The Merchant of Venice* renders explicit what in *Hamlet* is

registered only as a sort of underlying dream-work summoned forth—or as we might say, *excited*—by structural transformations of the social order. It was Schmitt himself who argued apropos of *Hamlet* that, 'even the dreams that the dramatist weaves into his play must be able to become the dreams of the spectators, with all the condensations and displacements of recent events' (36). But as Schmitt also argues, these 'recent events' include the opening of a *structural interregnum* that would not fully take shape in the lifetime of the London audience of Shakespeare's play. *Merchant* helps to identify the key historical forces at issue in this opening along with the semantic and symbolic transformations it brings in its wake" (59). I note now, for my later turn to Melville, that among the many citations that open *Moby-Dick* is one from *Hamlet*: "very like a whale." Herman Melville, *Moby-Dick, or, The Whale* (New York: Modern Library, 2000), xxviii. Hereafter, pages are cited in the text.

14. Lara Bovilsky, "'Racked ... to the Uttermost': The Verges of Love and Subjecthood in *The Merchant of Venice*," in *The Distracted Globe: Worldmaking in Early Modern Literature*, ed. Marcie Frank, Jonathan Goldberg, and Karen Newman (New York: Fordham University Press, 2016).

15. Recent work on the play has done much to scramble, reconsider, and reallocate these seemingly structuring binaries. See especially Harry Berger on the manipulative mercies of Antonio in *Fury in the Words: Love and Embarrassment in Shakespeare's Venice* (New York: Fordham University Press, 2012) and Bovilsky,"'Racked ... to the Uttermost.'"

16. No one in the play thinks the pound of flesh figures "a value that can be extracted ... materially abstracted—from a living body." Shylock's bond is a death sentence for Antonio and Antonio (even discounting his melodrama) knows it.

17. On this, Sheldon Wolin's "The People's Two Bodies," *Democracy* 1, no. 1 (1981): 9–24, may be pertinent.

18. Portia: "It must not be, there is no power in Venice,/Can alter a decree established." Shakespeare, *Merchant*, 4.1.218–19. The Duke has a certain soft power, however, or so one may infer from the fact that the Venetian currency of the ducat derives its name "from Medieval Latin *ducatus* 'coin,' originally 'duchy,' from *dux* (genitive *ducis*) 'duke'" (*Online Etymology Dictionary*, s.v., "ducat," accessed August 3, 2014, http://www.etymonline.com). It may be worth noting that Melville himself notes the power of the Duke in chapter 105 of *Moby-Dick* (in England, not Venice) and in that context comes close to gesturing to the doctrine of the King's Two Bodies: "On what principle [is] the Sovereign ... originally invested with" rights to any whale caught off the coast? The answer comes from Edmund Plowdon [sic: Plowden]: 'Says

Plowdon, the whale so caught belongs to the King and Queen, 'because of its superior excellence'" (580). And that right can be delegated to any Duke by the Crown. Notably, it was this very Plowden who formulated (along with Anthony Browne) the theory of the King's Two Bodies, the very doctrine tracked by Ernst Kantorowicz and drawn upon by Santner. Kantorowicz argues that this doctrine dates to the 1560s, from debates over the status of the Duchy, to whom the right to the whale is granted, in *Moby Dick*. I discuss the Meville/Plowden/Kantorowicz connection in more detail in my own work in progress: *The King's Three Bodies: Lion, Leviathan and the Democratic Imagination Gone Wild*.

19. Though they may signify differently in the different context of biopolitics. On contemporary cutting in relation to ancient practices of self-laceration, see chapter 5 of my *Antigone, Interrupted* (Cambridge: Cambridge University Press, 2013). Debt bondage is a topic to which I return later.

20. That is, a reproductive crown that, if unmurdered, begets "scores" more pounds is a sign of usury; it is not just, as Santner suggests, a remnant of the other crown—i.e., the sovereign (which, it is worth noting, Franklin actually did have a hand in murdering, via the U.S. revolution).

21. Samuel Weber homes in on precisely this dimension: that of mortality and the effort to attenuate it through the redemptions of capital, as seen in Franklin. It is worth thinking about whether Franklin here, intentionally or not, is arguing not just in favor of moneyed futurity (as I note above) but also against religious practices of sacrifice, which give up this sort of futurity (of investment) on behalf of a different one—an afterlife—and this precisely by sacrificing animals (though not sows, exactly) and contributing money. If we ally the practice of sacrifice, which is deliberately nonreproductive and anti-profitable, with the sort of destituent forms that Agamben and Santner (in Lecture 2) identify with Sabbath and (Bartlebyian) inoperativity, then we may see the options here as follows: a certain secularity and related futurity (Franklin) versus Sabbath and a different futurity (Agamben, Santner) versus what I call "Sabbath-power" and a still-different democratic futurity, discussed later.

22. ANTONIO: "This was a venture, sir, that Jacob served for,/A thing not in his power to bring to pass,/But sway'd and fashion'd by the hand of heaven,/Was this inserted to make interest good? Or is your gold and silver ewes and rams?" SHYLOCK: "I cannot tell; I make it breed as fast." Shakespeare, *Merchant*, 1.3.89–94.

23. Jacques le Goff, *Your Money or Your Life* (Cambridge: Zone Books, 1988), 29. The position of the usurer at the bottom of the social ladder is underlined when Hannah Arendt, in what seems an unfortunate choice of words

given the historical association of usury with Jews, says in a letter to Jaspers that human beings were equally innocent "in the face of the gas chambers" and that even "the most repulsive usurer was as innocent as a newborn child." Quoted in Shoshana Felman, *The Claims of Literature* (New York: Fordham University Press, 2007), 359.

24. Historically, there was another exception, too. Slavery provided the human livestock that could make one's investment grow, (un)naturally—i.e., reproductively: The advantages were considered by Thomas Jefferson, whose cooling to the idea of emancipation, is traced by Henry Wiencek to 1792. "As Jefferson was counting up the agricultural profits and losses of his plantation in a letter to President Washington that year, it occurred to him that there was a phenomenon he had perceived at Monticello but never actually measured. He proceeded to calculate it in a barely legible, scribbled note in the middle of a page, enclosed in brackets. What Jefferson set out clearly for the first time was that he was making a 4 percent profit every year on the birth of black children. The enslaved were yielding him a bonanza, a perpetual human dividend at compound interest. Jefferson wrote, 'I allow nothing for losses by death, but, on the contrary, shall presently take credit four per cent per annum, for their increase over and above keeping up their own numbers.' His plantation was producing inexhaustible human assets. The percentage was predictable.... In another communication from the early 1790s, Jefferson takes the 4. percent formula further and quite bluntly advances the notion that slavery presented an investment strategy for the future. He writes that an acquaintance who had suffered financial reverses 'should have been invested in negroes.' He advises that if the friend's family had any cash left, 'every farthing of it [should be] laid out in land and negroes, which besides a present support bring a silent profit of from 5. to 10. per cent in this country by the increase in their value.'" This "silent profit" is the sound of money growing. Henry Wiencek, "The Dark Side of Thomas Jefferson," *Smithsonian Magazine*, October 2012, http://www.smithsonianmag.com/history/the-dark-side-of-thomas-jefferson-35976004/?%3Cau&no-ist. In *Moby-Dick*, such calculations will be applied to young black Pip, who is charged with becoming their carrier, and not just their object, when Stubbs tells him not to jump overboard again: "'Stick to the boat, Pip, or by the Lord, I won't pick you up if you jump; mind that. We can't afford to lose whales by the likes of you; a whale would sell for thirty times what you would, Pip, in Alabama. Bear that in mind, and don't jump any more.' Hereby perhaps Stubb indirectly hinted, that though man loved his fellow, yet man is a money-making animal, which propensity too often interferes with his benevolence'" (597).

25. Hence Antonio's objection, which Santner and other critics see as a charge of a kind of verbal usury: Shylock is said to wrest extra meaning out of the biblical text. Of course, usury once connoted punning as well. (See Shell, *Money, Language, and Thought*).

26. In one such "busybody" column, Franklin chides those who dig for gold, hoping to stumble undeservedly on some unlikely treasure. He cites Agricola's words to his son, bequeathing him land: *"I give thee now a Valuable Parcel of Land; I assure thee I have found a considerable Quantity of Gold by Digging there; — Thee mayst do the same. — But thee must carefully observe this, Never to dig more than Plow-deep."* Benjamin Franklin, "The Busy-Body, No. 8," *The History Carper*, accessed August 3, 2014, http://www.historycarper.com/1728/06/30/the-busy-body-no-8. See also Franklin, *Silence Dogood, The Busy-Body, & Early Writings* (New York: Library of America, 2002).

27. The move to Melville was further licensed by the live lectures in which Bartleby was mentioned approvingly more than once. Bartleby reappears briefly in Santner's Response in this volume: "there is a psychoanalytically relevant cause only where some element in our psychic household begins to assume . . . that zero-level status or office whose uncanny ways we have come to know under like names like Bartleby and Odradek" (270). And, of course, Melville's character played a role as well in Santner's *The Royal Remains*, where Bartleby is said to be "the harbinger of a new sort of 'divine comedy' of creaturely life, one created out of the troubles that plague the office of the human" (247) and where the character's famous words —"I prefer not to"— are Santner's own closing words (252).

28. See Rossello, "Creature and the Sovereign."

29. *If* he did successfully secure meaning, once upon a time, as it were: the Kantorowiczian claim that sovereignty "worked" in this way does not mean it succeeded. This was its operation. Santner's earlier work on crises of investiture (*My Own Private Germany* [Princeton, NJ: Princeton University Press, 1996]) does call attention to the failures or vulnerabilities of political theology and not just its successes and strengths. Also, when he calls the liturgical in Lecture 2 a "performative," he invites a consideration not just of its natal magics but also of its constitutive failures or misfires.

30. See, for example, Santner's powerful reading of the Terri Schiavo case ("Terri Schiavo and the State of Exception," *University of Chicago Press*, March 29, 2005, http://www.press.uchicago.edu/Misc/Chicago/05april_santner.html).

31. Santner is aware of a possible rapprochement between his view and the new materialists. He cites Julia Lupton's argument that the assemblage

of hospitality presupposes assemblages of the sort that Bennett writes about, drawing on Deleuze. See Julia Reinhard Lupton, "Hospitality," in *Early Modern Theatricality*, ed. Henry Turner (Oxford: Oxford University Press, 2013), 423–41. But Santner does not open the question of the animal as a site of flesh and glory (leviathan?), a juncture of somatic and normative.

32. I mention illumination because whale flesh is what lighted the homes of the East Coast until 1859, when petroleum was discovered and the whaling industry was undone, only eight years after Melville wrote *Moby-Dick*—which turned out to be whaling's swan song: "If the financial crisis of 1857 signaled the beginning of the end of whaling . . . the discovery of petroleum in 1859 quickly provided a new series of far cheaper substitutes for all the products derived from sperm whale oil." Cesare Casarino, *Modernity at Sea: Melville, Marx, Conrad in Crisis* (Minneapolis: University of Minnesota Press, 2002), 82. It is worth noting that whaling waned, but it did go on. As I put the final touches on this essay, I stumbled on a childhood book, *The Reader's Digest Junior Omnibus* (Montreal: Reader's Digest Association, n.d.) featuring the story "I killed 'Moby-Dick'" (by Amos Smalley, as told to Max Eastman). In 1902, Smalley, a Native American born in Gayhead, Massachussets, and working out of New Bedford, killed a white whale. He only found out 35 years later, when he was interviewed by a history professor named Marcus Jernegan, about "the story that whalers used to tell some fifty years before my time, of a white sperm whale that raged around the Pacific Ocean and was more ferocious than anything ever met on land or sea" (36). In 1956, Smalley was invited by John Huston and Gregory Peck to attend the opening of the film *Moby-Dick*, and he was introduced as the man who killed Moby-Dick. Smalley was not so sure: "I don't know if it was Moby-Dick I killed. I do know, though, that whales sometimes move from ocean to ocean. I also remember Captain McKenzie saying when he examined the worn-down teeth of my white whale: 'He's at least a hundred years old and might well be two'" (36).

33. I have found only one critical reference to the two together: Kenneth Gross says: "Shylock, like Meville's Ahab, has here set himself beyond any rational calculation, rejecting any fear that the real cost of pursuing what he himself calls 'a losing case' might be greater than its imaginary gain." Gross, *Shylock Is Shakespeare* (Chicago: University of Chicago Press, 2006), 72. The only other connection I found between these two great characters is Orson Welles, who seems to have played both (see Geoffrey O'Brien, "Encore: Too Much Johnson," *Film Comment*, January/February 2014, http://www.filmcomment.com/article/review-too-much-johnson-orson-welles/print). And, of course, it seems worth noting that in 1849 Melville bought a collected

edition of Shakespeare's works and his reading of the plays led him to introduce a new character to his whaling story: Ahab. See Nathaniel Philbrick,
Why Read Moby-Dick? (New York: Penguin Books, 2013).

34. The term "landscape" was in the live lectures.

35. "[S]o at nightfall, the Nantucketer, out of sight of land, furls his sails,
and lays him to his rest, while under his very pillow rush herds of walruses
and whales" (93).

36. Davide Panagia, review of *Aisthesis: Scenes from the Aesthetic
Regime of Art* by Jacques Rancière, *Critical Inquiry*, June 4, 2014, http://criti-
calinquiry.uchicago.edu/davide_panagia_reviews_jacques_ranciere/.

37. On left theory's turn to Bartleby, see Kevin Attell, "Language and
Labor, Silence and Stasis: Bartleby Among the Philosophers," in *Political
Companion to Melville*, ed. Jason Frank (Lexington: University Press of
Kentucky, 2013). In the live lectures, Santner followed Agamben in naming
Bartleby as the figure for a desirable inoperativity, what I am calling here
a kind of unbusied-body. In Santner's work, Odradek often stands in for
Bartleby. In Santner's Response, the two are coupled.

38. Remarking on the novel's not always heeded assertion of an *un-busied
body* type of temporality, and linking it to the body, through blood, if not
flesh, David Gilbert says: "You cannot read this book for speed. It is designed
for the long haul, the chapters never too long, naps seemingly built into the
text. It is, dare I say, a voyage. When in doubt, or simply in need of something, the something uncertain, a scratch like the scratch Ishmael feels in
those opening lines, instead of the sea I will take to *Moby-Dick* and turn to a
random page and read a few paragraphs out loud, my voice hauling forth the
words like a net full of squirmy fish. It gets in your blood. It is your blood."
Quoted in Joe Fassler, "The Endless Depths of *Moby-Dick* Symbolism,"
The Atlantic, August 20, 2013, http://www.theatlantic.com/entertainment/
archive/2013/08/the-endless-depths-of-i-moby-dick-i-symbolism/278861/.

39. It may be worth adding that in turning from *Merchant* to Melville, we
also turn from Jacob, the chosen one, to Ishmael, the unchosen.

40. Antonio's substitute for pistol and ball is arguably Shylock. It is a kind
of suicide by proxy when he makes himself vulnerable to Shylock, whom he
has goaded into a murderous fury. On the affective investment here, Bovilsky
drily observes: "No one cares about Shylock more than Antonio does."
(Bovilsky, " 'Racked . . . to the Uttermost.' ")

41. "Is it that by its indefiniteness it shadows forth the heartless voids and
immensities of the universe, and thus stabs us from behind with the thought
of annihilation, when beholding the white depths of the milky way? Or is it,
that as in essence whiteness is not so much a color as the visible absence of

color; and at the same time the concrete of all colors; is it for these reasons that there is such a dumb blankness, full of meaning, in a wide landscape of snows—a colorless, all-color of atheism from which we shrink? And when we consider that other theory of the natural philosophers, that all other earthly hues—every stately or lovely emblazoning—the sweet tinges of sunset skies and woods; yea, and the gilded velvets of butterflies, and the butterfly cheeks of young girls; all these are but subtle deceits, not actually inherent in substances, but only laid on from without; so that all deified Nature absolutely paints like the harlot, whose allurements cover nothing but the charnel-house within; and when we proceed further, and consider that the mystical cosmetic which produces every one of her hues, the great principle of light, for ever remains white or colorless in itself, and if operating without medium upon matter, would touch all objects, even tulips and roses, with its own blank tinge—pondering all this, the palsied universe lies before us a leper; and like wilful travellers in Lapland, who refuse to wear colored and coloring glasses upon their eyes, so the wretched infidel gazes himself blind at the monumental white shroud that wraps all the prospect around him. And of all these things the Albino whale was the symbol. Wonder ye then at the fiery hunt?" (282–83).

42. Santner refers on 51 to "[t]he shift from the political theology of sovereignty to the political economy of the wealth of nations [which] is . . . a shift from one 'epochal' mode of shaping our life in the flesh to another."

43. Casarino notes in *Modernity at Sea* the conflation of these in the comparison of the Pequod tribe to the ancient Medes. As I noted above, Franklin may be out to extinguish the distinction.

44. Though in this he may be more Greek than Jew, more Sophocles's Ajax than the biblical Abraham, in fact, for the sacrifice Ahab seeks is in vengeance *against* and not in gratitude *to* the deity.

45. Thus Melville's novel follows in the wake of Shakespeare's play, which, as Santner says, "finally offers us the figure of a value that can be extracted . . . *materially abstracted*—from a living body and weighed in the balance" (55). This is precisely what Melville describes as the business of whaling while leaving open and plural what such material extractions/abstractions can *mean*. Melville also exceeds Santner's frame in that *Moby-Dick* calls attention to the sensorial dimensions of the experience of the flesh, the taste, the smell, the visions, the touch of it. Relatedly, see my discussion of the "sensorial synagogue" in Heine (in Bonnie Honig, *The Laws of the Sabbath (Poetry): Arendt, Heine, and the Politics of Debt*, 5 U.C. Irvine L. Rev. 461 (2015). The sensorial is a register to which the new materialists are more attuned.

46. Hubert Dreyfus and Sean Dorrance Kelly, *All Things Shining: Reading the Western Classics to Find Meaning in a Secular Age* (New York: Free

Press, 2011), 149. In his Response (269), Santner quotes Laplanche, whose reflection on the enigmatic signifier calls to mind these workings of whiteness (and the whale): "We know *that* it signifies, but not what it signifies.... Lacan suggests the image of hieroglyphs in the desert, or of cuneiform characters carved on a tablet of stone.... It ... means that the signifier may be *designified*, or lose what it signifies, without thereby losing its power to signify *to*." (Jean Laplanche, *New Foundations for Psychoanalysis*, trans. David Macey [Oxford: Basil Blackwell, 1989], 44–45.)

47. See Toni Morrison, "Unspeakable Things Unspoken: The Afro-American Presence in American Literature," *Michigan Quarterly Review* 28, no.1 (2000): 1–34.

48. As Jason Frank says in a powerful Nietzschean reading not just of Ahab but also of his crew: "Ahab's 'dismemberment' and his quest for vengeance is a synecdoche, then, that gives articulation to the deeply felt but inchoate grievances and resentments disseminated among the crew; it taps into their 'unconscious understandings,' stimulates 'the subterranean miner that works in us all' ... and imbues their suffering with shared significance while affectively orienting their collective actions to overcome it [even if in a doomed way]. Ahab's quest identifies the enemy on which they can unleash their wounded hate, and offers a cause vivified by a sense of shared injury and shared vengeance. Even Ishmael, the novel's embodiment of fair-minded common sense and liberal tolerance, is not immune to the lure of this collective fantasy." (Frank, "Pathologies of Freedom in Melville's America," in *Radical Future Pasts: Untimely Political Theory*, ed. Romand Coles, Mark Reinhardt, and George Shulman (Lexington: University Press of Kentucky, 2014), 451–52.

49. To be fair, Starbuck is less driven—or, perhaps better, differently driven—than Ahab. Starbuck wants profit and he is willing to die for it. He finds a useful sublimation in the commercial adventurism of whaling, which, after all, has a bit of the old (the aristocratic world: Melville calls the whaling men "knights" and "squires") and a bit of the new (market and money-life).

50. There is a legal history of putting animals on trial for committing wrongs; see Darren Oldridge, *Strange Histories: The Trial of the Pig, the Walking Dead, and Other Matters of Fact from the Medieval and Renaissance Worlds* (London: Routledge, 2004). The practice is medieval, but recently it has been reactivated with animals positioned as potential plaintiffs against unethical, cruel treatment by humans. See Charles Siebert, "Should a Chimp Be Able to Sue Its Owner?," *New York Times*, April 23, 2014, http://www.nytimes.com/2014/04/27/magazine/the-rights-of-man-and-beast.html?_r=0.

51. He is not idiosyncratic. Unique only on board ship, on land he would have had more company: "Ahab had purposely sailed upon the present voyage with

the one only and all-engrossing object of hunting the White Whale. Had any one of his old acquaintances on shore but half dreamed of what was lurking in him then, how soon would their aghast and righteous souls have wrenched the ship from such a fiendish man! They were bent on profitable cruises, the profit to be counted down in dollars from the mint. He was intent on an audacious, immitigable, and supernatural revenge" (270). Of course, as we shall see, the people who stay on land are made of different stuff. Indeed, it was for a time the ones who set out to sea who emblematized the new nation as a global power: in the early nineteenth century, "whaling in the open ocean was rapidly becoming the young Republic's strongest claim to global preeminence and indefatigable enterprise. . . . By the 1840s some 600 American whaling vessels were plying the Pacific, vanguards of U.S. geopolitical ambitions, and a major source of national wealth," says D. Graham Burnett, *Trying Leviathan* (Princeton: Princeton University Press, 2010), 6. My thanks to Anna Bialek for referring me to this book.

52. In the end, Ishmael decides, the pleasure is too great and must be sublimated: "Would that I could keep squeezing that sperm for ever! . . . [But] in all cases man must eventually lower, or at least shift, his conceit of attainable felicity; not placing it anywhere in the intellect or the fancy; but in the wife, the hearth, the bed, the table, the saddle, the fire-side; the country; now that I have perceived all this, I am ready to squeeze case eternally. In thoughts of the visions of the night, I saw long rows of angels in paradise, each with his hands in a jar of spermaceti" (601–602).

53. See Frank's introduction "American Tragedy: The Political Thought of Herman Melville," in *Political Companion to Melville*, ed. Jason Frank (Lexington: University Press of Kentucky, 2013), 1–20.

54. This is the name of a book by Jason Frank: *Constituent Moments* (Durham, NC: Duke University Press, 2010).

55. On the question of whether Melville invented sperm squeezing, or reported on it, see Caleb Crain, "Did Melville Invent Sperm-Squeezing?" *Steamboats are Ruining Everything* (blog), September 9, 2010, http://www.steamthing.com/2010/09/did-melville-invent-sperm-squeezing.html.

56. The idea of easy gliding suggests to me that, in Melville's terms, Bennett can be said to write from the perspective of loose fish and Santner from the perspective of fast fish (caught fast). The distinction sticks with the reader because it is one of the powerful places (in one of the supposedly "boring" chapters) where Melville stops to address the reader directly and animalizes us: "And what are you, reader, but a Loose-Fish and a Fast-Fish, too?" (576). On the "boring" bits of *Moby-Dick*, see Jennifer Doyle, "*Moby-Dick's* Boring Parts: Pornography's Allegorical Hothouse," in *Sex Objects* (Minneapolis: University of Minnesota Press, 2006), 1–14.

57. To say the flesh is not pure is to note that it surely enchants and/or is enchanted by its proximity to vengeance or trade. On the significance of its aroma, I am grateful to James Martel.

58. The undecidability of whale flesh, or of whales more generally, were matters for trial earlier in the nineteenth century. The trial, which was to decide the status of the whale as fish or mammal, was almost certainly mocked in *Moby–Dick's* cetology chapter. On the trial, see Burnett, *Trying Leviathan*.

59. True, under the condition of "rise of the social" this "inter-est" could relapse into what is merely a rather old self-interest: the traffic in flesh. Thus, the question for Arendt is always how to hold the charge of the "inter-est" so that it electrifies and vitalizes the everyday, rather than succumb to (what she sometimes seems to see as) its deathless repetitions. That is, her question is Lear's question and Santner's question: how to secure a possibility for new possibilities? For more on this, see Arendt, *The Human Condition* (Chicago: University of Chicago Press, 1998). On Arendt as a kind of rethinker of political theology, between Franz Rosenzweig and Carl Schmitt, see the fine work of John Wolfe Ackerman, for example, "The Memory of Politics: Hannah Arendt, Carl Schmitt and the Possibility of Encounter," in *Concentrationary Memories*, ed. Griselda Pollock and Max Silverman (London: I. B. Tauris, 2014), 31–46.

60. That is, I want to read this in a way that is more fleshly than Frank's reading. Frank's reading stays with the men and highlights (C. L. R. James style) the importance of shared work to their experience of collectivity while underrating the importance to that experience of the uncontaminated perfume of the whale's boiled flesh.

61. Thus, thinking about the politics of the flesh through the whale arguably does more than the vibrant or spectral materialisms of Bennett and Santner, respectively, to undo the image-knot that true democracy must undo if it is to alter the world of possibilities and not just add a possibility to the world of politics and rule. That image-knot is that of the Hobbesian head over body, the image of rule. Santner's weighty flesh risks leaving the head intact, but Melville's whale flesh perspective (which includes head and/as body) shows us how it just melts away. Indeed, why not wonder whether it may not be Hobbes who is mocked (along with so many others) when Melville has Ishmael say that the Greenland whale, until now taken by scientists as exemplary of whales, "is an usurper upon the throne of the seas. . . . Reference to nearly all the leviathanic allusions in the great poets of the past days will satisfy you that the Greenland whale, without one rival, was to them the monarch of the seas. But the time has at last come for a new proclamation. This is Charing Cross; hear ye! Good people all, – the Greenland whale is deposed, – the great

sperm whale now reigneth!" (192). Elsewhere Melville is more direct: he cites the opening lines of Hobbes's *Leviathan* in the opening pages of *Moby-Dick*. And there is a clear allusion to Hobbes in chapter 87, "The Grand Armada," when a herd of whales seen from afar is described as "sometimes embracing so great a multitude, that it would seem as if numerous nations of them had sworn solemn league and covenant for mutual assistance and protection" (552). These references are noted, too, in Joseph Adamson, *Melville, Shame, and the Evil Eye: A Psychoanalytic Reading* (New York: State University of New York Press, 1997).

62. On this point, I am grateful to George Shulman, whose essay, "Chasing the Whale: Melville's *Moby Dick* as Political Theory," tracks the figure and the work of "Leviathan" through Job, Hobbes, and Schmitt (in Frank, ed., *Political Companion to Herman Melville*, 70–108).

63. For the sake of argument, I assume here the more conventional readings of Hobbes rather than the provocative, intelligent commentaries of those who see Hobbes as a defender of individuality. (Examples of the latter are Michael Oakeshott's "Introduction to Leviathan" in Oakeshott, *Hobbes on Civil Association* [Indianapolis: Liberty Fund, 2000], 1–79; and Richard E. Flathman's *Thomas Hobbes: Skepticism, Individuality and Chastened Politics* [Newbury Park, CA: Sage Publications, 1993].)

64. Thus, when Santner says that "how one comes to understand this third element [between the somatic and the normative that he often calls flesh] and whether it needs to be cured, policed, quarantined, put to work, put into play" (51), he comes close to Melville who records the play of flesh, as it were, but always as an excessiveness to the curing, policing, quarantining, possibly, as Santner also anticipates, "autoimmune," but possibly also an emergent alternative to this whole (Pauline/Freudian) way of thinking about the "needs" of flesh, as such.

65. "[H]e can never see an object which is exactly ahead, no more than he can one exactly astern." It is as if for a human our ears were our eyes and we could see only from the side, even if "your bitterest foe were walking straight towards you, with dagger uplifted in broad day" (476).

66. And he is thus rendered surely incapable of the ferocious wronging of which Ahab accuses him. Given Hobbes's choice to orient Leviathan from reasoning to willing, the whale's declared vulnerability to a "helpless perplexity of volition" seems significant. In *Leviathan*, Hobbes establishes willing as the last appetite in deliberation (a point since left behind by deliberative democratic theory): "In Deliberation, the last Appetite, or Aversion, immediately adhering to the action, or to the omission thereof, is that wee call the WILL; the Act, (not the faculty,) of *Willing*. And beasts that have *Deliberation*, must

necessarily also have *Will*. The Definition of the *Will*, given commonly by the Schooles, that it is a *Rationall Appetite*, is not good. For if it were, then could there be no Voluntary Act against Reason. For a *Voluntary Act* is that, which proceedeth from the *Will*, and no other. But if instead of a Rationall Appetite, we shall say an Appetite resulting from a precedent Deliberation, then the Definition is the same that I have given here. *Will* therefore *is the last Appetite in Deliberating.*" Thomas Hobbes, *Leviathan*, ed. Richard Tuck (Cambridge: Cambridge University Press, 2003), 44–45.

67. Significantly, the idea that the whale is vulnerable to action in concert by ordinary men might have suggested to Ishmael that so, too, was Ahab, whom Leon Harold Craig takes to represent Hobbes's sovereign. It may be his awareness of this sovereign vulnerability that causes Ishmael to wonder at his own submission to Ahab's mission. Writing from a different perspective, Leon Harold Craig documents many of the apparent allusions to Hobbes's *Leviathan* in Melville's great novel: "Suffice it to say, there is no shortage of features woven into *Moby-Dick* that are suggestive of Hobbes' *Leviathan*." Craig, *The Platonian Leviathan* (Toronto: University of Toronto Press, 2010), 21. On Hobbes and Melville, see especially "A Melvillian Coda: *Moby-Dick* as Fourfold Allegory", *Platonian Leviathan*, 499–524.

68. Following Jessica Whyte on Agamben, we may say that these encircled men are "ungovernable" but contra Whyte and Agamben, they are not for that reason necessarily unproductive and workless. See Whyte, *Catastrophe and Redemption: The Political Thought of Giorgio Agamben* (Albany: State University of New York Press, 2013), 166.

69. This vexes but does not undo an aspirational sentence from my *Emergency Politics: Paradox, Law, Democracy* (Princeton: Princeton University Press, 2009), mocked anonymously (as one of many "pearls of wisdom") on a political science blog. The sentence reads: "we may find that we, the people, are the sands of time. Those grains that slipped through the court timekeeper's glass in Goethe's Italy could do so only one at a time. Bound together, they would have stopped time. Similarly, the people when bound together can arrogate to themselves the rights of states: The people can make time stop too" (111). Wrenched out of context, such aspirational lines can seem cringe-worthy (even, or especially, to their author!). But, in the context of US racial politics right now, we have seen some people bind themselves together to make the ordinary time of racial policing stop or slow down: Black Lives Matter has arrogated to itself the task of police accountability, racial equality, and more. Ordinary people (sometimes on their own, sometimes led, inspired, frightened by others) acting in concert can stop the smooth running of sovereign time, and they can stop the all-powerful Leviathan, too. Or at

least these are among the hopes intimated by Franz Rosenzweig (examined in *Emergency Politics*) and Herman Melville (examined here). That quoted sentence is mocked, in particular, for its supposedly soap-operatic quality: it seems the figure of *sands of time* reminds that reader, though not this author, of a line from *The Days of Our Lives*. The figure, however, is Goethe's, not mine. He notes the working of sovereign power in a trial timekeeper's practice of holding the defense to its time limitations while stopping time's hourglass flows for the prosecution and the judge. Hundreds of years later and thousands of miles away, Black Lives Matter tracks such operations of justice in the US carceral system. The question for democratic theorists is always how to appropriate that power of resource allocation (assume for a moment that time is a resource) for agencies seeking to promote greater equality rather than to protect the status quo. Although melodrama was not yet on my mind in *Emergency Politics*, anonymous blog posters may find yet more to mock in my effort to open readers to that genre in *Antigone, Interrupted*. There the aim is actually to dethrone tragedy from its privileged genre status and treat it in relation to others, such as melodrama, that are usually cast as low culture and unworthy of scholarly attention in political theory. Democratic theory's reasons to take an interest in low-culture genres seem obvious and are compatible with the Cambridge School's move from great texts to contexts, from the great supposedly timeless treatises read in isolation to a broader archive that includes pamphlets of the day.

70. Thanks to James Martel who also says that we can therefore read the whale as a messianic figure in Benjamin's sense, disrupting the fetishes we project onto it. Martel's own work on fetish and Benjaminian messianism is very useful here. Martel, *Textual Conspiracies: Walter Benjamin, Idolatry, and Political Theory* (Ann Arbor: University of Michigan Press, 2011). I should add that this idea of literalizing or materializing the symbol or the fetish (e.g., the flesh) in order to work our way out from under it may well be taken to guide my own reply to Santner, whose use of the term "flesh" varies.

71. That *Moby-Dick* takes us full circle is appropriate because it is best read as a circle, such that the end is the beginning and the beginning the end.

72. On the homophobic nature of futurism, the ideology of futurity, see Lee Edelman, *No Future* (Durham, NC: Duke University Press, 2004). Edelman's critique, to which I am indebted, is of an ideology—futurism—not the tense of the future.

73. Notably in Santner's *My Own Private Germany*.

74. That is, my view is not far from Jason Frank's, but I insist this possibility is always already implicated in, and perhaps amplified by, the enthusiasm and calculation from which Frank distinguishes it. Moreover, I think the flesh

of the whale, to which Frank does not attend, and to which Santner, as I read him, inadvertently calls us to attend, is key.

75. It was this very unplugging that I earlier suggested Franklin was working *against* when he opposed the killing of the otherwise reproductive sow and the murder of the otherwise reproductive coin. The Sabbath and the sacrifice are what 24/7 capitalism cannot countenance. But this is true for them not only as destituent power but also as constituent power. What is striking in Agamben and Santner, who seems to follow him in this, is that the essentialization of man as a sabbatical animal suggests it is fundamentally inhuman or corrupt to orient around productivity and that productivity as such (not just its neoliberal form) is corruption. Jessica Whyte provides a great reading of Agamben on precisely these points in *Catastrophe and Redemption*. She explains that for Agamben, Bartleby, in effect a figure of "Sabbatism," is important because his worklessness represents a politics of pure means and a redemption that consists in the "free use of human capacities" (165). Whyte notes, too, that Agamben treats Bartleby in the context of a formalized messianism drawn from Benjamin, "yet stripping it of its content" (115): hence, potentiality.

76. Whyte notes, drawing on material of special relevance to these lectures, that Agamben's idea of the messianic as inoperativity, modeled by Bartleby, treats Bartleby as a "new creature." Whyte explains that the new creature Agamben "has in mind here is no doubt the one that appears in Paul's epistles," twice, one of which refers to the new creature as that which "remains after Paul has nullified the divisions of the law: 'For in Jesus Christ,' he writes, 'neither circumcision availeth anything nor uncircumcision, but a new creature' (Gal. 6:15)." (Whyte, *Catastrophe and Redemption*, 119.)

77. Whyte in *Catastrophe and Redemption* notes one seemingly uncharacteristic reference by Agamben, approving, to the idea of constituent power, in the context of an interview about Greece and the politics of austerity (161). Agamben's more characteristic commitment to inoperativity is connected to his embrace of pure potentiality. I find in Anne-Lise François's *Open Secrets* a similar preference for inaction or "affirmative passivity" over agency, indeed, a certain suspicion of agency as always complicit with that which we would like to oppose. Like Santner, she criticizes the busied body of contemporary life. If she does not invoke Bartleby, but turns rather to Dickinson and Wordsworth, that is because her ideal of "recessive action" is different from Agamben's—less messianic. See François, *Open Secrets: Literature of Uncounted Experience* (Stanford, CA: Stanford University Press, 2008). As Pieter Vermeulen points out, moreover, François affiliates Agamben's work with "the current theoretical compulsion to radicalise negativity."

(Vermeulen, "The Future of Possibility," *Postmodern Culture* 18, no. 2 [January 2008]: 64. Thanks to Kevis Goodman for calling Vermeulen's essay to my attention. Of course, Agamben thinks inoperativity precisely escapes negativity.) Whatever their differences, however, and they are not insignificant, both seek to undo or relinquish the demands for perpetual busy-ness and not, as I do here, to rework or reorient that busy-ness on behalf of something else. For my engagement with François's book, see my "Corpses for Kilowatts?," in *Second Nature: Rethinking the Natural through Politics*, ed. Crina Archer, Laura Ephraim, and Lida Maxwell (New York: Fordham University Press, 2013), 61–82. Santner connects his critique of the busy body to Agamben and to Bartleby, but he does not locate his critique in the context of this literature, some of which refers explicitly to Bartleby and some of which is significantly silent on the figure.

78. For a more detailed account of the Sabbath alternatives and an account of what I am calling "Sabbath-power," see my "The Laws of the Sabbath (Poetry)."

79. If we turn to the idea of "possibilities for new possibilities," coined by Jonathan Lear, cited by Santner, we may see the Sabbath of destituent power as a new possibility that falls short of that standard. See Lear, *Happiness, Death, and the Remainder of Life* (Cambridge, MA: Harvard University Press, 2001), 129. Agamben sometimes refers to such destituency or inoperativity as law that undoes law. I will discuss that formulation and the questions raised by it in detail elsewhere.

80. On randomness as a principle of justice, see Honig, "By the Numbers" in *The Jewish Political Tradition*, vol. 3, ed. Michael Walzer et al. (New Haven: Yale University Press, forthcoming). On the current creditocracy, see Andrew Ross, "Welcome to the creditocracy, where your debt piles up forever," *Guardian*, March 4, 2014, http://www.theguardian.com/commentisfree/2014/mar/04/household-debt-relief-creditocracy.

81. Thanks to James Martel on this point. I note that this is something like what L.T. Hobhouse struggled to do in response to unemployment in *Liberalism* (Oxford: Oxford University Press, 1964).

82. Richard Dienst, *The Bonds of Debt* (New York: Verso, 2011), 183–84.

83. Shaun McVeigh called my attention to Whitefriars. Nigel Stark focuses on the Mint, the "last surviving debtors' sanctuary . . . which stayed beyond the law until 1723. The Mint occupied both a physical space close to the center of London, and a place in ongoing debates about the liberty of debtors who faced imprisonment for non-payment and the property rights of creditors. At a time when the force of English law was relied upon to defend liberty and property, the continued presence in London of an area the law could not reach

was highly problematic." "Fugitive Meanings: The Literary Construction of a London Debtors' Sanctuary in the Eighteenth Century," *British Journal for Eighteenth-Century Studies* 24, no. 2 (2001): 175.

84. The debtors' prison is the third, usually unnoted, context of *The Merchant of Venice*, beyond the commerce of Venice and the hearth of Belmont: "Jailer, look to him," Shylock says, demanding that Antonio be taken away (3.3.1). We may note that Antonio has played something like the role of Strike Debt, not exactly buying and forgiving debts randomly and anonymously, but lending or giving to those in need of remedy without charging usury ("I oft deliver'd from his [Shylock's] forfeitures, /Many that have at times made moan to me," Antonio says [3.3.22–23], and Shylock complains that Antonio has thus brought "down /The rate of usance here with us in Venice" [1.3.44–45]). But Antonio does not act in concert and his antagonism is not to the structure of debt as such but, rather, it seems, to Shylock in particular. (That is why his debt forgiveness cannot be a "grace-event" but Strike Debt's might.) Antonio delivers sufferers from *"his"* (i.e., Shylock's) forfeitures, but not, as Bovilsky points out, from those of other Jewish lenders like Tubal, whose funds Shylock calls upon to make the loan he cannot quite afford to Antonio. Hence Lara Bovilsky's claim (noted earlier) that "[n]o one cares about Shylock more than Antonio does." Also, as noted earlier, Berger argues persuasively that Antonio's help always comes with strings attached. Never really debt-freeing, it is, on the contrary, debt-inaugurating.

85. "How often are debtors arrested across the country? . . . No national statistics are kept, and the practice is largely unnoticed outside legal circles." One observer says the "debt collection industry does not want the world to know these arrests are happening, because the practice would be widely condemned" (Robert Hobbs, deputy director of the National Consumer Law Center in Boston, quoted in "In Jail for Being in Debt," Chris Serres and Glenn Howatt, *Star Tribune*, March 2014). Cf. Michael Edwards, "Debtor's Prison Making a Comeback? Our Future in Chains: The For-Profit Debtors' Prison System," *Pragmatic Witness* (blog), September 30, 2010, http://white-wraithe.wordpress.com/2010/09/30/debtors-prison-making-a-comeback/. See also Jonathan Turley, "The Rise of 'Debtors' Prisons' in the U.S.," *Jonathan Turley* (blog), April 7, 2013, http://jonathanturley.org/2013/04/07/the-rise-of-debtors-prisons-in-the-us/. Turley cites *The Outskirts of Hope: How Ohio's Debtors' Prisons Are Ruining Lives and Costing Communities*, a report by the ACLU of Ohio, April 2013, and NPR's report "Supreme Court Ruling Not Enough to Prevent Debtors Prisons," May 21, 2014, http://www.npr.org/2014/05/21/313118629/supreme-court-ruling-not-enough-to-prevent-debtors-prisons. On the impact of new (Orwellian named)

"offender-funded" probation companies, see Hannah Rappleye and Lisa Riordan Seville, "The Town That Turned Poverty into a Prison Sentence," *The Nation*, April 14, 2014, http://www.thenation.com/article/178845/ town-turned-poverty-prison-sentence#. Finally, events in Ferguson Missouri after the police killing of Michael Brown in August, 2014, culminating in a U.S. Justice Department report, have exposed that town's reliance on money raised from its African-American residents, put into debt by policing practices that create the conditions for fines that cannot be paid, then imprison people for debt, and then charge them, for their time in jail. The word "charged" connoting demands for money, laying of accusation of law-breaking, and the electrified frisson of flesh covers a lot of ugly territory here (http://www.justice.gov/sites/default/files/opa/press-releases/attachments/2015/03/04/ferguson_police_department_report.pdf).

86. See Honig, *Emergency Politics* (Princeton: Princeton University Press, 2009) for more.

87. Lear, *Happiness, Death, and the Remainder of Life*, 129.

88. *My Own Private Germany* is the book by Santner most focused on this issue, but the topic recurs throughout Santner's work since. It seems to be what underlies his interest in Kantorowicz as well.

Secularization, Dialectics, and Critique

PETER E. GORDON

I want to begin by thanking Eric Santner for his stimulating lectures. I have known Eric for many years now, and his uniquely searching intellect never ceases to impress me. It is therefore an honor to comment on his work, though I must confess it is also a challenge, in part because the species of theoretical discourse to which Eric has contributed lies at some remove from my own habitual terrain. Whether I can offer constructive insights into Santner's project is an open question. What I *can* do, perhaps, is make explicit some of the underlying premises of that project, and maybe in doing so I can mark the point at which our paths diverge.

It may help to sketch some of the broader streams of contemporary theory in which his work is situated. If I understand him correctly, Santner stands somewhere within the contested field defined by the recent intersection of post-Marxism and political theology, with the added complication that his work draws instruction from both psychoanalysis and modern literature. His style of theoretical discourse operates in relative autonomy from disciplinary constraints and borrows freely, and with remarkable creativity, from a wealth of social-theoretical and literary texts, with a notable emphasis on Agamben, Lacan, Benjamin, Scholem, Žižek, Badiou, Kantorowicz, Freud, Peterson, Foucault, Derrida, and Marx, further embroidered with references to the work of the art historian T. J. Clark, alongside literary readings of, *inter alia*, Shakespeare, Goethe, Robert Walser, Gottfried Keller, and Kafka.

The result is a speculative work of densely woven intertextuality, the argument retaining its integrity thanks chiefly to the powerful analogical skills of the author himself. More specifically, Santner participates in, but also extends, the new post-Schmittian trend that articulates a critique of bourgeois civilization by alerting us to the spectral persistence of political-theological powers within the mechanism of liberal democracy. The argument draws much of its inspiration from Ernst Kantorowicz's 1957 masterpiece, *The King's Two Bodies*, which detailed the complex passage of the Christological distinction between the *corpus naturale* and *corpus mysticum* into the medieval political-theological doctrine of double sovereignty, as illustrated, most famously perhaps, in Shakespeare's *Richard II*, and ritualized in the slogan: "The King is Dead, Long Live the King." Kantorowicz himself proposed the ingenious idea that the theme of an eternal sovereignty survived the age of the great monarchs and took up a new home in the emergent early-modern and modern discourses of popular sovereignty. This idea also inspired the theoretical inquiries in Santner's last book, *The Royal Remains: The People's Two Bodies and the Endgames of Sovereignty* (from 2011). This project now continues in the Tanner lectures presented in this volume.

To be sure, Santner dissents from the classical literature on political theology in many respects. For Schmitt, political theology furnished a critical instrument for revealing the occluded but constitutive moment of authoritarian decisionism internal to liberal structures of power. Schmitt was keen to reveal this quasi-theological dimension because, in his view, its presence showed that political power even in a democratic regime cannot wrest itself free of an authoritarian core in the manner that liberal apologists imagined. When Schmitt said that modern concepts of the state were *secularized* theological concepts, this dictum aimed to expose the *myth* of a purely secular liberalism. To mark the theological provenance of secular political concepts was implicitly to criticize the self-professed autonomy of liberal-rationalist theories of state. For Schmitt, the rationalist pretension of Kant's self-legislative ideal is thereby exposed as the modern precipitate of a medieval metaphysics. Authoritarianism turns out to be the animating core of self-authorization, and the theological genealogy of modern political concepts thus calls into question the legitimacy of the modern age.

Santner approaches this argumentation from the left. He performs a critique of the persistent political-theological structures that, in his view, continue to underwrite modern capitalism. At the same time, Santner follows Marx in claiming that the fetishistic hold of the commodity is due to its metaphysical or quasi-theological form. The prooftext for this idea is the well-known analysis of commodity fetishism from *Kapital*, where Marx observes that the commodity is "a very strange thing, abounding in metaphysical subtleties and theological niceties (*ein sehr vertracktes Ding ... voll metaphysischer Spitzfindigkeit und theologischer Mucken*)."[1] For Santner, this passage is a key for exploring the historical and analogical passage from medieval and early-modern religion to modern capitalism. Bringing the political-theological critique of modernity into dialogue with the critique of political economy, Santner concludes syllogistically that we can only understand capitalism if we trace out the continuities that link modern political economy to the political theology of the *ancien régime*.

The union between these two modes of critique produces a certain dissonance in Santner's argument. It is not insignificant that political-theological critique insists on the autonomy of *the political* as the privileged sphere of human meaning. In the closing pages of his 1922 monograph on *Political Theology*, Schmitt explicitly condemns Marxism as a symptom of a metastasizing economic reason that threatens authentic political existence from all sides. Historical materialism, meanwhile, *denies* precisely the autonomy of the political and even condemns its theoretical isolation as another specimen of bourgeois fetishism. It is therefore unclear if one can sustain the bond with Marxian theory if one also identifies the distinctively medieval idea of Christological kingship as the unique structuring force behind all social order.

To be sure, Santner departs from both Schmitt *and* Kantorowicz insofar as his argument must characterize the theological inheritance of modernity as something illicit. In homage to the Marxist critique of commodity fetishism, Santner wishes to expose *not* the theological logic that constitutes all sovereignty but merely a theological *mystification* that should ideally be overcome. Originally, the political theological critique of liberalism was meant to expose the *impossibility* of any modern political order that tried to suppress its dependency on quasi-divine decision. The Marxist critique, by contrast, aims to dissolve the last residues of enchantment. The alliance between political-theological analysis and Marxian critique is therefore perturbed, insofar as historical genealogy in the mode of political theology works to solidify the very continuity between past and present that materialist criticism aims to disrupt. What political theology sees as an eternal structure of theological authoritarianism in all social arrangements is from the Marxian perspective a mystifying and historically contingent ideology that humanity could under the proper conditions leave behind.

One could ask whether this dissonance is productive or disabling; but this is a question for which I have no certain answer. Still, it is worth noting that for Santner, theology itself appears to retain something like an eternalized hold in the logic of modern capitalism. This eternal quality is evident insofar as Santner draws upon a remarkably heterogeneous array of religious sources and illustrations, some medieval, some modern: just how these sources and religious motifs, drawn from over centuries of theological debate, all cohere into one religious legacy remains uncertain. While paying homage to Kantorowicz, Santner also appeals to Weber's argument that early-modern capitalism draws energy from a *Beruf,* or vocation. The Calvinist reformers demanded that one live and work *"ad majorem Dei gloriam,* with the consequence that, as Santner deftly explains, work itself becomes a form of what we might call *"the doxology of everyday life"* (49, 119). But here too the history of theology may challenge the view that modern capitalism is haunted by a doctrinally unmarked Christology. Santner detaches this Weberian insight from the broader theory of disenchantment in which it was originally embedded. We might recall that, according to Weber's argument, it was not the teaching of Calvinism itself but, rather, its specific social-historical modification by later Calvinist preachers that enabled the sacralization of capitalist action. This point reminds us that theology never enjoys the self-identical immunity from time as its apologists claim, but is instead subject to human transformation and reconstruction. To occlude history in political-theological analysis grants too much power to the Schmittian view of modernity as fatally in thrall to an eternal God (or, more precisely, to its this-worldly analogue).

Nor should we neglect the thesis of world-rationalization that Weber worked out in far greater detail elsewhere—for example, in the various texts on the sociology of religion published only in the decade following *The Protestant Ethic and the Spirit of Capitalism*, especially in the *Zwischenbetrachtung*, or "Intermediary Reflection" (1915), and in "The Economic Ethics of the World Religions" (the methodological prolegomenon for his sociology of religion). In the former, Weber laid out his general theory concerning the pluralization or separation of value-spheres, a theory which militates *against* the claim that the ghost of religion retains its erstwhile role, even in modern life, as the coordinating principle across all domains of social action. In fact, Weber explicitly denied this. He believed that once the trial of rationalization had run its course, religion would shift "into the realm of the irrational."[2]

For Weber, in other words, religion no longer functions as the comprehensive doctrine or organizing metaphysical framework for all facets of modern life. Rather, religion has passed through the very same trial of differentiation and marginalization as all the other value-spheres of the rationalized life-world, alongside aesthetics, law, natural-scientific reason, and so forth. Santner may disagree with this facet of Weber's historical sociology. But it is important to note that Santner borrows from Weber only those themes that would seem to confirm the thesis of religious persistence while he leaves to one side the Weberian thesis of disenchantment and value-differentiation, presumably because this would conflict with the thesis of enduring theological-metaphysical enchantment.

Indeed, Santner is keen to note that this continuity describes a trial of secularization that is *not* disenchantment: the theological structure of the commodity reminds us that disenchantment has never happened, and that secularization has the meaning of transfer rather than dissolution. Secularization for Santner—and these are his words—is "mutation" or "transition." Here the argument seems to echo not just Derrida's "hauntology" but also Weber himself, who observed that the theological idea of a "calling" or *Beruf,* has not disappeared entirely but, rather, prowls around in our lives like the ghost of a once-living belief. For Santner as well, theology haunts capitalism like an "inheritance" or an "afterlife." Theology, in other words, has never yet gone away; it merely underwent a process of diffusion into the capillaries of the capitalist market. The result is that peculiar *dis*order of the modern economic order, which Santner characterizes in a pathologizing language that joins Marxism to a mode of psychoanalytic or psychotherapeutic cultural criticism. Our ostensibly disenchanted world, Santner claims, "vibrates" with a certain surplus of demand. We are driven to work, or, more precisely, our corporal existence is overburdened with "busy-ness" and stress. We are, in Santner's phrase, "busy bodies."

This, if I understand Santner correctly, is our current predicament. Now, one should ask whether this original interpretation of contemporary life misses the rational-universalist structure of historical materialist criticism. Indeed, one might claim that Santner's analysis has not taken sufficient care to inoculate itself against the Schmittian critique of modernity, and it therefore permits the anti-modernism of this inheritance to vitiate the rational-universalist logic of Marxian critique. Specifically—and this is my chief argument later—one could argue that throughout his theoretical adventure, Santner places undue stress on only one side of this critique; he discerns the theological mystifications of bourgeois society but not its cognitive and political gains.

Here it may be instructive to recall the dialectical character of Marxian critique: it is simultaneously a theory of truth *and* a theory of illusion, a theory of disenchantment *and* a theory of mystification. This is already evident in the famous lines from *The Communist Manifesto*, where we are told that the bourgeoisie has played a revolutionary role in history, precisely because it has "drowned the most heavenly ecstasies of religious fervor . . . in the icy water of egotistical calculation. . . .[F]or exploitation, veiled by religious and political illusions, it has substituted naked, shameless, direct, brutal exploitation." The bourgeoisie, Marx concludes, "has stripped of its halo every occupation hitherto honored and looked up to with reverent awe," and it has liquefied the fixed or "fast-frozen" relations of the *ancien régime*. In fact it is only with bourgeois modernity that the "holy is profaned" such that we can at last face "with sober senses" our "real conditions of life."[3]

This (admittedly rhetorical) passage underscores a key principle in the Marxian theory of history, according to which the cognitive and social advances of bourgeois society are historically indispensable. In the passage from feudalism to capitalist modernity, our civilization undergoes a trial of disenchantment and value-differentiation, one that separates out civil society as an intermediate field of transaction, formally distinct from both the affective structures of the family, on the one hand, and the legal-political structures of the state, on the other. Humanity can at last confront the "real conditions of life." With this theory (which borrows a great deal from Hegel's *Philosophy of Right*), Marx thereby distinguishes himself as a child of the Enlightenment for whom the historical achievements of bourgeois society cannot be dismissed.

My disagreement with Santner hinges chiefly upon how we are to understand the critique of commodity fetishism, and what role that critique occupies within the broader framework of critical theory. First, note that Santner reads the idea of commodity fetishism as a *corrective* to the classical theory of secularization:

> The shift from the fetishism of persons—above all that of the singularly representative person, the *Staatsperson* or sovereign—to that of things takes place in the context of a long process of secularization that ostensibly drains the shared institutions of the public sphere of transcendental resources of legitimation; it is a process that, so the story goes, disenchants the world more generally, and evacuates from all aspects of life the last vestiges of otherworldly, animating spirits, be they divine or demonic. *The critical thrust of Marx's theory of the fetishism of the commodity has been to demonstrate just how wrong this story is.* (80, my emphasis)

Incidentally, Santner notes that even Max Weber, known for his grand narrative of disenchantment, did not subscribe to the theory of secularization in any straightforward sense. This is so because Weber tracks the *afterlife* of the Protestant Ethic into the secularized ethos of capitalism's collective institutions and internalized individual dispositions. But as I have already noted above, it is crucial to recall that Weber does *not* affirm the *persistence* of the Protestant ethic but only diagnoses the pathologies it leaves in its wake; indeed, the crucial lesson of his historical sociological study was precisely that the institutional-behavioral imperative *survives the collapse of its spiritual supports.* The theological animus behind capitalist action is not "dispersed" (Santner's term); rather, on Weber's view, it is *evacuated.* And this explains the spiritually hollow sense of compulsion—of specialization without a spirit—that according to Weber lends a distinctive imprint to our own modern age.

But let us leave Weber to one side. Most of all, Santner wants to explain how the Marxian theory of commodity fetishism belies any simplistic story of disenchantment. This is so because the commodity carries forward the "immaterial stuff" or "surplus carnality" (Santner's terms for the congealing of abstract or homogenous labor) that was once found in the king's royal flesh: As Santner explains, "What Marx characterizes as the 'dual character of the labor embodied in commodities' is, in a word, a two-body doctrine transferred from the political theology of the sovereign to the realm of political economy" (46). A few pages later Santner repeats this claim as follows:

> My concern continues to be the ways in which what had been, to a large extent, localizable in early modernity, invested within the sphere and "physiology" of the traditional master or sovereign, disperses into the texture of the social space at large—into the life of the People—and so into the very soul of the modern citizen-subject. Marx's theory of the fetishism of the commodity is, I am suggesting, above all a contribution to an understanding of that process of dispersion. (85–86)

If I understand Santner correctly, he therefore wants to claim that (a) the commodity is a site in capitalist modernity in which we may discern the persistence of pre-modern theological-doxological motifs; and (b) because Marx diagnoses this doxological persistence, his theory does not endorse but actually contests a conventional historical-sociological narrative of world-disenchantment. Santner thus concludes that "It is no surprise" that in *Capital* Marx claimed to have discovered " 'metaphysical subtleties and theologicial niceties' in the midst of our life with commodities" (90). Indeed, this occluded theological-metaphysical debt constitutes nothing less than " 'the religious structure of capitalism' " (Santner, 120, citing Benjamin "Capitalism as Religion," 288).

The textual evidence for (a) is uncertain. As I have noted above, the Marxian theory of history is, in part, a theory of *de*sacralization whereby "all that is holy is profaned" and the acid of the economic order begins to dissolve all prior forms of institutional and cultural cohesion. The rise of bourgeois modernity occupies a pivotal place in this narrative insofar as it serves as the preparatory stage of desacralization in which all earlier forms of cohesion lose their salience, leaving behind no other medium of social interaction than the "cash nexus" (which supplants not only feudal hierarchical norms but also the traditionalistic bonds of the guild and the affective ties of the family as well). We find this theory not only in *The Communist Manifesto*. It informs Marx's argumentation in the *Economic and Philosophic Manuscripts of 1844*, but also in the analysis of commodity fetishism in *Capital*.

We can begin by examining the chapter on "Private Property and Labor" from the *1844 Manuscripts*, an important site in which Marx was developing the theory of the fetish in connection to the history of religion. In the following passage, Marx first singles out Adam Smith as the political economist who identifies the labor theory of value, and then (in a self-reflexive gesture that typifies the Marxian theory of ideology) argues that this mode of classical political economy is the subjective expression of its own epoch. It is "the independent movement of private property become conscious of itself":

> The subjective essence of private property, private property as activity for itself, as subject, as person, is labor. It, therefore, goes without saying that only that political economy which recognized labor as its principle (Adam Smith), and which therefore no longer regarded private property as nothing more than a condition external to man, can be regarded as both a product of the real energy and movement of private property (it is the independent movement of private property become conscious of itself, it is modern industry as self), a product of modern industry, and a factor which has accelerated and glorified the energy and development of this industry and transformed it into a power belonging to consciousness.[4]

With this theory we can see how Marx has already taken up a Hegelian strategy of dialectical reading whereby thought itself—or a particular form of thought, namely Smithian political

economy—is said to be *its own time reflected in consciousness.*
More surprising, however, is the way Marx (appealing to Engels)
develops a religious comparison, where the debate between mercantilism and classical political economy is said to correspond to
the contest between Catholicism and Lutheranism. Because we are
accustomed to thinking of the "fetish" as an idea that attaches to
the critique of "primitive" and nonmonotheistic religion, it is especially interesting to note how Marx deploys the concept to distinguish between these two competing types of Christian theology:

> Therefore, the supporters of the monetary and mercantile system,
> who look upon private property as a purely objective being for
> man, appear as *fetish-worshippers,* as *Catholics,* to this enlight-
> ened political economy, which has revealed—within the system
> of private property—the subjective essence of wealth. Engels
> was, therefore, right to call Adam Smith the Luther of political
> economy. (In Engels's 1843 "Outlines of a Critique of Political
> Economy," 147)

Notice here that, in the eyes of their critics, the advocates of mercantilism "appear as *fetish-worshippers,*" or as Catholics ("*Als
Fetischdiener, als Katholiken erscheinen*" [79]), whereas Smith
exercises a critique of this fetishism analogous to Luther's critique
of Catholicism. The analogy holds insofar as Catholicism is characterized as fetishistically cleaving to external sources of the sacred
(priestly intervention, for example, and the salvific status of works),
whereas Lutheranism locates salvation only within "the inner essence
of man." More generally, of course, the inter-religious comparisons
provide an analogy for the way that the mercantilist cleaves fetishistically to money as the source of wealth, whereas the classical political
economist recognizes that wealth derives only from man himself:

> Just as Luther recognized religion and faith as the essence of
> the external world and, in consequence, confronted Catholic
> paganism; just as he transcended external religiosity by making

religiosity the inner essence of man; just as he negated the idea of priests as something separate and apart from the layman by transferring the priest into the heart of the layman; so wealth as something outside man, and independent of him—and, therefore, only to be acquired and maintained externally—is abolished [*aufgehoben*]. i.e., its external and mindless objectivity is abolished inasmuch as private property is embodied in man himself and man himself is recognized as its essence—but this brings man himself into the province of religion. So, although political economy, whose principle is labor, appears to recognize man, it is, in fact, nothing more than the denial of man carried through to its logical conclusion: for man himself no longer stands in a relation of external tension to the external essence of private property [*einer äußerlichen Spannung zu dem äußerlichen Wesen des Privateigentums steht*]—but rather he himself has become the tense essence of private property [*dies gespannte Wesen des Privateigentums geworden ist*]. What was formerly being-external-to-oneself, man's material externalization, has now become the act of alienation—i.e., alienation through selling [*Veräußerung*]. (147–48, German 79–80)

This analogical contrast—between the Catholic-mercantilist "fetishism" of money and the Lutheran-Smithian emphasis on the human being as the sole source of value—means that political economy takes on the status of an unprecedented cosmopolitanism: it possesses a "universal energy" that "breaks through every limitation and bond," and it is ultimately forced "to cast off its hypocrisy." The argument anticipates the well-known lines from *The Communist Manifesto* (quoted earlier) about the *desacralizing* effects of bourgeois society:

This political economy, therefore, starts out by seeming to recognize man, his independence, his spontaneous activity, etc. Since it transfers private property into the very being of man, it can no longer be conditioned by local or national features of private property as something existing outside it. It (political economy) develops a cosmopolitan, universal energy which breaks through every limitation and bond and sets itself up as the *only* policy, the *only* universality, the *only* limitation, and the *only* bond. But then, as it continues to develop, it is forced to cast off its hypocrisy and step forth in all its cynicism. (148)

That Smith's labor theory of value can appear as a casting off of hypocrisy and the "stepping forth in all its cynicism" (*"in ihrem ganzen Zynismus hervortreten"* [80]) should strike us as signifi-cant: it means that classical political economics offers a certain truth about economic relations and, indeed, represents an advance beyond the "fetishism" of the "Catholic" mercantilist order. But Marx is no less quick to observe that this so-called advance into full-blown cynicism is also a movement into contradiction, because the truth of the labor theory of value is developed in a fashion that is "one-sided" and (ultimately) "anti-human": "This it does, without troubling its head for one moment about all the apparent contradic-tion to which this doctrine leads, by developing in a more one-sided way, and, thus, more sharply and more logically, the idea of labor as the sole essence of wealth, by showing that the conclusions of this doctrine, unlike the original conception, are anti-human" (148). The result is a twofold movement—a critique of fetishism that becomes simultaneously a new mode of estrangement:

Not only does political economy become increasingly cyni-cal from Smith through Say to Ricardo, Mill etc., inasmuch as the consequences of industry appeared more developed and more contradictory to the latter; the latter also became more estranged—consciously estranged—from man than their prede-cessors [*sondern auch positiv gehn sie immer und mit Bewußtsein weiter in der Entfremdung gegen den Menschen als ihr Vorgänger*]. But this is *only* because their science develops more logically and more truly [*aber nur, weil ihre Wissenschaft sich konsequenter und wahrer entwickelt*]. Since they make private property in its active form the subject, thereby making man as a non-being [*Unwesen*] the essence [*Wesen*], the contradiction in reality corresponds entirely to the contradictory essence which they have accepted as their principle. The discordant reality of industry, far from refusing their internally divided principle, actually confirms it. [*Die zerrißne Wirklichkeit der Industrie bestätigt ihr in sich zerrißnes Prinzip, weit entfernt, es zu widerlegen.*] Their principle is in fact the principle of this division. (149, German 80–81)

Here Marx puts his dialectical reasoning boldly on display: the critique of mercantilist fetishism creates a new mode of candor (that labor is the source of wealth), which then develops into an inhuman principle of estrangement. But this one-sided truth corresponds precisely to the one-sided estrangement of the economic order itself. If their principle is "discordant" or marked by diremption (*Zerrissenheit*), this is only because it is an accurate expression of the diremption of reality itself. Bourgeois economics is the truth of an untrue world.

The passage analyzed above has important consequences for any understanding of the Marxist idea of fetishism. For we can see that Marx (relying on Engels) here deploys the term "fetishism" to indicate an ideological construct that is destined to collapse as the capitalist economy comes into its own. Whether "Catholicism" accurately describes the fetishism of the mercantilist order merits further consideration. It would be easy to dismiss it as merely a fanciful analogy. But if we accept for a moment that it plays a more than analogical role in Marx's analysis, we should then recognize that classical political economy stands (ironically) in greater proximity to "reality." It represents truth insofar as it offers a truthful corrective to mercantilism, and it represents reality insofar as its one-sided understanding of economics *just is* the one-sidedness of the economic order it describes. But it is also false precisely because it is one-sided: its estrangement is both truth and untruth.

This dialectical conception of bourgeois ideology (for classical political economy according to Marx is the quintessence of bourgeois ideology) reappears in *Capital* itself when Marx turns to the famous analysis of commodity fetishism. In the following passage Marx explains just why the commodity, when analyzed properly, stands revealed as "a very queer thing, abounding in metaphysical subtleties and theological niceties":

> A commodity is therefore a mysterious thing, simply because in it the social character of men's labour appears to them as an objective character stamped upon the product of that labour; because the relation of the producers to the sum total of their own labour is presented to them as a social relation, existing not between themselves, but between the products of their labour. This is the reason why the products of labour become commodities, social things whose qualities are at the same time perceptible and imperceptible by the senses.[5]

In trying to explain just why the "appearance" of a commodity is so misleading, Marx first appeals to the theme of optical perception (a commonplace in epistemology). But he is immediately dissatisfied with the analogy because, in the case of optics, there is an "actual passage of light from one thing to another," whereas, in the case of commodities, the value-relation among the commodities has "no connection with their physical properties":

> In the same way the light from an object is perceived by us not as the subjective excitation of our optic nerve, but as the objective form of something outside the eye itself. But, in the act of seeing, there is at all events, an actual passage of light from one thing to another, from the external object to the eye. There is a physical relation between physical things. But it is different with commodities. There, the existence of the things *qua* commodities, and the value-relation between the products of labour which stamps them as commodities, have absolutely no connection with their physical properties and with the material relations arising therefrom. There it is a definite social relation between men, that assumes, in their eyes, the fantastic form of a relation between things. (165)

It is only when Marx feels dissatisfied with this optical analogy that he reaches to religion. But notice that he does so with some embarrassment, because the illusory independence of the commodity-relation seems to demand such an illustration:

> In order, therefore, to find an analogy, we must have recourse to the mist-enveloped regions of the religious world. In that world the productions of the human brain appear as independent beings endowed with life, and entering into relation both with one another and the human race. So it is in the world of commodities with the products of men's hands. This I call the Fetishism which attaches itself to the products of labour, so soon as they are produced as commodities, and which is therefore inseparable from the production of commodities. (165)

The importance of this passage should not be missed. When Marx suggests that "fetishism" (a term of religious critique) may prove itself an apt analogy for the status of the commodity in the capitalist system, he does not suggest that the commodity has become an actual repository for religious values or gestures from the past. He is offering what he takes to be a helpful illustrative device so that the reader might better unlock the otherwise perplexing status of the commodity form. Nothing in the passage above suggests that the fetishistic understanding of the commodity actually *derives from* the fetishism of religion. On the contrary, Marx has just demonstrated that the fetishism of commodities is the objective effect of the economic order itself in which social labor can be alienated from its producer and represented *as if* it were the vessel for a nonsocial value.

Now, Marx obviously believes that commodity fetishism amounts to a new kind of mystification. But mystification can take many forms and religion is only one of them. The singular power of the bourgeois capitalist order is that it develops a form of mystification that corresponds precisely to its very own functionality.

Fetishism, in other words, is an analogy, not a sign of historical derivation.

It is crucial that we recognize this point because otherwise we can make little sense of Marx's own critical task in *Capital*. When he appeals to the theme of fetishism in the passage quoted above, Marx is clearly trying to move the reader toward a better understanding of the "mystery" of the commodity-form. To call a commodity a *fetish* is quite simply a way of alerting the reader to the erroneous gesture that can be conceptually annulled *in and through the critique itself*. Needless to say such a critique would hardly suffice to abolish capitalism in its objectivity. But the purpose of *Capital* is that of critical analysis, and as such it is an exercise in demystification.

Marxism, in other words, is both a theory of mystification and a theory of demystification, and it is both of these at once; indeed, it must be both at once because it comprehends the structure of historicized social relations in a *dialectical* form that resists one-sided mythologies of both apologetic rationalism and religious fatalism. Its critical stance is also self-reflexive: Marxism absorbed the historical principle of demystification into its own practice by making the profanation of social relations the historical precondition for Marxian theory itself. The critique of political economy becomes a historical possibility *only once* the economy has emerged as a distinctive sphere.

Now, as I understand him, Santner wants to trace not just the transition from political theology to political economy; he also wants to trace out this transition into a modern *theological-politico complex*—that is, which emerges once the theological is sublated into the economic. The relation is not one of *replacement* but *infusion*. The energies society once invested in the body of the king and the glory of this-worldly sovereignty are "dispersed" or distributed into the bloodstream of the exchange economy and results in what Santner calls the "vibrations" of commodity fetishism.

Santner, in other words, takes literally—as a theological inheritance—what was for Marx an analogy in the service of demystifying capitalism's internal and *structural* effects. The ambiguity in this argument, in my view, derives from its attempt to effect an unlikely synthesis of Marxian critique with political theology. The homage to historical materialism borrows from political theology a strain of anti-modernism that denies the moment of enlightenment that belonged to historical materialism as its rightful inheritance. To be sure, no historical materialism worth that title can simply endorse progress without recognizing (with Benjamin) the suffering that makes progress possible. And this is precisely why historical materialism exhibits a dialectical structure: without reducing either of these two moments, it articulates *both* a theory of mystified social relations *and* a principled view that rational critique can help to dismantle just that mystification. It comprehends *both* a critique of Enlightenment ideals *and* a drive to realize the Enlightenment's own unrealized ideal of a life beyond the *ancien régime.* In Habermasian terms, the ideals of bourgeois society are at once *ideology and more than ideology.*[6]

This, incidentally, was also the dialectical core of "On the Jewish Question," where Marx understands bourgeois legal-political emancipation as *both* freedom and unfreedom, both a release from mystified feudal tutelage and a reinforcement and naturalization of capitalist tutelage. Marx's unqualified endorsement of Jewish emancipation is otherwise unintelligible. Hence the celebrated distinction between "political" emancipation and "human" emancipation, and Marx's crucial claim that the "political revolution . . . *abolished* the political character of civil society." Thanks to this abolition, the contradictions of civil society become *demystified,* losing their feudal political character, and the fact of economic exploitation becomes self-evident for the first time.[7] In this respect I would suggest that Santner has incorporated only one moment of the Marxian narrative, with the result that secularization is structured in his argument not as a dialectic but only as a reinforcement of capitalist unfreedom, a reinforcement that has solidified to such a degree it only reveals itself in our theoretical language with metaphors of embodiment, the biological, the somatic.

The somatic *stress* of capitalism as an experiential order gains in drama with the distress we may feel when Santner reminds us that our own bodies teem with micro-organisms. Still, the irony is that such language does everything to suggest not the social contingency of oppression but its *carnal finality*. (If this is not what Santner intends, then one might ask why the unusual reference to micro-organisms would be of any relevance. Presumably these creatures exemplify a constitutive feature of our creaturely life—that is, they are not merely a symptom of the capitalist present.) The proposal that we break from this condition of somatic unrest becomes nearly inexplicable except as a radical break that recapitulates the shock of theological revelation, but only in the inverted form as a sudden awakening *from* religion. The consequence is that theological critique becomes not just a precondition but also something like a *substitute* for economic transformation. The critique of political economy reverts back to the left-Hegelian critique of religion that Marx had tried to overcome.

It may be that there is something like an "obsessive compulsive doxology" that runs like an animating spirit through the channels of world capitalism today. Perhaps so. But whether this quasi-religious drive to "busy-ness" in our modern economic order is the late-modern precipitate of early-modern European religion strikes me as doubtful. For the truth is that capitalism as a *global* phenomenon, from South Asia to Brazil, and from the sweatshop to the call center, sustains its functionality chiefly because it exhibits a spectacular *indifference* to the past. Popular theologies abound, and especially so in the United States, which always serves as convenient counter-evidence for those who would contest the classical theory of secularization. But as the performance imperative has gained in strength, the promises once sustained in religion have lost much of their distinction, and faith has become a simulacrum of its former self. Capitalism does not preserve tradition, it liquefies it. It runs roughshod over variations of culture and convention, and the neoliberal imperative of constant expansion flattens out both the future and the past, just as a highway carries us forward across all terrain, taking little notice of customs, religions, or identities.

Before concluding, I must add a parenthetical remark. One might ask whether Santner's culturalist analysis of doxological inheritance hasn't also missed the emancipatory and rational content of religion itself. For Santner, religion names only the idolatry that was the original object of religious critique. But the line of critical theory that runs from Adorno and Horkheimer through Habermas would remind us that there may be more rational and emancipatory content in both bourgeois and religious principles than this definition allows. Disregarding this content, the political theological critique of political economy runs the risk of consuming its own energies, leaving us with little more than the quasi-therapeutic discourse of "unplugging" from our too-busy lives.

Whatever our views on theology, we would do well to remember that the left-Hegelian critique of theology may be a necessary, but it is surely not a sufficient, condition for the dismantling of the commodity form. To fix our attention to an excessive degree on the *theology* of capitalism is (as Adorno once observed) to reify the critique of reification itself. It misreads social and economic pathology as psychopathology, and leaves the former intact even while it devotes itself (with great erudition) to theorizing the extravagant neuroses of the bourgeoisie. I am struck by the fact that the critique of commodity fetishism has been detached here from the analysis of economic exploitation—a sign, perhaps, of the diremption in bourgeois experience (and in the experience of all theorists) between the realm of exchange and the labor, which, occluded from our eyes or exported overseas, makes this exchange possible. One is tempted to say that this theoretical demarche symptomizes what has happened not only in the history of capitalism but also in the history of readings of *Capital*. If the exploitation of labor is sent to the margins of theory, the idea of fetishism is itself fetishized, dissociated from the economic injustice it was meant to explain. At the end of the day (though there is never an end of the day to such discussions) this line of argumentation turns us away from the critique of political economy and allies us, once again, with the left-Hegelians who confined their energies to the critique of religious consciousness. But that is where Marx first came in.

Notes

1. Karl Marx, *Capital: A Critique of Political Economy. Volume One,* trans. Ben Fowkes (New York: Vintage, 1977), 163. German from *Das Kapital: Kritik der politischen Ökonomie. Erster Band* (Berlin: Karl Dietz Verlag, 2008), 85.

2. Weber, "The Social Psychology of the World Religions" originally published 1915-19 as "Die Wirtschaftsethik der Weltreligionen," in serial form in the *Jafféschen Archiv für Sozialwissenschaft,* published in full in the *Gesammelte Aufsätze zur Religionssoziologie,* vol. 1 (Tübingen: J.C.B. Mohr Verlag, 1922–23), 237–68.

3. Karl Marx and Friedrich Engels, "Manifesto of the Communist Party" in *The Marx-Engels Reader,* ed. Robert C. Tucker (New York: Norton, 1978), 476.

4. "Economic and Philosophical Manuscripts," in Karl Marx, *Early Writings,* ed. and trans. T. B. Bottomore (New York: McGraw-Hill, 1963), 147. German quoted from Karl Marx, *Ökonomisch-philosophische Manuskripte.* ed. Barbara Zehnpfennig (Hamburg: Felix Meiner, 2005). Hereafter pages cited in the text.

5. "The Fetishism of the Commodity and its Secret," in *Capital: Volume One,* 163. Hereafter, pages cited in the text.

6. Jürgen Habermas, *Strukturwandel der Öffentlichkeit: Untersuchungen zu einer Kategorie der bürgerlichen Gesellschaft* (Suhrkamp: Taschenbuch Wissenschaft, 1990), 106.

7. "On the Jewish Question," in Marx, *Early Writings,* 28.

The Exercise
of Paradoxological Thinking

HENT DE VRIES

My comments will not rehearse Eric Santner's subtle reasoning, telling examples, and overall claims in the beautifully articulated lectures, whose modified and expanded versions one finds in this volume.[1] Instead I begin *in medias res* and address—so as to eventually also challenge—just a few premises underlying Santner's argument, if we can say so, *as a whole*. That these lectures form an integral part of an even larger body of thought and writing, and one for which I have developed the highest respect, not least because it analyzes problems with which I often felt I was deeply familiar, only to realize that they could be recast in a stunningly original register that forced me to revisit so many of my own long-held assumptions and all too hastily drawn conclusions—all this goes without saying. And so does my appreciation of the unique kind of writing and singular idiom that we have all come to recognize as Santner's signature style across an ever expansive and increasingly influential body of work.

I

What I aim to discuss and question is the guiding thought that organizes these lectures, namely that there is such a thing as an "afterlife of political theology in secular modernity" and one whose distinctive, if not necessarily *metaphysical* or *theological*, features we can begin to delineate here, in this most recent installment of Santner's larger project as it moves one step beyond the argument of *The Royal Remains* and, perhaps, already in *On Creaturely Life*, to the vestiges of a "political economy" (in his words, a going about our business more broadly, "somatically" and "normatively") that has become the hallmark of modern and, increasingly, contemporary life. It is this "political economy" that is now seen as relentlessly secularizing and transforming the fundamental traits of the "political theology" of old—to the point of substituting for it with virtually *no remains left*. What henceforth determines our "forms of life," whether we realize and appreciate or resist this or not, is a new dispensation, an epochal shift.

Following Karl Marx rather than Max Weber, Santner observes: "it is not that secular society remains secretly bound to transcendence but, rather, that our ostensibly disenchanted world vibrates with a *surplus of immanence* that profoundly informs our dealings in the world, makes us into 'busy bodies' trying to discharge an excess of demand ... that keeps us driven even when we are ostensibly 'idling'" (80–81). Indeed, he adds, according to Marx's well-known analysis in *Das Kapital*, "[i]t is not so much *we* who continue to engage in metaphysics and theology but, rather, our *busy bodies*" (81). With this, Marx, like Freud, puts his fingers on an "uncanny mode of stress," identifying the new locus of "ideology" and its technically partial but nonetheless subliminal and "sublime object"; the theologico-political, on this view, is subject to a peculiar "mutation" that diminishes nothing of its original driving and organizing symbolical force, even though the latter should, perhaps, no longer be understood in either all too blatant or elusive mystical and metaphysical terms. As so often in Franz Rosenzweig's footsteps, in the (live) lecture Santner proposes a "new thinking" that ventures beyond the well-known historical and conceptual controversies between faith and reason, theology and modern science.

Neither the political theologies of old nor the "vibrant matter, actants, and assemblages of the new post-humanist materialisms"

(81), Santner suggests, truly capture the "surplus of matter" or "spectral materiality"—"*die gespenstische Gegenständlichkeit*," "vitality," and "animation," supposedly "immanent" to what Marx, in *Capital*, calls the "commodity form"—that forms the new "subject-matter" of political economy as it has come to replace the medieval and early-modern conceptions of monarchical sovereignty, embodied in the king's two bodies. No longer a *corpus mysticum*, the modern body politic has democratized, dispersed, indeed exorcized—naturalized, but not neutralized—what was left of the age-old obsession of political theology, of "the royal remains." Yet, what takes its hovering place is more terrifying and differently pervasive than the authority it dethrones. The natural and historical immanence that has come to reduce all transcendence—not only the theological and metaphysical dualisms of political Manichaeism and Gnosticism but also of the biblical earthly and heavenly kingdom, of this world and the next—incorporates or introjects the very impetus it thus overcomes. Its immanence is itself not enough and requires, if not creates, its own surplus in excess of its apparent—naturalist or, in our context, economist—premise. And, if the theological vocabulary were not too misleading, one might say that, once again, a certain "passion" overtakes the language of "interest," reintroducing an incalculability that escapes every attempt to suppress and control it. So much for the logic of market and the pursuit of happiness. An invisible hand, but not the one we have come to bank on, keeps us adrift, on the move, whether we like—and know—it or not. Divine providence, double predestination, historicist determination, in ancient, medieval, and modern times, paradoxically, offered more leeway and (if one can say so) freedom than that.

But how, exactly, do we picture the "spectral materiality" or, rather, "objectivity"—the "*gespenstische Gegenständlichkeit*"— that Santner, following the Marxian turn from Hegelian idealism and German ideology in its historicizing critique of theology and anthropology, is after? What, in other words, is the proper "object" of a "political economy" no longer restricted by the more general economy (divine *oikonomia*, as we will see)—that is to say, the political theology that in previous centuries, well before the full-blown expansion and exponential growth of industrial and financial Capital and its contradictions emerged on the scene, had relegated conditions of material production to a second-order phenomenon? Marx started his *Critique of Political Economy*, the subtitle of *Capital*, with a study of the commodity in its proper light, in which it revealed itself as a very strange thing, abounding in "metaphysical subtleties and theological niceties," as Santner reminds us (81, citing Marx, 163). Are we certain, after Marx, that such aura and nuance fades out? Or does a dimension of depth, if not transcendence, continue to haunt our every day, perhaps, ever more so? If this were the case, there would be little hope for political *economy* to leave political *theology* forever aside. Put differently, it would be impossible for economy and its theoretical no less than its social, juridical, and financial apparatus to rid itself from the older—and, metaphysically, indeed, theologically deeper—sense that this term once carried. And the same may well be true of the object of so-called libidinal economy that Santner's second main interlocutor here, namely Freud, adds to the equation. Perhaps, the "surplus"—whether immanent or transcendent, the difference matters little—is nothing if not metaphysical, as so-called mystical postulates of human no less than divine authority tend to be: *"that the king reigns without governing"* (52, my emphasis), that his power is valid but no longer has any meaning, as any negative dialectic of the political quickly reveals, is a direct (here, textual) confirmation of this overarching view. Yet, paradoxically, this view is best—that is, most adequately and strategically—described in theologico-political terms.

If there is a beyond (or before) of the theologico-political (*concesso non dato*), then it may not be so easy to delineate where it begins or ends or even what forms it takes. Moreover, there is little, perhaps nothing, that surrounds the theologico-political register and idiom, its archive and apparatus, about which this historical tradition with its own peculiar logic, rhetoric, and imagery has not had something to say, or for which it does not hold something *in stock*. And, if this is the case, notions such as reserve, debt, and gift (which are eminently economical terms in their own right) may be more pertinent to the analysis of the theologico-political legacy (including its political economical "afterlife") than the Marxian insistence on commodification, reification, fetishization, and the like, upon which Santner builds much of his argument. In short, the cultural logic of capital—the more than historical and ontological, but deeply theological, as well as quotidian weight that it imposes on us—is, well, not that of *Capital* in the reading that Santner proposes of its basic tenets and its lasting contribution to understanding our world today: "metaphysical subtleties and theological niceties," citing Santner citing Marx, sit too much in the way.

I am not quite sure how one could develop this more fully or rigorously than Jacques Derrida did in *Specters of Marx* and elsewhere, when he replaced "ontology," including the guiding presuppositions and methods of historical materialism, determinism, and secular humanism of the late and early Marx, with the "haunting" meandering of its concepts and practices with no further *fundamentum in re*. But while Santner points out that Derrida's conception is subtle and measured, its implications are not always emphasized in every context. In citing *Specters of Marx* and referring to Derrida's later *Le toucher* (*On Touching*), Santner makes this is abundantly clear: "The specter is a paradoxical incorporation, the becoming-body, a certain phenomenal and carnal form of the spirit. It becomes, rather, some 'thing' that remains difficult to name: neither soul nor body, and both one and the other. For it is flesh and phenomenality that give to the spirit its spectral apparition."[2] For reasons that I cannot fully explicate here, such an approach is very different from, say, Richard Rorty's provocative move that replaces epistemic, normative, and, more broadly, ontological claims by so-called cultural politics (to which I return briefly below). For while there is a pragmatist—or, one might say, "pragrammatological"—streak to his own considerations, Derrida's is a pragmatism that reaches as *deep* as it does *further out*, well beyond the historicisms and culturalisms, lingualisms and structuralisms, idealisms and materialisms, old and new, hung up as all are on unquestioned axioms and parameters. Revealed religion, in its most *global* of concepts, including its heterodoxies and mysticisms, knows of such depth and reaches beyond.[3]

Paradoxically, part of this depth can be seen in the way Derrida portrays the impossible overcoming of previous strata of thought and of action, insisting instead on paleonymy—that is, on the infinite substitution of infinite concepts (and of the Infinite, to begin with). Nothing is left behind, which is precisely why deconstruction is not destructive or, for that matter, why Martin Heidegger came to privilege the Old German *Verwindung* over and against the more supersessionist language of *Überwindung*, whose vain promises are the very disappointments of so many philosophical schools (e.g., phenomenology in its early, scientific aspiration, spearheaded by Edmund Husserl, but also logical empiricism, led by Rudolf Carnap and others).

With this in mind, I am not convinced that the semblance of a definitive move beyond "hauntology"—the very term and discipline that Derrida substitutes for ontology, old and new—is not exactly the very relapse into yet another "dogmatic image of thought" (as Gilles Deleuze would have called it) that one had hoped to avoid. In other words, another reification, conceptual idolatry, or representationalist naturalism here, in Santer's lectures, takes the guise of a political economy discarding its theological counterpart (and legacy), even while it is clearly in no better position to support its theoretical claims or practical effect than the "metaphysical subtleties and theological niceties" of old.

Santner is certainly right when he surmises that the recent turns to "vibrant matter," perhaps, do not cut it and hardly succeed in capturing the spectral objectivity of which we spoke earlier. This would, of course, merit a longer debate than we find in these lectures, with scholars such as Jane Bennett and others receiving a far more generous hearing than they are given here.

Yet, for all my appreciation of Santner's deeply original project, I am not so sure that the alternative concept or trope he banks his argument on, namely that of "creaturely life," fares any better in diagnosing the remaining critical impetus in both life and world that our time has lost more and more sight of. What generates general and more restricted forms of "stress"—whether semantic, psychic, societal, or political—is surely not externally imposed on life in its most creative aspects, just as it does not merely hamper the vibrancy of all things material. There is a paradoxicality to life and matter itself that is situated at a much deeper and more disturbing level, and not only defies Freudo-Marxist interpretation (and, *a fortiori*, the language of political economy) but also does not let itself be resolved in any therapeutic or dialectical fashion or in any foreseeable future. But, then, this paradoxicality may be perceived within this tradition as well, whereas the so-called new materialisms tend to forget it—and this is for a simple reason, which is that the former remains steeped in a specific Western theological archive. As Santner notes, "the Marxist project—along with that of psychoanalysis—operates within a Judeo-Christian tradition for which the *creatureliness* of human life ... is inseparable from being subject to normative pressures of various kinds the generic source of which is our life with language" (82). Instead of emphasizing the animist or, later, Spinozist tendency of locating, while "dispersing," normativity in presumably "self-perpetuating patterns" of either "organized matter" or beings' *conatus*, Santner takes his lead from a different element in what he calls "the subject-matter of political economy." His claim is that "what is studied under the heading of political economy—its subject matter in the conventional sense—demands a special sort of materialism, one attuned to the strange matter or materiality generated by the emergence and sustenance, under ever-changing historical conditions, of human subjectivity" (43).

Whereas the new materialisms aim to capture the relatively recent "sensitivity to the liveliness and agency of nonhuman animals, things, 'actants,' and environments," together with "the flows, fluxes, and intensities ... of capital in our everyday life" (44), the Freudo-Marxist insistence on Judeo-Christian creatureliness does not lose sight of the subject matter that matters: it names and defends what resists the seemingly irrevocable processes of which these tendencies and intensities are both the driving force and the result.

This said, does any one of these recent approaches—that of the new materialism or vitalism, on the one hand, and that of Santner's own "psychotheology" and political economy, on the other—ultimately succeed in capturing and theorizing the true formal (I am tempted to say, global) nature of the "virtual real" of which these lectures speak here as well? Do they offer a possible answer, perhaps even a political challenge, to the havoc it wreaks? Alternatively, do they sufficiently appreciate and evaluate the potential—and, at once, material and spiritual—emancipatory effects that virtual materiality, accompanied by a whole theologico-political "archive" and "apparatus," may have on offer as well?

Addressing the "metamorphosis of the king's royal flesh into the spectral materiality of the product of human labor, into the substance of value qua congelation of abstract, homogeneous labor" (46), Santner takes Marx's transposition of the political theological "two-body doctrine" into the schema of political economy as generative of a profound difficulty for the "theory and practice of revolution" (47). The reason is that Marx, for Santner, so much as acknowledges a simple, incontrovertible truth: "a revolutionary, too [like the advocate of political theology], *must strike something other than what's there*." The wording (which is Santner's, citing Slavoj Žižek citing Jacques Lacan) is well chosen and explains some of the recent (or ongoing) appeal of the messianic and messianicity in the wake of Walter Benjamin's "Critique of Violence" and Derrida's *Specters of Marx*. It underscores also, Santner suggests, the enduring relevance of the psychoanalytic model and method: *"Striking something other than what is there* would seem to be a task located at the intersection of political and libidinal economy, a zone that very clearly resonates with tensions vital to the messianic tradition of religious thought and action" (47). But this raises two questions already: First, should we assume that "something other than what is there" is, thereby, necessarily or primarily libidinal (or at least to be found "at the intersection" of the libidinal and political—of their economy, that is to say)? And, second, does not the very language of "resonance"—as in "resonates with tensions vital to the messianic tradition of religious thought and action"—imply that we can no longer speak of a one-directional and, hence, irrevocable transition or shift or metamorphosis of political theology into political economy at all? Is there resonance across a temporal divide? Or should we differentiate between the *messianic* part of religious tradition (its thought and action) and this tradition more generally? Does reference to "something other than what is there" and, by extension, to the "messianic," not immediately conjure the traditional—religious and theological—archive and apparatus *as a whole*? This much one could say (as Santner, in his first lecture, interestingly does): "The famous 'metaphysical subtleties and theological niceties' [*voll metaphysischer Spitzfindigkeit und theologischer Mucken*] that Marx discovered in the realm of commodities once belonged to the realm of the king" and thus Kantorowicz's *King's Two Bodies* is essentially a study of those very "metaphysical subtleties and theological niceties" in their sovereign form, in the realm of the political theology of the sovereign (46). The dual-body image or metaphor, then, travels forwards and backwards, left and right, with no historical law determining its emergence (it pops up, sometime, somewhere, somehow) and its relevance well in advance of or even after the fact. It is somewhat of a *generic* and *generative* notion that is productive of much beside itself, the ancient and modern political economy no doubt included.

The sovereign king's "surplus body" and the capitalist commodity "surplus value" both invariably inhabit the logic of the "surplus," no matter what transmutation between the two may have occurred (or still occurs). In such transmutations, however, the "enigmatic jointure of the somatic and the normative that defines human life" (50) is, arguably, just one epochal moment, as the reference to "the human" hardly condenses or limits the logic of surplus. And this is a logical—perhaps, deeply metaphysical—consequence, not the surreptitious reintroduction of the so-called new (de-subjectivized and, in that sense, anti-humanist) materialism per se. By the same token, according to this view, the "generic site" of surplus can hardly be libidinal—that is, sexuated—as Freud and, with him, Santner assume. But then, while the "shift from the political theology of sovereignty to the political economy of the wealth of nations is . . . a shift from one 'epochal' mode of shaping our life in the flesh to another" (51), the Freudian conception of flesh qua libido is itself (here Santner reiterates an insight from Jacob Taubes) "already prefigured" in the letters of Paul (*Romans 7*, in particular), in the apostle's "conception of the flesh as an amplification of human sentience" (75)—that is to say, of a paradoxicality not just of sexual desire, but of the will in its broadest, quasi-infinite scope. One is tempted to conclude that if the duality of discourse (of "flesh" and its putative other) is seated this deeply in the history, texture, and, well, body of our Scriptures and literature (from Shakespeare to Kafka and Rilke, at a minimum), then there is little justified in the fear that—in the transformation from the King's Two Bodies to the People's Two Bodies—the latter will end up being "manag[ed] . . . by way of political-economic calculations" (55).

II

We all intuit that in the exponential growth of economic markets and new technological media over the last decennia there lurks what (following Dutch Hollywood director Paul Verhoeven's 1990 science fiction action movie) one might designate a *total recall*, one that is accompanied by disturbing, dystopian forms of total submission, memory control, and correlative memory loss.[4] The bleak latter-day apocalyptic and political Marcionites (among whom one might certainly count the later Heidegger and the current Giorgio Agamben) miss out on the former (i.e., the mechanism of recall) while exaggerating the latter (i.e., the mechanization of psychic and social submission). There is little doubt that Santner's diagnosis of, if not remedy for, contemporary existence and culture in the pervasive busy-ness of the capitalist world system has its dystopian—hence, Marcionite—resonances. And only another thinking, close reading, and patient working through of the signs of these times seems to offer any solace, albeit one that deliberately falls short of the redemptive promises of past messianic movements, whether religious, mystical, and theologico-political in their premises and eschatology or naturalist, materialist, and secular in their axioms and teleology. No dialectic—much less paradoxology—of capital and its psycho-social analogies is here invoked.

Yet, one might counter that there is a precise, if peculiar, sense in which the global "culture of make-belief," as sociologist Manuel Castells aptly puts it, is in the end also one of "belief in the making," and this not only or primarily because religions react against the onslaughts of modernity and against the contours of the information age and network society, more specifically.[5] There are intrinsic or structural reasons why what Henri Bergson summarized as "mechanics" and "mysticism" presuppose—and revert into—each other. And that is not always a bad thing to happen. Even the looming perspective of an increasingly "global"—expansive and worldwide, as well as vague and generic—religion *retains*, indeed, *gains*, moments and thereby momentums of "small, nonsensical hope," just as much as such "global religion" may well be an exponent, if not a sure sign, of further oppressions. After all, everything is or can be. Global religion's globality and abstractive vagueness go hand in hand, rendering the worst of its legacies virtually innocuous, while mobilizing its very best for the good that can only now be envisioned. This, at least, is a standing possibility—or, paradoxically put, an always possible, if currently often apparent impossibility—which by no means denies or forgets that the conditions of the good, the better, and the best and those of the bad (or worse, evil) are and remain virtually the same.

One should add that there is nothing "partial" about this redemptive "metamorphosis" of "make belief" into "belief in the making" that subjects and societies may or may not undergo. For it is not "some part or aspect" or "partial object" that is surreptitiously salvaged in the "substance of value of commodities" when and where this so happens, but tradition—read: the theologico-political archive and apparatus—*in toto*. Indeed, this is the *total social fact* (to echo Marcel Mauss) that we have barely begun to fathom in its pragmatic depth and widest of reaches.

As a consequence, both more and less than a "shift from one form of fetishism to another, from the fetishism of persons to that of objects of exchange" (45), is at stake in modern capitalism. In fact, much more and much less than the transition from pre-modern to modern sovereignties and subjects keeps us unsettled and "busy" as well. Strictly speaking, then, sovereignty and *its* subjectivation are no longer the issue. For good or for ill, different forms of commonality and selfhood enter the fray, some of them unprecedented, others foreshadowed in the deeper recesses of our imagination (archived and not).

There can, currently, be no point in locating the "immaterial stuff" of sovereignty (royal and other) in some "new, thingly location" that is the one highlighted by the "labor theory of value" (46). Precisely from a theologico-political view—under an infinitizing, eternal aspect, *sub specie aeternitatis*, as it were—all things and locations, like all ideas and movements, souls and bodies, in their possible roles as stepping stones and stumbling blocks, are equally close and distant from their being salvageable or forlorn, redemptive or destructive, vehicles of peace or of war, plus or minus. And whatever remains of the category of metaphysical or ontological "substance" in the reality and understanding of "value," its abstractive quality is, perhaps, no longer one of "congelation."

If one says that "the metaphysical subtleties and theological niceties" that Marx discovered in the realm of commodities once belonged to the realm of the king—that they are composed, that is, of royal remains, the breakdown products of the political theology of sovereignty—then one is assuming a solidity and divisibility where there may well be none. And, while it is one thing to say that modern or contemporary political formations are *fully describable* in terms of the archive and apparatus of what preceded them, it is quite another to assume that the present is somehow (somewhere, sometimes) *pieced together* with parts—including literal, spiritual, and mystical body parts—of the past.

The latter, genealogical claim is problematic for yet another reason: it relies on a scheme of before and after, cause and effect, of their proportionality, that is to say, of there being no more of, say, substance and sovereignty, subject-matter or surplus-"stuff," in the last phase than there is in the first—as if substance and sovereignty could only diminish, displace themselves, but never accrue, never return *with a vengeance*.

III

Santner speaks of a "prior displacement, murderous or not, of the *sovereign* of the realm by the *coin* of the realm," adding that it is, paradoxically, "prefigured by the imprint of the sovereign's own figure on coins" (48). With reference to Benjamin Franklin's observation he further notes: "We can murder a crown in Franklin's sense—perform *economic regicide*—only if the political theology of sovereignty has already been largely absorbed by and translated into the terms of the political economy of the wealth of nations, only when the stuff of the king's 'surplus body' has been transformed into that of surplus value, the product of a certain mode of human labor." As so often, then, what comes after, as a matter of historical fact and of principle, came before, even though what came before it "prefigured" the ulterior "figure." In other words, the conditioned conditions what conditions it, thus subverting any logic of transcendentality, causality, historicity, or of any other linear directionality, as—on second glance—everything co-exists here and is, hence, co-extensive with everything else. So much for any remnants of the secularist assumption, and, without it, the language of "afterlife"—here, the life of political economy's "metaphysical subtleties and theological niceties" that presumably follows upon, even if it is not directly caused or occasioned by, the political theologies of old—ceases to lose most of its explanatory or descriptive function.

But the alternative model, if one can still say so (it is a *mobile* of ever-moving elements, rather than "parts," first of all), is hard to reconcile with the language of "absorption" or even "displacement" (as in "the displacement of royal by popular sovereignty"); it further resists any logic of presupposition, of "transformation" and "transfer" (whether that of secularization, naturalization, or democratization), and, in sum, of metamorphosis, mutation, mediation, and all the rest.

For complex reasons, the story of a different *mediatization*—in Derrida's "hauntological" terminology, of *dissemination* and *diffusion*, together with the *artifactuality* and *actuvirtuality* that come with it—still provides us with a more plausible account of how certain given discourses and dispositions (archives and apparatuses) come to alternate and inhabit—indeed, haunt as well as outdo and outwit, each other. Rethinking and reinventing a "historicity without historicism," that is to say, a genealogy without teleology, a series or seriality and "seriature" without sequence or consequence, is what is called for. What matters is not whether, provisionally and strategically, one speaks here of "'messianicity' without messianism," or opts for an altogether different, say, secular idiom. Indeed, speaking, as Santner does with reference to *The Merchant of Venice* and *Hamlet*, of the emergence of a *spectral* materiality out of the *spirit* of kingship comes remarkably close to what I am suggesting here. But, then, there is a problem of conflicting metaphors if this alternative formulation is taken to illuminate what "absorption" and its conceptual and figural analogues fundamentally mean.

IV

If this above, alternative view is correct, then there is something wrong with the *picture of embodiment*, the "fleshly form [*Leibesgestalt*]" of which Santner speaks with reference to Marx's *Capital*, just as there may well be something fundamentally off in identifying the Hegelian "*Reflexionsbestimmung*, or reflexive determination, as the key to this sort of relational identity" (45). Moreover, there may be something mistaken with the very assumption that there is such a thing as a "sovereign *form*" or, for that matter, "commodity *form*," just as there may well be no "mediation," properly speaking, that can be said to organize the "social" in its most fundamental "dimension." Again, an altogether different *dialectic* seems *at work* between all these concepts and practices, figures and pictures, and it is only through it (mounting the ladder before discarding it, as we will see) that a whole system of divinely and humanly economic relations can be rendered "inoperative," here and there, for a moment or two. And, perhaps, "dialectics" is not even the term we are in search of here. A more fluid, call it erotico-political, interpretation of subjective and popular desire as it divests monarchical power of its sovereignty, while incurring some fatally attractive power and imagined sovereignty of its own in the process, may be of use in further explicating the restricted and general economies of political—and, I would add, undiminished theological or theologico-political—significance.

Already Claude Lefort's phenomenal essays on the "irreducible" element of the political and in politics, centered on the "permanence of the theologico-political" (with, in his text, a question mark added) and on "the future of immortality," respectively, undo all too *corporeal* or *corporealistic*—philosophically speaking, all too ontic—determinations (reflexive or not).[6] They substitute for them an at once more elusive and robust ontological or, rather, phenomenological model. Lefort's use of the "flesh of the world," indeed, of mere and brute "being"—"*l'être brut*"—enables a very different take on these matters that resonates with several of Santner's deepest concerns in these lectures.

There may well be an "ultimately enigmatic jointure of the somatic and the normative that defines human life" (50), as Santner suggests. But the Merleau-Pontian motif of the "flesh," underlying the Lefortian idea of "erotico-politics"—not unlike the Spinozist-Bergsonian-Deleuzian refrain of the "we do not know what the body can do"—strangely *disincarnates* the localized and compartmentalized ("busy") body and the life that comes with it as much as it gives it fluid forms—should we say, giving its spectral body—a novel and divided place in the general economy of all things material and spiritual.

And, if already in Marx's conception of the "spectral materiality of the commodity" this apparent immateriality is "the value abstracted from the body of the worker and transferred ... to the product of labor qua commodity"(56), then there is no reason to assume that things—that is to say, the circulation and dislocation of value—will stop right there. Ironically, the "way of all flesh" is "registered" not only—or not even primarily—as "the *weight of all flesh*" (56), as if the value of "value" ("the substance of value") had the last word in all matters. Paradoxically put, the value of value is not itself, in turn, *a* value (or, perhaps, even *of* value). It has neither "substance" nor "essence," whether that of common and proper use or that of surplus. Values are variables—they have not just a value; as we say, they have value—in the grander scheme (and, who knows, the larger scheming and dialectical ruse) of all things seen and unseen. That's just how things *are*.

What seems at least just as important as the *"weight of all flesh,"* then, is the apparent *weightlessness* of things circulating in markets and media (the formation and very form or format of information and disinformation, for starters) and the eventful, quasi-miraculous, special effect this takes on all "forms of life" (both human and other). This is how I take the passage Santner cites from Derrida's *Specters of Marx* that differentiates the "spectral historicity of Europe from other histories of the 'European Spirit'" (59–60) and introduces the "dimension of the flesh," the "paradoxical incorporation, the becoming-body," that materializes itself in "neither soul nor body" or, what comes down to the same, that phenomenalizes itself in both. Only thus, things acquire an unmistakable *"phenomenality,"* albeit one that has little in common with the *corps-sujet* about which the existentialist phenomenalists, the early Merleau-Ponty among them, mused for so long.[7]

V

Following and countering the way of all flesh, what can or should be our mode of proceeding, if not our method? In other words—Santner's own—what, precisely, is "paradoxological thinking," notably in the "modes of engagement with glory" (120)? Or what, as in Franz Kafka's case as recalled by Santner, are genuine "exercises in paradoxological thinking"? Are they a thinking in paradox or in paradoxes? But, if so, which one or which ones, exactly?

There is no doubt that Santner's lectures introduce an "enigmatic signifier" by adopting this terminology of "paradoxology"—and one that, he says, "gets under the skin." But why and how does paradoxicality, more than any other procedure, experience or experiment, illuminate the very "subject-matter" at hand here and, most notably, its fragile ontological status (or, should we say, complete "lack" thereof, as if ascribing even a negative metaphysical or, say, apophatic, mystical theological absence to it were still saying too much)?[8] Moreover, in what sense, precisely, can paradoxology explicate, indeed, unfold the logic of capital and the apparent ways in which it ushers in a transition—possibly or presumably irreversible—from the theologico-political regime of sovereign monarchical power to the democratized and interiorized "busy-bodyness" of popular sovereignty and its political economy? For one thing, one might have expected the concept and practice ("exercise") of paradoxology to be *prima facie* more fitting to tackle the "metaphysical subtleties and theological niceties" of the Divine economies of old, those that Agamben, in Michel Foucault's footsteps, tracks all the way back to the Church Fathers (suggesting that discursive apparatuses find their origin and justification, if not in prehistorical man uttering the first word, then in the biblically inspired theologies of Divine Providence and the Trinitarian logic—of Father, Son, and Holy Spirit—that underlies them).

As an apparent contradiction, "paradox" introduces a however slight but essential disjunction between the position or method adopted (e.g., that of the theologico-political archive and apparatus in its "afterlife," as we saw) and the very same position or method when taken as such, in its historical context and conceptual rigor. As a merely apparent source of true value—that is to say, as a presumably indisputable *arche* or *telos*, principle, or end term of all possible thinking and acting, rather than a merely discursive ladder to be discarded, like Ludwig Wittgenstein's logic, once one has climbed all the way to the top (or, in any case, high and far enough to see and move well beyond), thus reaching a different (if, in Santner's sense, still "immanent") plane—the historical theologico-political construct, call it metaphysics as we know it, must come unhinged. Yet, as we enter this novel terrain, a salutary plane-ness lies also in waiting. It is one that can be stated in the plainest of conceptual and figural terms and thereby, paradoxically, offers yet another (and far more profitable) "surplus" of that very immanence than could be imagined or ever hoped for within the language and thinking of old. In Santner's words, the reversal of perspective that is thus brought about "involves an effort to reach into the doxological machine—the machine that sustains the religious structure of capitalism—and pull its plug, if even for a fleeting moment of Sabbatical inoperativity in which, perhaps, something new might be spelled out by, precisely, *spelling out the spell* cast by the doxology of everyday life" (120).

Interestingly, Santner equates this motif of inversion, which entails nothing short of a conversion, or *Umkehr*, with the Benjaminian figure of the metamorphosis of life into *Schrift*, although the reasons for this identification remain somewhat unclear in the finale of these marvelous lectures.[9] For is this to say that "everyday life" *only* *thus* becomes *legible* once again—that is to say, once we awaken from the "dreamless sleep" (to cite Bob Dylan's album *Time Out of Mind*) into which we were lulled by the Sirens' songs of prehistorical myth? There is no doubt that such myth exerted its power in the dubious glory of the Christian-theological "resonance machine"—of religion as capitalism—of which William Connolly (albeit in an altogether un-Benjaminian register, I should add) has spoken compellingly. But is this the only actual or potential working and effect it must or might have on us, here and now?

Needless to say, to associate *"spelling out the spell"* with a turn toward *Schrift*—call it the turn or return to language at its deepest (and that means also at its most plane and poetic rather than purely liturgical or doxological) of levels—opens up a whole field of study, namely the "literary practice and theory of the paradoxology" (120). Such interpretative exercise, Santner seems to intimate, might one day come to supplement, even though it will therefore not necessarily supplant, the Foucauldian-Agambian "archeology of glory," with its somewhat one-sided obsession with biopolitical and cultic or pastoral "power."

VI

But this is not all: paradox or paradoxology may further signify "near-aporetic"—that is to say, the practice or exercise of espousing two contrasting and alternating viewpoints—to the point of contradiction. Such *coincidentia oppositorum* reminds one of Wittgenstein's theory of dual aspect seeing, of the duck or rabbit that *now you see, now you don't*; in other words, it recalls the co-extensiveness of two visions that one may need or want to subscribe to even though one cannot hold them simultaneously, in one single moment, just as one cannot *mediate* or *negotiate* between the two. Paradoxology, thus defined, implies that their very alternation does not yield a metamorphosis, mutation, substitution, translation, transformation, or transfer of one into the other, no matter how often we may be tempted to *take one for the other,* to *reduce the other to the one.* Like the logic of presupposition, that of supplanting one perspective by the other is not *de rigueur.*

But then, paradoxology is not just the speaking in paradoxes; it is also the expression of statements that *seem* self-contradictory, absurd, or false, but at a deeper or more factual, as well as speculative, level contain a possible truth. Paradoxology, thus conceived, is speaking truth to the power of "doxology," the praise that surrounds, announces, and anoints or baptizes sovereign power, whether royal or popular. Besides, like *parapraxis* in Freud's *The Psychopathology of Everyday Life,* it does not speak to power directly, but quite literally *changes the subject* and, as it were, "slips" right beyond it (belittling the sovereign lord—*Signorelli,* as Freud keeps forgetting—and who- or whatever takes his place).

VII

To say this has several consequences. If Agamben—and earlier Benjamin, and through him, Kafka as we now understand them—is indeed right, as Santner suggests, should we not ask whether the question of "power," including that of bio-, cultic, and pastoral power, is, perhaps, not the key to the political? After all, it may not offer the first or last word on the theological, either. Rather, it is toward a rethinking of so-called *weak* or even *soft* "power"—in Jean-Luc Marion's recent terms, of "unpower" (*impouvoir*),[10] by assuming a lack (contingency, fragility, and givenness) at the very foundation of sovereignty, whether royal or popular, reigning or governing—that all these thinkers and, I suspect, Santner himself, must somehow be under way.

Now, if this is indeed the case, this would be yet another lesson that the religious-theologico-political archive and apparatus may continue to teach us, in its enduring "afterlife," so to speak. The very paradox of the *"doxology of everyday life"* that Santner discusses with reference to Max Weber consists in the fact that even the democratized materialism of busy, self-interested bodies (*pace* Alain Badiou) may thus offer yet another, unexpected testimony *ad maiorem Dei gloriam*. Such that even the progressive withholding of divine grace—even though there remains a minimal rather than royal theology in place, free to manifest or reveal itself as an invisible, if often intangible, force *everywhere, at anytime*—still or, in fact, more and more counts as the very proof of what it would seem to negate: the less than empirical and more than ontological haunting of a "hidden God," whose secret workings are not so much providential or predetermined—for good or ill—but, in their worldly or practical effect, nonetheless strangely "economical" (in every historical, broadly ecclesial, and modern, political sense of this term).

Just as on Santner's reading of Foucault "the subject matter of political economy includes an *un-economic subject matter*," whose "disruptive force" derives from elsewhere, and whose "theological roots" can be " 'extended and moved back in time' " all the way down (or is it up?) to the "semantic field" of divine *oikonomia*, so also Santner's suggestive analysis of "creaturely life" is "one that seems to push thinking in the direction of theology" (84). And, by "theology" we must, at this point, simply mean the assumed, if not observed, "ultimate *lack of foundation* for the historical forms of life in which human life unfolds."

VIII

Santner's lectures and much of his published work, then, are what I would like to think of as theoretical or, perhaps, spiritual exercises in (or of) *"ontological vulnerability"* through which a distinctively human "precariousness"—including that of its "biological life"— becomes, as he says, "potentiated, amplified, by way of exposure to . . . radical contingency" (84).

How this "anarchic 'potentiation'" of our forms of life and the very "space of meaning" that they constitute—our "natural history," as Wittgenstein with Benjamin might have said here—can, in turn, be *historical*, as Santner insists, is, however, far from clear. The anarchical, as that which opens up to historical life forms, precisely, by exposing us to them, is radical and ineradicable, ontological and generic, is neither ontic nor empirical, but meta-material and, come to think of it, something spiritual. And, if this is the case, then neither human existence nor language, neither the "somatic" nor the "normative" (nor their inflammatory point of intersection of which Santner makes so much) may be its sole or even privileged locus. This much one would need to grant the *new* materialism. But, as we know, it is also the deepest of theological insights.

What the old and new materialisms no less than the "archeology of glory" (in its Foucauldian-Agambian variety) get wrong is the belief—in Santner's words, "the small, nonsensical hope" (118)— that one could ultimately avoid and overcome, undo or profanize, the "archaic [or, technically speaking, sacred] sphere in which religious and juridical action and speech [have and will always] become indistinguishable" (95). The more important question to be asked, therefore, is not "Why does power—heavenly or earthly—need glory?" but "Why would glory—divine or human—need 'power'"? Indeed, the "modes," modalities, and moods of *glory* may well be the *via regia* of everything (every "thing," the very "thing in itself" or, in the Heideggerian diction, *"das Ding"*) that cannot be "produced," "circulated," or "consumed." Glory may well just *work out*, but there is little in or to it that we can *work toward* in advance, much less *work through* after the fact. Glorious "acts," if we can say so, reveal what is either *more* or *less* than the ontological *"weight"* that, Santner agrees with Kantorowicz's *Laudes Regiae*, "cannot be measured by legal standards." They carry a "weight" that is non-criteriological and, hence, not just that of "all flesh"[11] (in any conceptual, materialist, psychoanalytic or, for that matter, phenomenological determination of that term).

IX

This brings me to my conclusion. If there is, as Santner writes, "a missing task or *telos* proper to human life"(101), if this is our fundamental vulnerability, exposure, and answerability to the world and everything (everyone) in it—our ontic-ontological lack or "flesh wound," as he adds—then it must necessarily follow that neither "inoperativity" (the "sabbatical *otium*," *"what does not work"*) nor even its virtual opposite (for example, Bonnie Honig's understanding of "Sabbath-power" and its secular functional equivalents) can be it—that is to say, "central to human life," the aspired opposite of its Freudian *It*.

It seems metaphysically as well as empirically false to claim, as Agamben does (and Santner endorses), that man is "in essence … completely devoid of work, because he is the Sabbatical animal par excellence." There is good reason why the Bible pairs and contrasts six days of work with one day of Sabbath (and does not, like capitalism, "eliminate the distinction between workday and holiday, workday and Sabbath" [119], nor, by contrast, endorse "Sabbatical power"). We are, precisely, not asked to be *either* operative *or* inoperative all the time, as if either one of these two modes, modalities, and moods could, all by itself, be or become the "center of the human," the "political 'substance' of the Occident."

Paradoxically, this *bipolarity* is *of the essence*—indeed, *off* the essence (and thus much more of a theological than a metaphysical significance, if we define matters strictly, "essence" not being a theological but at best an onto-theological category and hardly among the nonpredicable Divine Names one can pray to).

But then, such dual aspect of our individual and multiple being—the difference matters little—also means that generically, in our species and specific being, we are neither this nor that, whether "in essence" or "par excellence." This is another way of saying that we may well be deeply *indebted*, such that there is, indeed, a *"sovereignty of debt* over human life and its possibilities" (119), as Heidegger's language of "thrownness," "falling," and "originary guilt" aptly captures. Yet this does not mean that such indebtedness is moral or financial, much less genetic, per se.

Emmanuel Levinas once remarked that behind the "weight of Capital" there lies a "weight in Being," without any further ontic determination or historical determinism. We might call this the very "value of value," its "self-valorization," its *conatus essendi*, preceding any distinction or intersection of the "somatic" and "normative" that we can—and, perhaps, must—subsequently introduce in our description and interpretation of things that surround us. And the very concept and meaning of "Being" is certainly one of those later, belated determinations, not to be taken for granted but hard to avoid. From a deep pragmatic standpoint, the late Rorty was absolutely right: ontology is and must be seen or redefined as "cultural politics"—that is, in ways and words, without *fundamentum in re*, that are coined, adopted, or otherwise introduced, and that we and others with (and after) us must nonetheless somehow own up to and deal with.

X

Paradoxology, in its ongoing engagement with the tradition of political theology or political economy—and, one would hope and expect, much else instead—dispenses with the residual humanism and, if you like, ontological existentialism that, like royal or popular sovereignty, are merely some of the values we find among the *theological remains*. But it does so in the full knowledge that such dispensation *partly* reinstates and reaffirms what it thus—correctly and justly—also sets free and, thereby, loosens up. Santner's "paradoxologies" are a brilliant exercise in that they bring out this *dialectic*. When all is said and done, "dialectic" is the very term that comes to mind here, especially if taken in its open-ended—that is, negative—understanding and exercise, reminiscent of Theodor W. Adorno's "metaphysical meditations," which, lest we forget, were originally conceived as a "theory of spiritual experience (*Theorie der geistigen Erfahrung*)." Yet, strangely enough, it is the very concept in the Hegelian-Marxian archive and apparatus that is largely absent in the lectures presented in this volume.

How such an eminently rhetorical, yet deeply pragmatic, dialectic—which is both abstract and singular, and indeed, movingly personal ("rereading one's own existence")—translates into concrete political subject matters (inducing a "general strike," contributing to "class struggle" or plain reform) remains, I think, an open question in Santner's overall work. But it is a question for which we are now, thanks to his profound and compelling "exercises in paradoxological thinking," so much better prepared.

Notes

1. I would like to thank the members of the Tanner Lectures Committee, Eric Santner, and my two fellow commentators, Bonnie Honig and Peter Gordon, for the wonderful occasion to discuss these exciting lectures with them at Berkeley. My deep appreciation, as always, goes to Martin Jay for his kind words of welcome and introduction during these days. It was an honor to be part of the conversations that ensued and I remain grateful for the provocative thinking to which we were invited to respond with our own thoughts in mind.

2. Jacques Derrida, *Specters of Marx: The State of the Debt, the Work of Mourning, and the New International,* trans. Peggy Kamuf (New York: Routledge, 1994), 6; Santner, 60.

3. Cf. my "Introduction: Why Still 'Religion'?," in Hent de Vries, ed., *Religion—Beyond A Concept* (New York: Fordham University Press, 2008), 1–98.

4. The script for Verhoeven's film *Total Recall* was partly based on Philip K. Dick short story "We Can Remember It for You Wholesale," published in the April 1966 issue of *The Magazine of Fantasy & Science Fiction.*

5. For a discussion, see Hent de Vries, "In Media Res: Global Religion, Public Spheres, and the Task of Contemporary Comparative Religious Studies," in *Religion and Media,* ed. Hent de Vries and Samuel Weber (Stanford, CA: Stanford University Press, 2001), 3–42.

6. Claude Lefort, "La permanence du théologico-politique?," in Lefort, *Essais sur le politique: XIXe-XXe siècles* (Paris: Éditions du Seuil, 1986), 275–329; Claude Lefort, "The Permanence of the Theologico-Political?," trans. David Macey, in Hent de Vries and Lawrence E. Sullivan eds., *Political Theologies: Public Religions in a Post-Secular World* (New York: Fordham University Press, 2006), 148–87. See also Claude Lefort, "Mort de l'immortalité?," in *Essais sur le politique,* 330–64; Claude Lefort, "The Death of Immortality?," in Lefort, *Democracy and Political Theory,* trans. David Macey (Minneapolis: University of Minnesota Press, 1989), 256–82. See my " 'The Miracle of Love' and the Turn to Democracy," *CR: The New Centennial Review,* vol. 8 (2009), no. 3, 237-290.

7. Santner cites the introduction to Sara Melzer and Kathryn Norberg, eds., *From the Royal to the Republican Body: Incorporating the Political in Seventeenth- and Eighteenth-Century France* (Berkeley: University of California Press, 1998), 10–11: "With democracy the concept of the nation replaced the monarch and sovereignty was dispersed from the king's body to all bodies. Suddenly every body bore political weight.... With the old

sartorial and behavorial codes gone, bodies were less legible, and a person's place in the nation was unclear." Structures of power, it would seem, thus became ever more elusive, weaker, and softer. Yet Santner makes it clear that his own emphasis is less on the often intractable "transformation of social codes" than on the "agitation of the 'flesh'" brought about by this shift, "the nature of the 'matter' that accounts for the new 'political weight' of every citizen" (Santner, *The Royal Remains: The People's Two Bodies and the Endgames of Sovereignty* [Chicago: University of Chicago Press, 2011], 4–5). While his earlier writings focused on the regulatory practices that Foucault grouped together under the heading of *biopolitics*, his current interest lies elsewhere, centering as it now does on "political economy as a site where this weight begins to be taken into account by, precisely, efforts to weigh it, reckon with it, subject it, as it were, to double-entry bookkeeping without ever really grasping the real nature of the "double" involved" (31).

Whereas Foucault would tie in the political economical aspect of biopolitics under the rubric of "governmentality," Santner thinks that it is not so much the mantra of biopolitics but, rather, the clinically based theory of psycho-analysis that offers the necessary conceptual tools for interpreting the chang-ing nature of the king's and now people's two bodies. For these are deeply interwoven with the individual and collective fantasies of subjects and citi-zens, fantasies Santner takes to be the privileged means to negotiate their sense of self and place within the new historical landscape.

The difference between this psychoanalytic approach and the plethora of so-called new materialisms is precisely that the former is not inclined to "dispense" with the very subject-matter—in Santner's words, with "the spec-tral materiality proper to human subjectivity, one with distinctive '*flesh and phenomenality*'" (61) —that one should keep in view. The *"its"* may "out-number the *me's*" and we may well be made up of *"an array of bodies"* (as Jane Bennett, invoked in these lectures, aptly reminds us) but, for Santner, this is no reason to resort to "a kind of multiculturalism at the cellular, or even molecular level" (61). Such proclamations of a "newish self" do not all by themselves inhibit the violence that modern societies still and increasingly have to deal with and that they cannot hope to resolve in any other way than to patiently and systematically *work them through.* Such therapeutic relief, Santner insists, requires facing what Freud called the singular "*It*," not some fantasmatic multitude of "its," not least because it is so difficult to name.

Yet Santner does find several words to circumscribe this virtual mate-riality underlying, constituting, and pervading the subject—as its very subject-matter, that is—for example, when he continues by saying that we should think of it as a "complex disorder of the 'tribe,'" as "a disorder that in one way or another—and psychoanalysis is the effort to understand those ways—congealed as the uncanny cause of . . . desire, the 'un-economic' dimension of . . . libidinal economy" (62).

By contrast, the new, "post-humanist" materialisms that center around "vibrant" and "vital" materiality tend to result, in Santner's view, in a problematic homogenization of alterity, now undertaken in the name of multiplicity and heterogeneity, a theoretical move in which too much gets lost to warrant the very "moral and political wager" with which such new materialism are proudly advocated.

But, if this is all pertinent, how can Santner nonetheless side with the Marxian verdict that in the commodity form it is "not so much *we* who continue to engage in metaphysics and theology but, rather, our *busy bodies*" (81)? The answer seems to hinge on the assumption that our bodies' "*busy-ness*" must, first of all, be seen in a *Freudo*-Marxian perspective, namely as an "uncanny mode of stress," one that is strangely coupled with "the afterlife of political theology in secular modernity—essentially its mutation into political economy" (81). But a further presupposition is that such busy-bodyness entertains an intrinsic and intimate relationship with the very subject (indeed, human subjectivity and erotico-material subject-matter) that cannot but matter most to us all. This is what I am tempted to call Santner's *residual humanism* or *ontological existentialism*, to distinguish it from the new materialists' anti-humanism, on the one hand, and from the existential phenomenology of similarly subject-oriented thinkers (such as Claude Lefort and, via him, Maurice Merleau-Ponty), on the other.

8. By the way, the concept of "subject-matter" is not the only one that merits further discussion here. For what, precisely, is the meaning of "matter" or "mattering" that is "in the wrong place" (43), as Santner suggestively claims? Moreover, what to make of the locution "surplus of immanence," which recalls Jürgen Habermas's expression "transcendence in immanence," which, likewise, is virtually indistinguishable from the "transcendence of transcendence" whose register the theological archive or apparatus masters all by itself, without the assistance of secular or, for that matter, political economical thought? Finally, is it fully clear what Santner means when he explains "animation" in Marx's sense with what is "ultimately deadening—or rather, *undeadening*—for human beings, something that drives them while holding them in place . . ." (81)? Confronted with the new materialisms of late, why would such reference to "petrified unrest [*erstarrte Unruhe*]" equal a "deanimation of undeadness" in which we are justified to put critical hopes?

9. What "inversion" might mean in these matters, I have tried to analyze in "Inverse versus Dialectical Theology: The Two Faces of Negativity and the Miracle of Faith," in *Paul and the Philosophers*, ed. Ward Blanton and Hent de Vries (New York: Fordham University Press, 2013), 466–511.

10. Jean-Luc Marion, "L'impouvoir," in *Revue de Métaphysique et de Morale* 4, no. 4 (2009): 439–45; Jean-Luc Marion, "Unpower," in Hent de Vries and Nils F. Schott, eds., *Love and Forgiveness For a More Just World* (New York: Columbia University Press, 2015), 36–42.

11. There is a further difficulty here. If we follow Santner's bold interpretation "that what Kantorowicz later elaborated under the heading of the King's Second Body is a *sublimate* of . . . a sonorous mass, a *congelation of its vibrant doxological matter*" (98), then it becomes all the more clear that the body and its flesh comes neither first nor last in the catalogue (archive and apparatus) of theologoumena that the discourse of sovereignty in its monarchical and republican variety continues to draw on, whether it knows it or not. Unless, of course, one takes the "sonorous mass of acclaiming voices," the language of the angels of which Erik Peterson speaks in his *Theological Tractates* (trans., Michael J. Hollerich [Stanford, CA: Stanford University Press, 2011]) as somehow itself a body and not just embodied, that is to say, as the underlying "vibrant matter" of the "flesh," its substantive part, itself.

The timbre and rhythm of jubilant voices, in their very tonality and sonority, would themselves have attained the role of a vibrant, vital, indeed, spectral materiality, namely that of the flesh, without there even being a body—say, a human body—in sight. But would this not simply lead to one further step on the path taken by the new materialists, who altogether jettison the—first and second—human and spiritual body (or *corpus mysticum*) without whose serial incarnation, it is often assumed, no body politic worthy of mentioning could ever be conceived, founded, let alone maintained (or, in Santner's striking choice of terms in this context, "fleshed out")?

A further passage confirms this reading. Speaking of the "archeology of glory," Santner writes: "Agamben's insight is that there is no political theology of sovereignty without a theological economy of glory, no constitution of *Herrschaft* without the doxological production of *Herrlichkeit*. . . . What might at first appear to be a superstructural feature of a ruling state apparatus is, essentially, its *economic base*, one that produces the glorious flesh of the social bond" (98–99). Here, as well, the divine or theological conception of glory conditions, upon second glance, what, at first, seemed to condition it in turn. It forms, informs or forms itself in the very matter or mattering of whatever subjects and citizens, as living and working humans, can further be or eventually become. The *subject*-matter, the flesh—tied as it is, for Santner, to the human form, to the eminently and however contingent and forever vulnerable human forms of life, exposed to the "lack" of their world—would thus, again, seem to come second. Crudely put, it is the *explanandum*, not the *explanans* at all. Belated, constituted after the fact, as it were, the human body and *its* flesh could hardly be claimed to play a pivotal role in the general economy of things, the point of departure or return of any analysis that tracks the transition (if, indeed, it is one) from royal to popular sovereignty. Indeed, a critique of sovereignty, across the spectrum of political formations and the forms of life that sustain them, would have to begin and end elsewhere: in the questioning of "power" in its very practice, no doubt, *and* its concept. There are *glorious* examples in the theological archive and in the present day and age that aptly—I would say, *economically*—demonstrate that such inquiry need and must not play the power game of old, nor follow the theoretical fixation on political or bio-, cultic, pastoral, and, now, doxological power per se.

Reply to Commentators

Idle Worship

ERIC L. SANTNER

I

Before commenting on the three "official" responses to my lectures offered by Bonnie Honig, Peter Gordon, and Hent de Vries, I would like to say a few words in response to Katharina Kaiser, a philosopher at Berkeley who, in the informal discussions that followed the final seminar in April 2014, expressed concerns about my use of the word "flesh." The word was, on the one hand, too vague—resisted being properly fleshed out, as it were—and, on the other, too historically and, above all, too theologically overdetermined, too saturated with sacramental, eucharistic sense, to be available for the sort of conceptual work I wanted it to do. As Kantorowicz made eminently clear in *The King's Two Bodies*, such sacramental sense is what opened the way for the political theology of sovereignty in the first place, for the elaboration, that is, of a sublimely carnal dimension of kingship, the virtually real substance of royal legitimacy. For Kantorowicz, the story of political theology in Europe begins with—and in a certain sense never fully leaves behind—a conception of "Christ-centered kingship" in which the sovereign's double nature is modeled on the logic—or as Agamben has emphasized, the *oikonomia*—of the incarnation. The two natures of Christ are transferred to the king, who is thus seen to have not only his own mortal body but also to *enjoy by grace*—an enjoyment made manifest and effective in the liturgical practices of consecration and acclamation—a sublime body in and through which he appears as the "type and image of the Anointed in heaven and therewith of God." As Kantorowicz puts it, here "the vision of the king as a *persona geminata* is ontological and, as an effluence of a sacramental and liturgical action performed at the altar, it is liturgical as well."[1] My own work over the last years has involved repeated attempts to "reduce" the sacramental senses put to work in theology and political theology to their basic elements or, to put it more accurately, to track the historical process of their real reduction to a sort of "base materiality" or subject-matter. The historical name of that historical process is, of course, *secularization*. My argument has been that modern secular societies have come to elaborate this subject-matter, *put it to work*, in largely biopolitical and political economic ways, that these two realms of modern life thereby provide the crucial "haunting grounds" of what had previously been configured within a political theology of sovereignty as, precisely, the doctrine—or perhaps better, the *doxa*—of the King's Two Bodies. I have furthermore argued that both Marx and Freud each in his own way caught a glimpse of this subject-matter in quasi-pure form, in a form at least potentially uncoupled from its various modes of elaboration, of being put to work. Their stroke of genius was to seize the dimension of the flesh, to *freely associate with it* where it began to come loose from meaning, purpose, and (surplus) value, where it could finally go "on strike."

The result of such "free associations" is the view of the flesh I have been proposing here. Taking my orientation from both of these thinkers—as well as from various modernist writers and artists—I have been using the word in an attempt to locate for thought a spectral carnality that forms at and as the unstable jointure of the somatic and the normative dimensions of human life, a sort of a *negative protuberance* or navel marking the birth of the human animal into the conflict-ridden space of normativity, a space in which we are invested with various kinds of authority and responsibility for what we do and say. I understand this birth moreover as that of an emphatic sense of creatureliness, of being continuously subject to creative (and destructive) historical forces that posit and de-posit forms and norms of communal life. Our biological life is amplified, "inflamed" by its inscription in historical forms of life, forms that must always at some level come to terms with—give some shape and meaning to—this very inflammation. In both *The Royal Remains* and in these lectures I have attempted to track a major transformation of those terms in the transition from royal to popular sovereignty, a transition accompanied by a significant transfer of governmental powers to economic "laws."[2]

To repeat the basic contours of the argument regarding that transformation, my claim has been that a social fantasy belonging to the realm of political theology and sustained by a variety of juridical and, above all, liturgical practices—that of the King's Two Bodies—comes to be displaced into the realm of political economy where the double nature of the *Staatsperson* morphs into that of the commodity. The sublime dimension of the royal person bleeds, as it were, into the commodity where it "coagulates" as the social substance of its Value. This substance is sustained, in turn, by the perpetual conversion or doubling of useful labor into what Marx characterized as abstract, homogeneous labor. The *real* product of commodity-producing labor is, as Marx puts it, a *gespenstische Gegenständlichkeit*, a spectral materiality that, as it were, keeps the economy humming. At some level, Marx had grasped that commodity-producing labor had inherited the charge formally discharged in the acclamations and doxologies—the *liturgical hum*—sustaining the political theology of sovereignty. This background hum perhaps never fully loses a eucharistic aspect insofar as what is fundamentally at issue there is the way in which human bodies enter into, are libidinally inscribed in, normative "corporations," even if they are no longer officially regarded as instances of a *corpus mysticum*.[3]

Over the course of our conversation, Katharina and I tried to think of alternative words and concepts for "flesh." As one alternative I proposed a German term that my colleague in Chicago, David

Wellbery, had coined in another context: *das Leiblich-Imaginäre*. The term, which might be translated as the corporeal-imaginary or the carnal-imaginary, captures the dimension of the imagination that reaches into our condition of being embodied, as well as our capacity—and perhaps tendency—to imagine our varied social and political bonds and relations by way of corporeal and corporate metaphors. More importantly, the word *leiblich* evokes something more than *körperlich* or corporeal, namely the sense or feeling of *Leben*, life, vitality. It connotes, that is, not only the dimension of organicity and so a certain mode of organization—that of an internally differentiated and functional unity—but also a certain quality of self-feeling accompanying such unity, the *Selbstgefühl* immanent to the unified flux of lived experience. One might think of it as the first-personal feeling of *being alive* that comes with *being-a-Leib*.

The richness of what this term, *das Leiblich-Imaginäre*, evokes—its own set of overdeterminations—has, in my view, been most thoroughly explored in the writings of various French phenomenologists who, following the lead of Merleau-Ponty, take as their point of departure Edmund Husserl's use of the terms *Leib, leiblich, leibhaft*, and perhaps most importantly, *Ichleib*. This tradition returns us, however, to our original terminological dilemma insofar as its leading figures have chosen to translate *Leib* as *chair*, as "flesh." It would seem, then, that both *flesh* and *Leib* "live" off of the very overdeterminations that risk generating confusion. I'd like to discuss briefly Jacob Rogozinski's exemplary work in this area, *The Ego and the Flesh: An Introduction to Egoanalysis*, a work that deploys the richness of these notions in compelling and exciting ways, ways that ultimately deepen my own commitment to remaining with the word "flesh."[4]

What is especially intriguing about Rogozinski's study is that it polemically offers itself as a mode of philosophical resistance to what he characterizes as *egocidal* tendencies in modern thought, above all those of Heidegger and of numerous, mostly French, post-Heideggerian thinkers. What these "egocidal thinkers"—and Rogozinski is thinking of a broad spectrum of post-structuralist, Lacanian, and Deleuzian theorists—have in common is the insistence on decentering or deposing the self of modern individuality, dismantling its pretenses of sovereignty by, precisely, *subjecting* it to various instances of a big Other, and thereby dislocating its sense of being a real, self-certifying locus of thought, feeling, and action. Rogozinski's fundamental argument is that the *alterity* of an Other—God, Being, another human being, a master, an institution, a symbolic tradition, culture, language, the impersonal flux of life, vibrant matter, even Merleau-Ponty's "flesh of the world"—presupposes the background of an *originary givenness of the self to itself*, an eternally recurring event of auto-affection or self-donation that constitutes the *ego-flesh* qua sensorium of any and all feeling that can be called *mine*. Alienation in the Other has no meaning, could never be suffered, without a more primary sense of self-givenness. In essence, Rogozinski presents the so-called Copernican turn of modern thought as a sort of revolutionary terror bent on the annihilation of the last bastion of human sovereignty, the individual ego, which ends up being deposed to the level of an empty subject, a sort of puppet in a game run by operations of ultimately impersonal signifying activity.[5] But without the sensorium of ego-flesh, without a living locus of sensation and affectivity *that I am*—and for Rogozinski, this remains Descartes's enduring insight—concepts like alienation, deposition, or captivation would lose their meaning; what they name could never be experienced as in each instance *mine*, as *jemeinig*, to use the Heideggerian locution. Much the way that Kant insists that for *sapient* human beings all representations must be accompanied by the "I," by the transcendental unity of apperception, Rogozinski argues that for *sentient* human beings, all feelings must be accompanied by the *me*, the immanent unity of ego-flesh.

Rogozinski's work along with that of the psychoanalysis he would like to supplant by "egoanalysis" belong, in my view, within the genealogical story I have been telling here. Again, the basic plot of the story runs something like this: once the form of life and symbolic apparatus that allowed for the figuration of the flesh as the substance of sovereign splendor—as the sublime object of majesty—were dismantled, once the political theology of sovereignty was displaced by the political theory of popular sovereignty along with the doctrines and practices of capitalist political economy, the locus of the flesh shifted to the two focal points of the life of the People identified by Foucault—living individuals and populations. Rogozinski's work—and prior to that, Freud's (above all, his writings concerning the notion of primary narcissism)—no doubt stand in some sort of correlation to the modern and postmodern developments of this story. It is, in a word, difficult not to see a correlation between Rogozinski's spirited defense of the ego and the radical individualism of liberal and neoliberal societies in which it becomes each individual's singular responsibility to invest his or her own "human capital," the unique store of value each "ego" harbors within. One could say that neoliberalism, in particular, with its totalization of the principle of self-interest and the market logic based upon it, is the political economic doctrine correlative to the *historical reduction* of the individual to being not so much the sovereign as the entrepreneur of his or her own ego-flesh; we are all, so to speak, *charged with investing ourselves* in the most productive way possible.

Against this background it makes a certain sense that critical thinking would be tempted by "egocide," which could then be grasped as the effort to return the flesh to the "Commons," to restore it to its status of what Merleau-Ponty called the "flesh of the *world.*" Deicide, regicide, and egocide would represent the three crucial stages on a path toward what might be thought of as a communism of vibrant matter in a shared space of pure immanence (some of Bonnie Honig's remarks go in this direction). But this would be, I think, to miss the real force of Rogozinski's critical stance with respect to "egocidal thinking" and the originality of "egoanalysis," which posits this dimension—the ego-flesh—as the true source of any genuine communitarian project, as the very medium in and through which—we might say, in the midst of which—the "truth event" of a communitarian politics could emerge. Egoanalysis functions for Rogozinski not only as a safeguard against egocide, not only as, additionally, a source of "anti-bodies" to fusional modes of incorporation that would efface all traces of singularity. Egoanalysis is, in the final analysis, the true locus of the "weak Messianic force" invoked by Walter Benjamin in his famous theses on the concept of history. For Rogozinski, only *a new thinking of the flesh* alerts us, turns us toward, the narrow gate through which the Messiah can at each moment enter to *resurrect* what has been *egocidally mortified*, to open a new dispensation of a purely immanent and fully common glory, the glory of what is held in common. Egoanalysis is conceived, that is, as an exercise—we might even say as a spiritual exercise—in what I have referred to as *paradoxology*—one that, of course, as yet lacks the crucial dimension of liturgical practice. It would thus perhaps be more accurate to say that egoanalysis provides something like the "germ cell" of what could then be more fully elaborated paradoxologically.

What Rogozinski does, in effect, is phenomenologically reduce the dimension of the flesh that we have explored up to now in various historical formations (along with the "work" in which it has been enlisted as a *herrlich* support of various forms of *Herrschaft*) to its "basics," as, precisely, an irreducible dimension of human life. My argument has been that it is precisely the *historical reduction* of the flesh to a political economic dimension of ego-value that makes its *phenomenological reduction* not only possible but also necessary and urgent. We saw this same process at work in visually stunning form in David's *Death of Marat*. There the abstract material out of which the upper half of the painting is made was shown to emerge out of a representational deadlock generated by the passage beyond the political theology of sovereignty. The task of painting is thereby transformed to that of *figuring out abstraction*—how to model, how to work with this seemingly new abstract materiality, how, as it were, to reinvent painting on the basis of its newly basic/base material. My worry, however, is that it is precisely *this overlapping of the historical and the phenomenological* that Rogozinski misses in his otherwise compelling introduction to the field of egoanalysis. Put somewhat differently, he is a theorist of the subject-matter we have been tracking at the very historical point at which it seems to shed its own historicity. This shedding shows up as the view—really, the fundamental axiom of Rogozinski's project—that the virtually real dimension of the flesh that I have presented as arising out of the knotting or jointure of the somatic and the normative has always already taken place within the somatic as a radically immanent process of self-organization that gives birth to the ego as a unified flux of sensation. For Rogozinski the field of the Other—the "transcendental" space of normativity—is secondary, arrives on the scene as a secondary supplement to the work of self-synthesis already well under way in—or better, as—the *Ichleib*, the ego-flesh. This returns us, in the end, to a view of reality as in itself already complete—without gaps, remainders, or constitutive conflicts—and to which the ego must adapt on the basis of the plasticity of its flesh.

To put it somewhat differently, Rogozinski's project could be understood as yet another attempt to "return to Freud," to rewrite Freudian metapsychology but now primarily from the perspective of Freud's writings on the ego. In a word, egoanalysis represents an effort to begin anew the development of that branch of psychoanalytic theory that became ego psychology but now framed by a radical phenomenological *epokhe*. Rogozinski effectively returns to Freud's notion of primary narcissism according to which the ego is the original reservoir of libido from which object-cathexes are sent out the way an amoeba sends out its pseudopodia. Once Freud introduced his new topology of the mind he seemed to modify this view by relocating the original reservoir of libido to the id. The notion of ego-flesh is at some level meant to absorb Freud's wavering on this point, to collapse the ego–id distinction into a more fundamental phenomenon. We might note that in his own *Outline of Psychoanalysis* from 1938, Freud more or less does the same thing: "We picture some such initial state as one in which the total available energy of Eros, which henceforward we shall speak of as 'libido,' is present in the still undifferentiated ego-id."[6]

Before Rogozinski's acute phenomenological gaze, the ego-flesh presents itself as a self-organizing flux of sensation, a ramifying, endlessly iterated process of auto-affection in and through which my living body is synthesized as a self-identical locus of affectivity, as a field of sensations *in touch with itself* and so experienced as *jemeinig,* as in each case *mine.* Before a human subject can affectively engage in the social space of (mutual) recognition, to feel libidinally implicated in such intercourse—we might call it the capacity for *passionate partiality*—the "carnal poles" of its own flesh must engage in their own form of recognizant social commerce and knot themselves together into a synthetic unity. For Rogozinski, *tactility*—the ultimate source of what we mean when we say that we *feel* something—turns out to be the "agora" of such commerce:

> In the whole field of my perceptual experience, there is one sole case in which the perceiving ego is able to find in another pole the same perception it felt within itself: *when I touch myself....* When one of my hands touches the other, it perceives it first as the smooth and inert surface of a thing. But then this hand-thing senses itself being touched, and tactile impressions arise in it. It *becomes flesh,* a hand of living flesh touching the hand touching it.... At the same time and in one single gesture, each of the two poles is given as flesh to itself *and* to the other: what gives—my touching flesh—coincides with what is given. Each pole now recognizes itself in the foreign pole, recognizes it as the flesh of its flesh, as *another* pole of the *same* flesh. (151)

To characterize the fundamental matrix "whereby I am carnally given to myself by myself" (151–52), Rogozinski appropriates

Merleau-Ponty's term for this intertwining or knotting of the touching and the touched, one taken, in turn, from Plato's *Timaeus*: "chiasm." The carnal synthesis whereby the ego-flesh is constituted follows the *law of the letter* χ and so includes, though Rogozinski would never put it this way, a figural trace of the normative.

What for Rogozinski holds the place of this trace—and here he is attempting to deflect the charge of "haptocentrism" lodged by Derrida against earlier phenomenological projects dealing with the flesh—is what he calls *the remainder*. As the untouchable supplement of a gap—we might say, as the *being of a gap*—the remainder allows the two poles not only *to remain two* and, so, to endlessly iterate the exchange of properties across the cross of the chiasm without collapsing into a single mass (Rogozinski calls this the "horizontal synthesis"). The remainder furthermore allows this exchange to cross over to a new level of tactile sensation in which one pole of flesh recognizes the other pole not only as flesh but also as body (he calls this "transversal synthesis"). The *work of the remainder* pushes incarnation toward incorporation, carves the flesh—this peculiarly plastic medium—into an articulated body. Noting the resonances of this dynamic in numerous mythic traditions that render creation as a series of violent acts of cutting, sacrifice, and dismemberment of an original life substance—call them the mythic primal scenes of *das Leiblich-Imaginäre*—Rogozinski writes that "what is present in the phantasms and myths as a dislocation or a mutilation is the very movement of my incorporation, which transforms my flesh into a thing of the world—a very singular thing that never stops being flesh: my body" (158).

Egoanalysis is essentially an effort to work out the ramifications, at all levels of individual and social existence, of the original figure or "germ-cell" of the chiasm and its equiprimordial supplementation by/inclusion of the remainder. The massive ambition of the project indicates that Rogozinski is offering a rewriting not only of Freud's thinking about narcissism and the ego but also of his final theory of the drives, which Freud himself tended to portray as a quasi-cosmic antagonism between Eros and Thanatos, the life drive and the death drive. What Freud designated under the heading of Eros is essentially the tendency toward synthesis, the movement that Rogozinski distributes across various levels of auto-affective activity that aim at synthesizing a unified body of flesh. What Freud intended with the notion of the death drive is what Rogozinski analyzes as the work of the remainder, the splitting into two that keeps the chiasm up and running but that also sustains a zone of untouchability, of *not-me*, in the very tissue of the *ego-flesh* (readers familiar with German Idealism will hear the profound Fichtean resonances of this language). The remainder—the work of the negative in the flesh—renders the activity of synthesis always only *partial*. The ego, we might say, is always *remaindered*. Rogozinski's grand claim is that this coincidence of the simultaneously enabling and disabling aspects of the remainder generates what Freud tried to capture with the notion of the fundamental ambivalence of the drives, what Klein was after with her "good" and "bad objects," and what Lacan tried to capture with the duplicity of the *objet a,* the *partial object* that both attracts and repels, that functions as both object of desire and uncanny specter of anxiety. It is precisely this fundamental partiality of the ego that propels it into transcendence, causes it to "impart itself"—into the world, into the field of the Other—where it enters into new kinds of traffic in the flesh that, for Rogozinski, can take the form of enlivening "transfers" or "transferences" of carnal vitality, as well as mortifying projections of the untouchable, spectral remainder. Here Rogozinski again adopts a Freudian posture—I am thinking of Freud's notion of *Triebmischung* ("fusion of the drives")—by arguing that for the most part such traffic includes both dimensions.

What is, in the end, missing from Rogozinski's egoanalytical approach is a proper account of the way in which the flesh and its remainder get taken up into the space of the normative, a space that includes, as I have argued, its own sorts of remainders and surpluses. What Rogozinski presents as the remainder is, in my view, most

productively grasped as an *index* of the Other, as the insistent (re)
minder of a space of normativity that is itself always already troubled by gaps/remainders (I use the locution "(re)minding" here to
convey the unceasing process of coming to be "minded"). To put it
in terms that at least provisionally suspend judgment as to ultimate
priority, I would put it this way: the *ego*, which is always partial with
respect to the remainder of its flesh, and the *Other*, the unanchored
and so always partly (in)operative and antagonistic space of normativity, *overlap around the same subject-matter.* My argument in
these lectures has been that both Marx and Freud made the tracking
and understanding of this subject-matter into their own Cause, the
perpetual *Anstoss,* to use a Fichtean locution, of their thought.

II

In her response to my lectures, Bonnie Honig has effectively made
this subject-matter into her own Cause as well—one that, as she
argues, provides the very medium of a new democratic theory and
practice. Her key witness for the potential of the flesh as a medium
in which a new kind of democratic self-interest might emerge is
Herman Melville, whose *Moby-Dick* is offered as a kind of complementary fable to *The Merchant of Venice* and its now seemingly
rather modest preoccupation with a mere pound of flesh.[7] Honig
is, at some level, trying to yoke together Jane Bennett's evocation of a "newish" self of self-interest open to the vibrant matter of the world—an opening that ostensibly overcomes human
exceptionalism—with Hannah Arendt's understanding of a distinctively human capacity for the mode of acting in concert with others that constitutes the life of politics. Honig argues that Melville
bridges the apparent gap between Bennett and Arendt by way of
the encounter with the animal, or more precisely, by way of an
immersive engagement with the sublimely excessive, economically
and socially generative flesh of the sperm whale (whether we can

still use the word "encounter" here is, I think, rather questionable). For Honig, Melville offers us nothing less than the vision of a new democratic subject born out of the "spirit" of the flesh—out of the *Leib* and *Leibhaftigkeit*—of this sovereign beast, this Leviathan, of the oceans.[8] I take her argument to be a further contribution to the field I have been trying to adumbrate here in spite of some disagreements at the margins.

Honig reads the novel as a political allegory in which three forms of rule are juxtaposed in the persons of Ahab, Starbuck, and Ishmael. Each figure is seen as personifying the subject-position—and modes of enjoyment—correlative to, respectively, that of a tyrannical sovereign for whom his "people" are ultimately instruments serving his monomaniacal purpose, namely conquering a rival king/Leviathan; that of the utilitarian entrepreneur for whom heroic virtues like fortitude and courage are subordinated to sober economic calculations; and most importantly, that of a new personage whose fleshly experience of democratic sociality—perhaps one needs to say, homosociality—singularly survives in the first-person testimony of the novel, the very style of which manifests what Tony Tanner has characterized as an "eroticized and playful porousness to the wholeness of life."[9] For Honig, then, Ahab stands in for a more or less Hobbesian political theology of sovereignty, Starbuck for the modern political economy of the wealth of nations, and Ishmael for a democratic politics to come.

That the novel places us squarely in the realm of political theology is, of course, made rather explicit by way of the web of references generated by the names Melville chooses for his cast of characters, above all that of the *Pequod*'s captain.[10] The ancient Israelite king Ahab is generally seen to be among the most telling biblical exemplars of the dangers of royal sovereignty, most importantly that of breaking the covenant that places the One God at the center of creation. Kingship is clearly seen by the biblical authors to involve the risk of, and indeed perhaps even to be one of the essential modalities of, idolatrous backsliding from the ethical demands of monotheism.[11] The collection of citations that Melville gathers—I am tempted to say "curates"—to form a sort of textual antechamber to the novel proper furthermore contains numerous references to milestones in the semantic field of political theology, biblical and otherwise, including, of course, to Hobbes's *Leviathan*.

We might say that the novel sets out to explore, among other things, a specifically American set of engagements with *royal remains*, with the afterlife of political theology. All three figures—Ahab, Starbuck, Ishmael—would thus embody possibilities that belong to the space opened by the passage beyond the political theology of the sovereign, possibilities opened, that is, by the shift from royal to popular sovereignty. All three are laboring, in one way or another, not simply in the *hunting* but also in the *haunting grounds* of the figure of the Leviathan. Recalling David's *Death of Marat*, we might say that all three possibilities remain virtually present in the abstract materiality occupying the upper half of that painting as possibilities of new representations, new figurations of a life in the flesh opened by the revolutionary violence that "remaindered" the royal (Ahab is himself, of course, in a quite literal sense a remaindered sovereign).

That Melville is preoccupied with possibilities opened by the divestiture of kings is signaled throughout the novel—even Queequeg is marked as a deposed and dispossessed king—and most explicitly so in Ishmael's hymnic evocation of the ideal of democratic dignity, one he equates with "that immaculate manliness we feel within ourselves, so far within us, that it remains intact though all the outer character seem gone."[12] This dignity deposited at what would appear to be the most fundamental layer of human being—we will soon hear more about such "layers"—retains, nonetheless, a trace of the modern space of political economy insofar as it appears in some way linked to what Marx characterized as homogeneous human labor: "But this august dignity I treat of, is not the dignity of kings and robes, but that abounding dignity which has no robed investiture. Thou shalt see it shining in *the arm that wields a pick or drives a spike*; that democratic dignity which, on all hands, radiates without end from God; Himself! The great God absolute! The centre and circumference of all democracy! His omnipotence, our divine equality!" (126; my emphasis).

It's worth recalling in this context that the social space in which this dignity is brought to phenomenal presence is above all one of productive labor, and indeed labor performed in the service of a joint stock company run by business savvy Nantucket Quakers. The busy-ness of the crew, however egalitarian it might come to appear, is called forth by that business, is "inspired" by the spirit of capitalism (or perhaps better, driven by its specter). What distinguishes the labor performed on the *Pequod* from that of a modern factory—the resemblance is emphatically underlined in the *Try-Works* chapter—is perhaps first and foremost that its workers own shares or "lays" in the company, earning back a portion of the surplus value they produce for the ship's owners. Ishmael seems to acknowledge the entanglement of the dignified business of democracy with its shadowy specter by way of an explicit disavowal. He begins his evocation of the naked glory of democratic dignity—"the abounding dignity which has no robed investiture"—by way of a sort of protest: "Men may seem detestable as joint stock-companies and nations; knaves, fools, and murderers there may be; men may have mean and meager faces; but man, in the ideal, is so noble and so sparkling, such a grand and glowing creature, that over any ignominious blemish in him all his fellows should run to throw their costliest robes" (126).

Against this background, Ahab would seem to represent not so much a throwback to the figure of a traditional master or sovereign, whether understood on the model of Israelite king or Hobbesian monarch, but rather the prospect of a new kind of master, the charismatic and potentially totalitarian leader of "mass politics," a figure belonging to the historical space of the modern *demos* to which equally modern modes and relations of production belong. We might say he is a figure bent on fully mastering the royal remains, the dispersed flesh of the Leviathan. His consuming desire is to fully consume his rival and at some level to compel his men to enjoy in that consumption with him.

The paradoxical combination of seemingly archaic and explicitly modern features of his character—what Ishmael characterizes as "that certain sultanism of his brain" that becomes "incarnate in an irresistible dictatorship" (160)—is what allows Ahab to weld his men into a kind of fused political mass in the famous "Quarter-Deck" chapter, a mass that, as we have noted, at times functions as a well-oiled machine of (oil) production organized by way of a clear division of labor. It is here, as Honig notes, that the difference between Ahab and Starbuck is most clearly laid out as one between a monomaniacal passion for the real and the—only seemingly—more sober passion of capital accumulation. (Starbuck's background as a Quaker links him to the two owners of the *Pequod*, Captains Peleg and Bildad—Ishmael characterizes them, one will recall, as "Quakers with a vengeance" [82]—and therewith, perhaps, to that spirit/specter of capitalism that Weber locates in the Protestant ethic.) When pressed as to his commitment to the pursuit of the white whale, Starbuck replies, "I am game for his crooked jaw, and for the jaws of Death too, Captain Ahab, if it fairly comes in the way of the business we follow; but I came here to hunt whales, not my commander's vengeance. How many barrels will thy vengeance yield thee even if thou gettest it, Captain Ahab? it will not fetch thee much in our Nantucket market" (177).[13]

In his response—Honig cites the crucial passage at length—Ahab disdainfully rejects the law of the market and tries, instead, to compel Starbuck to assume his own more metaphysical take on the enterprise. As one descends to this "lower layer" of things, the white whale figures as a last point of access to an encounter with the real, that is, to an experience of what is no longer a possible object of human experience at the foundation of human experience. More precisely, Ahab experiences the whale as the inscrutable thing that—with seeming malice—both offers and blocks access to the noumenal Thing which, as Ahab admits, might be no-thing at all but rather a pure void which his demonic drive would ultimately encircle as the true aim of the enterprise. In the terms I have been developing here, one might say that at some "lower layer" or level the whale comes to figure for Ahab as the paradigmatic instance of what is at issue in the flesh, the void or gap in human being that insistently, disturbingly *remains* at the enigmatic jointure of the somatic and the normative. For Ahab, the white whale holds the place of that void and so serves, if I might put it that way, as the very incarnation of the flesh—or perhaps better, what in the flesh touches on the void. This Leviathan, too, in other words, has two bodies, and it is the second, sublime body that ultimately counts for Ahab as the real, as the only remaining subject-matter of his mad hunt.[14]

The central event of the chapter is the oath taken by the crew that binds them to Ahab's "cetocidal" enterprise in all its obscure, metaphysical ambition. The force of Ahab's will and charisma allows him to seduce the crew into believing, at least at a "lower layer" of psychic life, that the killing of this Leviathan will eliminate, offer a sort of "final solution" to, *what does not work* in human life, what remains recalcitrant to human purpose.[15] Ahab infects the crew with his vision, gets the men to identify with the gaze for which the white whale figures as "the monomaniac incarnation of all those malicious agencies which some deep men feel eating in them" (200). As Ishmael continues, "All that most maddens and torments; all that stirs up the lees of things; all truth with malice in it; all that cracks the sinews and cakes the brain; all the subtle demonisms of life and thought; all evil ... were visibly personified, and made practically assailable in Moby-Dick" (200). Call it *redemptive cetology*.

In the Quarter-Deck scene, Ahab choreographs a complex ritual—a sort of ad hoc liturgical action—consisting of communal drinking, the pronouncement of acclamations, and the crossing of weapons of the hunt. In and through these actions the crucial oath

254 · REPLY TO COMMENTATORS

is ostensibly made effective, or to use the narrator's metaphor of energy transfer, in and through their performance "the same fiery emotion accumulated within the Leyden jar of [Ahab's] own magnetic life" (180) is transmitted to the crew, who thereby assume, at least to some degree, the "charge" that drives him, one seeking, as Freud at times conceived the death drive, a sort of absolute discharge of tensions.[16]

The chapter called "Moby Dick" in which the white whale is presented as the incarnation of "that intangible malignity which has been from the beginning" (200), opens with Ishmael's confession of his own susceptibility to Ahab's charisma and will: "I, Ishmael was one of that crew; my shouts had gone up with the rest; my oath had been welded with theirs; and stronger I shouted, and more did I hammer and clinch my oath, because of the dread of my soul. A wild, mystical, sympathetical feeling was in me; Ahab's quenchless feud seemed mine" (194).[17] This confession should be kept in mind when we turn to the crucial episode of "A Squeeze of the Hand" (chapter 94) in which Honig has located a mode of collective *jouissance* that offers the promise of a new democratic sociality that exceeds (or we might say, *unctuously slips*) the grasp of an Ahab or a Starbuck. That is, Ishmael has already experienced another mode of collective *jouissance* that more closely resembles that of a crowd or mob that has not so much introjected the leader's ego-ideal as succumbed to the force of his superegoic voice.

As Honig has shown, this promise is born from the immersive engagement with the flesh. But this flesh—and this is where I differ from Honig—is not that of the animal in its creaturely kinship with the human but, rather, of that uncanny crossbreed of sovereign and beast that the tradition dubbed Leviathan. In all its sensual excess—or precisely because of it—this flesh remains at its "lower layer" fantasmatic, a sublime substance. To use Wellbery's term, it remains *leiblich-imaginär*. That the literal matter at issue here is the so-called *spermaceti* concentrated in the flesh of the whale's massive head would only seem to underline this fantasmatic aspect.

But again, it is precisely that aspect that allows it to function as a medium of sociality, as the *leiblich-imaginäre* dimension of a social bond that at least potentially exceeds that of the welded wills of the Quarter-Deck scene, as well as the bourgeois mode of sociality ostensibly formed from the interplay of individual wills guided by economic self-interest. Under the imperatives of that mode of sociality, the laboriously refined flesh is, of course, destined to be stored in *fleshpots*, something that, according to the biblical tradition that plays such a crucial role in the novel, is ultimately enslaving. I am suggesting, then, that we consider the flesh of the whale in "A Squeeze of the Hand" in relation to the abstract materiality swirling in the upper half of David's *Death of Marat*: this is the stuff of royal remains, the historical destiny of which remains in a degree of flux. In "A Squeeze of the Hand," this flux is, we might say, directly encountered and enjoyed as such.[18]

The chapter describes the process by which clumps of the now congealed oil taken from the head of the sperm whale—from the so-called spermaceti organ—are broken down for further processing and storage: "it was our business to squeeze these lumps back into fluid. A sweet and unctuous duty!" (455). The first thing to note is that in this process, performed here on an unnamed whale, Ishmael experiences a kind of relief from the pressures of the oath by which he joined himself to Ahab's cause, had made the object-cause of the latter's desire his own:

> As I sat there at my ease, cross-legged on the deck. . . . As I bathed my hands among those soft, gentle globules of infiltrated tissues . . . they richly broke to my fingers, and discharged all their opulence, like full ripe grapes their wine; as I snuffed up that uncontaminated aroma—literally and truly, like the smell of spring violets; I declare to you, that for the time I lived as in a musky meadow; I forgot all about our horrible oath; in that inexpressible sperm, I washed my hands and my heart of it. . . . While bathing in that bath, I felt divinely free from all ill-will, or petulance, or malice, of any sort whatsoever. (455–56)

Against the background of this temporary release from the bonds of the *demos* welded together by Ahab's proto-totalitarian leadership, another mode of collective sociality—and again, one feels compelled to say, homosociality—begins to emerge. It's worth citing the passage again in full:

> Squeeze! squeeze! squeeze! all the morning long; I squeezed that sperm till I myself almost melted into it; I squeezed that sperm till a strange sort of insanity came over me; and I found myself unwittingly squeezing my co-laborers' hands in it, mistaking their hands for the gentle globules. Such an abounding, affectionate, friendly, loving feeling did this avocation beget; that at last I was continually squeezing their hands, and looking up into their eyes sentimentally; as much as to say,—Oh! my dear fellow beings, why should we longer cherish any social acerbities, or know the slightest ill-humor or envy! Come; let us squeeze hands all round; nay, let us all squeeze ourselves into each other; let us squeeze ourselves universally into the very milk and sperm of kindness. (456)

At the end of this remarkable description in which the flesh of the Leviathan becomes the medium of a new social bond, it is the angels, those exemplary busy-bodies vibrating with doxological energy, who are seen as joining in this human liturgy rather than the other way around (recall Erik Peterson's characterization of the nature of the Christian cult cited in Lecture 2): "In thoughts of the visions of the night, I saw long rows of angels in paradise, each with his hands in a jar of spermaceti" (456). What Melville offers us in this scene is, I would suggest, a vision and language of what I have referred to as *paradoxology*.[19]

The homosocial—and, to a large degree, fantasmatic—dimension of the activity is underlined in the following lines in which life amid the familiar features of hearth and home is characterized as a lower form of happiness, one involving a sort of desublimating, thinning out of the flesh: "Would that I could keep squeezing that sperm for ever! For now, since by many prolonged, repeated experiences, I have perceived that in all cases man must eventually lower, or at least shift, his conceit of attainable felicity; not placing it anywhere in the intellect or fancy; but in the wife, the heart, the bed, the table, the saddle, the fire-side, the country" (456).

The homosocial dimension of "A Squeeze of the Hand" is further emphasized by way of its resonances with an earlier chapter, "The Counterpane" (chapter 4), in which Ishmael, who shares a bed with Queequeg in the Spouter-Inn, awakens to find his companion's arm thrown over him "in the most loving and affectionate manner" (28). "You had almost thought," the narrator continues, "I had been his wife." The patterns of the quilt are such that Queequeg's tattooed arm appears to merge with them. The experience triggers a childhood memory for Ishmael of being confined to his room by his stepmother for attempting to crawl up the chimney. At some point, in a state of half-sleep following a nightmare, his own hand encountered its spectral double: "Instantly I felt a shock running through all my frame; nothing was to be seen, and nothing was to be heard; but a supernatural hand seemed placed in mine. My arm hung over the counterpane, and the nameless, unimaginable, silent form or phantom, to which the hand belonged, seemed closely seated by my bedside" (29). Ishmael realizes that only a slight but crucial adjustment was needed to transform the ghostly double encountered in childhood—one first registered as an organ without body, as an only spectrally visible hand—into the beneficent second body of his bedmate: "Now, take away the awful fear, and my sensations at feeling the supernatural hand in mine were very similar, in their strangeness, to those which I experienced on waking up and seeing Queequeg's pagan arm thrown around me" (29). Delbanco characterizes the process through which "Ishmael feels himself dissolve into the flesh and fabric that are touching him" in the Spouter-Inn as a "process of divestiture," the very process, that is, that Ishmael invokes in his hymnic praise of the "abounding dignity which has no robed investiture" and which would seem to form the basis of true democracy.[20] There, too, one will recall, Ishmael links such dignity to what we might refer to as *bare masculinity*, "that immaculate manliness we feel within ourselves, so far within us, that it remains intact though all the outer character seem gone" (126).

It is beyond the scope of the present study to query the status of this "queer" masculinity in Melville's novel, though the author does give us at least one important clue as to how one might proceed, namely by way of a comedic turn with regard to the entire semantic field of symbolic investiture and divestiture, one that exposes even the most naked of bare masculinities as a sort of phallic imposture. I am thinking of the short chapter, "The Cassock" (chapter 95), in which, during the industrial process of the "post-mortemizing of the whale," the whale's phallus—it is referred to as "the grandissimus"—is turned into a kind of vestment or cassock giving its bearer the look of "a candidate for an achbisho*prick*" (460, my emphasis): "The mincer now stands before you invested in the full canonicals of his calling. Immemorial to all his order, this investiture alone will adequately protect him, while employed in the peculiar functions of his office" (460). We might say that all phallic attributes, even those of "immaculate manliness," constitute a kind of "cassock" proper to an office—to a *dignitas*—that thereby becomes the space of a certain sort of comedic play.

Indeed, I am tempted to say that all comedies are *office comedies* in the sense of playing with and in the space of symbolic investiture/divestiture. It's worth recalling, in this context, Kantorowicz's concise formulation concerning royal investiture cited at the beginning of this epilogue: "the vision of the king as a *persona geminata* is ontological and, as an effluence of a sacramental and liturgical action performed at the altar, it is liturgical as well."[21] Office comedies (and this goes, of course, for both the British and American versions of the television series *The Office*) play with such "effluence" at the point at which it has been, as it were, reduced to a kind of base materiality; this is the point where glory, the very stuff produced to cover a void—a sort of flesh-wound immanent to human life—along with all the busy work charged with sustaining it, go ostentatiously—or as I would like to put it, *paradoxologically*—to waste.[22]

I think, finally, that such paradoxological deployments of the "effluence of a sacramental and liturgical action" stand in a profound solidarity with what Honig refers to as "Sabbath-power," a kind of power she herself figures in the form of a (comedic?) *persona geminata*, in this case one composed of two of Melville's most famous characters, Ishmael and Bartleby. She suggests, that is, that one might grasp the nature of Sabbath-power by imagining that Bartleby's famous preference, his power *not-to*—Honig refers to this as "destituent" power (134, 159–60)—be put into practice as a certain sort of manual labor, a squeezing of the hands in concert with others that, as Ishmael's narrative suggests, *at least for a time*, slips the sovereign grasp of political theology, as well as the invisible hand of political economy (along with its temporalities of debt).[23] What is produced instead is, as Ishmael suggests, a profoundly carnal experience of *kindness*, which doubtlessly includes a sense of kindredness in the midst of difference.[24] And here we should be careful to add that it is narrative time itself, the time Ishmael takes to tell his story (and for us to read it) that provides the "time signature" for this Sabbath.

Both Honig and I, then, ultimately agree on the need for a new thinking of the flesh, along with ways to mobilize that thinking, that could help to navigate the difficult passage beyond the doxologies of mass politics—the glorious hunt for a "final solution" to "all those malicious agencies which some deep men feel eating in them" —as well as those of neoliberal busy-ness that serve and sustain, whether with worshipful devotion or not, the self-valorizing substance of Value, a process in which, as we have seen, the flesh is destined to end up in fleshpots. Against this background, my sense is that our disagreements are ultimately the stuff of (university) office comedy, the sorts of things that no doubt make academics into the sorts of busy-bodies they are but that do not, in the end, change the fundamental *subject-matter* that remains at issue.

III

My response to both Peter Gordon and Hent de Vries will be much shorter and less systematic than my response to Bonnie Honig has been. That is in large measure because of the three, only Honig ventured to elaborate an original contribution to what I refer to as a "new thinking of the flesh," a thinking linked, as we have both tried to show, to efforts to mobilize new engagements with the liturgical-doxological dimension of human sociality that has *officially* been "housed" in religion and politics. I have proposed the term *paradoxology* as a name that could, with further work, provide some orientation for such mobilizations. The urgency of this sort of work is generated by the fact that in modernity, the real home—or perhaps better, *home office*—of this dimension has become the global *oikos*, the economic sphere that is, contrary to Gordon's sociological assessment, not simply a sphere among many in a horizontal field of differentiated and competing value-spheres but, rather, if I might put it that way, the king of value-spheres, the provider of the general equivalent of what is of value in all those other spheres. That is the distressing glory of the neoliberal economic order that is, as Gordon himself admits, a global one.

I am tempted to characterize Gordon's critique as a *vegan* response to my work. It is rather remarkable that the word I use throughout the lectures, "flesh," to name the special, immaterial stuff that entered into the composition of the king's fantasmatic physiology—the "thing" that Kantorowicz so marvelously elaborated in his *King's Two Bodies*, and that, with the demise of the political theology of sovereignty, takes residence in and ramifies throughout economic life as what Marx called the spectral objectivity/materiality, *die gespenstische Gegenständlichkeit*, of value—it is remarkable that this word appears only once in Gordon's text and there only to preface a citation from my lectures. The closest he comes to the dimension at issue in my lectures is at the very conclusion of his essay where he misreads my argument in breathtaking fashion. He conflates my approach, namely, with the very sort of new materialism I take considerable pains to critique in my first lecture. Gordon writes,

> The somatic *stress* of capitalism as an experiential order gains in drama with the distress we may feel when Santner reminds us that our own bodies teem with micro-organisms. Still, the irony is that such language does everything to suggest not the social contingency of oppression but its *carnal finality*. (If this is not what Santner intends, then one might ask why the unusual reference to micro-organisms would be of any relevance. Presumably these creatures exemplify a constitutive feature of our creaturely life, that is, they are not merely a symptom of the capitalist present.) (201)

I don't think that I can put my distance from such a view any more clearly and vehemently than I have done in the fourth section of the first lecture (Honig, one will recall, takes me to task for the extremity of the critique and tries to offer ways to reach some sort of middle ground between my approach and at least some of the new materialisms). There I argue that Jane Bennett's notion of "vibrant matter" conflates the dimension of a properly "carnal materialism" with, among other things, the teeming bacterial flora populating the nooks and crannies of human bodies. Against this view, which strikes me as a sort of multiculturalism at the cellular level, I offer a Freudo-Marxist materialism of the flesh. Suffice it to repeat here what I say in the first lecture apropos of the Freudian aspect of my alternative to Bennett's "vibrant matter": "To put it simply, the 'intensities' that occupied—or better, *preoccupied*—the crook of the elbow, among other body parts, of Freud's hysterics were not caused by tribes of bacteria but, rather, by a complex disorder of the 'tribe' to which these hysterics belonged, a disorder that in one way or another—and psychoanalysis is the effort to understand those ways—congealed as the uncanny cause of their desire, the 'un-economic' dimension of their libidinal economy" (61–62).

And apropos of the notion of *creaturely life*, it's again perhaps best just to repeat here the remarks I made in the second lecture to illustrate just how far off the mark Gordon's criticism is:

> By "creaturely" I do not simply mean nature, living things, sentient beings or even what the religiously minded would think of as the entirety of the "vibrant matter" of God's creation—*deus sive natura*—but, rather, a dimension specific to human existence, albeit one that seems to push thinking in the direction of theology. It signifies a mode of *exposure* that distinguishes human beings from other kinds of life: not simply to the elements or to the fragility, vulnerability, and precariousness of our mortal, finite lives, but also to an ultimate *lack of foundation* for the historical forms of life in which human life unfolds.... This gap, this crucial *missing piece of the world*, to which we are ultimately and intimately exposed as social beings of language, is one that we thus first *acquire* by way of our initiation—Heidegger would say *thrownness*—into these forms of life, not one already there in the bare fact of our biological being....We could say that the vulnerability of biological life becomes potentiated, amplified, by way of exposure to the radical contingency of the forms of life that constitute the space of meaning within which human life unfolds, and that it is only through such anarchic "potentiation" that we take on the flesh of creaturely life.[25] (83–84)

The paradox I have tried to articulate in these lectures and in much of my other work is that a dimension of human embodiment—the dimension I have circumscribed with the term "flesh"—serves as an uncanny sort of birthmark of the very historical contingency (of forms of life) that Gordon wants to protect from the threat of what he calls "carnal finality."[26] But by retreating so reflexively from this dimension—and really from all that registers as uncanny, as *unheimlich*—Gordon remains stuck with, at least to my mind, a view of critique that allows him to say things like the following: "To call a commodity a *fetish* is quite simply a way of alerting the reader to the erroneous gesture that can be conceptually annulled *in and through the critique itself*. Needless to say such a critique would hardly suffice to abolish capitalism in its objectivity. But the purpose of *Capital* is that of critical analysis, and as such it is an exercise in demystification" (199). My argument has been that critique engages in and with a dimension of human life that can be broached neither purely through cognition and conceptual analysis nor purely through interventions into social organization, however revolutionary they might be or present themselves. As I've argued, Marx's crucial point concerning the fetishism of the commodity is that it is not so much we disenchanted, secular citizens, who continue to engage in the metaphysics and theology that constitute this fetish but, rather, our uncannily *busy bodies* that are ever more caught in the "floodlights" of a 24/7 economy.[27] The psychotherapeutic analogy to Gordon's position with respect to critique would be that of a therapist or analyst reporting to a patient a (perhaps perfectly correct) theoretical articulation of his or her symptoms and declaring them to be thereby "conceptually annulled." Early on, Freud himself seemed to believe in this *Enlightenment version of magical thinking*—thinking that attributes to thinking the capacity to "conceptually annul" a fetish (or any other sort of torsion of the flesh).

Freud, for his part, eventually developed the notion of *Durcharbeiten*, the often difficult, sometimes comical, and always repetitive emotional, cognitive, and practical re-elaboration of the lived and embodied ways in which one participates in one's own unfreedom, of the modes of busy-body-ness in which one's capacity for freedom is held in a sort of suspended animation. The Freudian sense of working-through as a *lived critical practice* has much in common with Bonnie Honig's notion of the Sabbath-power deployed by Ishmael and his compatriots in "A Squeeze of the Hand" episode of *Moby-Dick*. One will recall that it was in and through that remarkable and erotically charged exercise of manual labor that Ishmael was able to loosen the bonds of the oath he had taken—and to a large extent internalized—to join himself to Ahab's mad pursuit of the white whale—to accept, that is, the transfer of Ahab's charismatic charge along with all its attendant debts. What we bear witness to is thus at some level—at some "lower layer"—a scene of a collective working-through of a political theological transference—call it working-through in concert with others—at precisely the point where the center of gravity of the transference—its subject-matter—has begun to shift to the realm of political economy (Honig, one will recall, mapped this as a shift from the political "master" Ahab to the economic "expert" Starbuck). It is precisely at this turning point in the historical destiny of their subject-matter that Ishmael and his compatriots find themselves able *to freely associate with it*. That, too—paradoxologically—belongs to the performance of any critique that matters. To put it more simply, the critique of political economy (or of political theology, for that matter) must find ways to engage the "lower layer," as Ahab put it, of libidinal economy. It is this lower layer of the work of critique that has gone missing in Gordon's understanding of things; there is, for him, no *subject-matter* in the subject matter of critique.

Early on in his response to my lectures, Gordon suggests that my efforts to read the fetish of the commodity genealogically—that is, as a formation bearing the signature of the fetishism of persons that sustained the doctrine and liturgical practices of the "King's Two Bodies"—represent a misreading of Marx. Had Marx meant such a thing there would have to be, Gordon insists, more certain textual evidence for it. Marx's own explicit appeal to the logic of determinations of reflection as they function in the fetishism of persons to account for the production of the spectral materiality of commodities is, for Gordon, insufficient evidence to motivate a genealogical argument. I fully agree with Gordon on that. I have gone to considerable length to show how much work is really involved in making the genealogical argument plausible, work that involves an extended engagement with the two most important genealogical thinkers of our time, Foucault and Agamben. Gordon, however, ignores that central piece of the argument (which does, indeed, leave it looking pretty thin, pretty skeletal, insufficiently fleshed out). I hope, nonetheless, to have shown that the genealogical perspective gives us not only a richer understanding of Marx's critique of political economy but also a better grasp of what is at issue in its genealogical precursor, the political theology of sovereignty. The genealogical perspective allows thinking to move in *both directions,* the result of which is—or at least this is my hope—a better understanding of the ways in which societies have struggled to come to terms with the inflammatory pressures that can arise at the jointure of the somatic and the normative, those shifting sites at which man's being as animal and his being as locus of initiative in the space of reasons, commitments, responsibilities are knotted or sutured together.

I'd like to close my response to Gordon's remarks by returning to his use of *The Communist Manifesto.* Here, again, is Gordon's text: "The bourgeoisie, Marx concludes, 'has stripped of its halo every occupation hitherto honored and looked up to with reverent awe,' and it has liquefied the fixed or 'fast-frozen' relations of the *ancien régime.* In fact it is only with bourgeois modernity that the 'holy is profaned' such that can we at last face 'with sober senses' our 'real conditions of life.' "[28] Gordon elaborates further:

> In the passage from feudalism to capitalist modernity, our civilization undergoes a trial of disenchantment and value-differentiation, one that separates out civil society as an intermediate field of transaction, formally distinct from both the affective structures of the family, on the one hand, and the legal-political structures of the state on the other. Humanity can at last confront the "real

conditions of life." With this theory . . . Marx thereby distinguishes himself as a child of the Enlightenment for whom the historical achievements of bourgeois society cannot be dismissed. (189)

My argument here has been that from the perspective of *Capital* and the theory of the fetishism of the commodity, the claim that in capitalism humanity confronts "with sober senses" the "real conditions of life" can itself function as the most refined form of ideology, one that effectively serves to naturalize capitalism. Marx's crucial point is that the ostensible "sobriety" referred to in the *Manifesto*—the "reality principle" codified in classical political economy as the rational pursuit of one's self-interest—is sustained by an intoxication displaced into the life of capital itself—one that is, as our busy bodies know, infinitely demanding.

IV

The task of responding to Hent de Vries's essay presents its own unique challenges. There is a great deal in the essay that I simply do not really understand—long passages where the level of abstraction and generality, and at times even of syntactic complexity, simply escapes my grasp. There may, in the end, just be real limits to our capacities to make our thinking available to one another. I will, however, try to address a few general (and related) areas of disagreement or concern that I am able to discern in his response.

First, de Vries complains of being left unable to "picture"—this is his term—what Marx calls the spectral materiality of the value of commodities. This strikes me as an odd complaint given what I take to be de Vries's more general discomfort with what he sees as a tendency in my work to localize and concretize what is, as he puts it, "a paradoxicality to life and matter itself that is situated at a much deeper and more disturbing level" (210) than the languages of a Marx or Freud could ever capture. Or as he puts it even more boldly,

There can, currently, be no point in locating the "immaterial stuff" of sovereignty (royal and other) in some "new, thingly location" that is the one highlighted by the "labor theory of value" ([Santner] (46). Precisely from a theologico-political view—under an infinitizing, eternal aspect, *sub specie aeternitatis*, as it were—all things and locations, like all ideas and movements, souls and bodies, in their possible roles as stepping stones and stumbling blocks, are equally close and distant from their being salvageable or forlorn, redemptive or destructive, vehicles of peace or of war, plus or minus. (215)

I'm not really sure I understand what de Vries means here, but more to the point might be what he then adds concerning the various "states" of the (subject-)matter in question: "And whatever remains of the category of metaphysical or ontological 'substance' in the reality and understanding of 'value,' its abstractive quality is, perhaps, no longer one of 'congelation' " (215–16).

De Vries seems furthermore concerned with the way in which I use the notion of (spectral) "afterlife"—above all when I speak of the afterlife of political theology (there are echoes here of Gordon's discomfort with the genealogical approach). This concerns the larger question of the historicity of the subject matter of these lectures, the historicity, that is, of *subject-matter*. As he puts it, "And, while it is one thing to say that modern or contemporary political formations are *fully describable* in terms of the archive and apparatus of what preceded them, it is quite another to assume that the present is somehow (somewhere, sometimes) *pieced together* with parts—including literal, spiritual, and mystical body parts—of the past" (216). Finally, de Vries is left wondering just what is really meant by "paradoxology"—he refers to it as an *enigmatic signifier*—what its exercise might ultimately look like, or how, in a word, we might "picture" it.

I would like to make use of the notion of the *enigmatic signifier* as an entry point into my response to these areas of concern, confusion, and disagreement. The French psychoanalyst Jean Laplanche coined the term "enigmatic signifier" to capture what he considered to be the true source-objects of the drives in psychic life. He claimed that human infants and children are bombarded by messages from the adult world that not only convey the "official" content of their communications but also often secrete a secret, enigmatic message that transmits to the child an aspect of the adult's sexual life. For Laplanche, this adult secret, sexual in nature, remains for the most part a secret to the adult as well, emanating as it does from the unconscious. This is a case indeed where, to paraphrase Hegel, the enigmas of the Egyptians are enigmas for the Egyptians. According to Laplanche, every child succumbs to a sort of Egyptomania, the interminable effort to translate these messages into livable communications, to convert their "validity" into "meaning." For Laplanche, each human child is born to the universe of human sexuality as a sort of hermeneutic busy-body metabolizing enigmatic signifiers floating through the atmosphere of the minimal "body politic" of the family, however it might be organized. For Laplanche, human sexuality emerges as a sort of signifying stress largely orbiting around the body parts and orifices that provide key loci of transaction and negotiation between the child and the adult world (the bathing of a child is, for Laplanche, a site rich with the transmission of enigmatic signifiers). It's crucial, of course, that what gets transmitted here pertains to a field or dimension of human experience—sexuality—that is itself ridden with impasses and antagonisms, a field in which something fundamentally *does not work* in spite of the fact that the most important work of the species—its self-reproduction—transpires there. Sexuality begins, according to this story, by way of *pulsive theorizations* of something that does not work in human life.

In one of his many efforts to explain the notion of the enigmatic signifier—clearly itself one of its own species—Laplanche ends up portraying a world that closely resembles the Kafkan universe of court or castle officials:

What comes to the fore at certain moments is that aspect of the signifier which signifies to someone, which interpellates someone, in the sense that we can speak of an official signifying a court decision, or issuing a ... prefectoral decree. This foregrounding of "signifying to" is extremely important, as a signifier can signify *to* without its addressee necessarily knowing *what* it signifies. We know *that* it signifies, but not what it signifies. ... Lacan suggests the image of hieroglyphs in the desert, or of cuneiform characters carved on a tablet of stone. ... It ... means that the signifier may be *designified*, or lose what it signifies, without thereby losing its power to signify *to*.[29]

One is hard pressed not to think of Kafka's minimalist fable in which, after the end of the age of kings, the remaining messengers "race through the world and, because there are no kings, they call out to one another proclamations that have become meaningless."[30] Laplanche offers us something on the order of an "un-official" story of the birth of sexuality as an effort, lodged in the flesh of the human child, to discharge the signifying stress introduced into it by adults not quite living up to the charge of their office, their own mandate to be in charge. For Freud, this ultimately has to do with the fact that adult sexuality always secretes remainders of infantile sexuality, the fact, that is, that human sexuality is constitutively unreceptive to the Enlightenment demand to emerge from its "self-imposed immaturity" or *Unmündigkeit*, to use Kant's famous formulation.[31]

In her own engagement with the work of Laplanche, Alenka Zupančič makes use of a Lacanian formula to characterize the nature of the causality proper to the source-objects of the drives, *il n'y a de cause que de ce qui cloche*, or in Zupančič's translation, "there is but the cause of that which does not work, or which does not add up."[32] For Zupančič, too, a human child comes to be "minded" by coming to mind in a profound way, by taking *Anstoss*, or exception to, what does not work in the historical space of meaning into which it is inscribed. For Laplanche, "seduction" just means that the child has, at some level, incorporated this *Anstoss*, taken on its elaboration as its unique charge and destiny. In the terms I have been using, we might say that the child thereby takes on the flesh of a singularly busy body. For Zupančič, such busy-ness constitutes the fundamental activity of the unconscious:

> If the constitution of the unconscious does ... coincide with a cer-
> tain ("conscious") interpretation taking place, i.e., with a certain
> solution that is given to the enigmatic message of the other, that
> does not mean that the unconscious is simply what is left outside
> (not included in the interpretation); rather, the unconscious is that
> which *continues to interpret* (after the conscious interpretation is
> done). Even more precisely: it is that which only starts to interpret
> after some understanding of the enigmatic message is produced.
> For what it interprets is ... precisely the relationship between the
> given interpretation and its leftover. And it interprets from the
> point of view of this leftover. (40)[33]

With Lacan's formula in mind, we might say that there is a psycho-analytically relevant cause only where some element in our psychic household begins to assume the aspect of a good-for-nothing *clochard*, that zero-level status or office whose uncanny ways we have come to know under like names like Bartleby and Odradek. For Zupančič, the insistence (rather than existence) of this dimension in psychic life "refers to the fact that there is always '*quelque chose qui cloche*,' something that does not add up in the relationship between the subject and the Other, in the relationship between the (subject's) being and meaning—this relationship is built on an irreducible difficulty" (41). She goes on to emphasize that, "neither the subject nor the Other have this object, although it is related, linked to both. More precisely: it is what *relates or binds* the two in their very heterogeneity, in the inexistence of their common denominator" (41, my emphasis). I take this to be an alternative formulation of what I proposed at the conclusion of my discussion of Rogozinski's work: the *ego*, which is always partial with respect to the remainder of its flesh, and the *Other*, the unanchored and so always partially (in)operative and antagonistic space of normativity, *overlap around the same subject-matter*, a "substance" that, as Derrida has emphasized, falls under the auspices of *hauntology* rather than *ontology*. Which means, of course, that one cannot picture it (this is also what Zupančič means when she speaks of the "inexistence" of subject-matter, of the point of overlap between the subject and the Other).[34] That being said, I have tried, in my discussion of David's *Death of Marat*, to show how this dimension can nonetheless be *registered* in the visual field, can compellingly succeed, as it were, at not being pictured.[35]

As for the genealogical story I've been proposing here, my concern has been to show the historically mutable ways in which that which does not work is, precisely, *put to work* at the "lower layer" of our social mediation, the affective binding of subjects to their form of life and to one another (again, I am trying to introduce a new language and approach to what has heretofore been for the most part analyzed under the more familiar heading of the "critique of ideology"). What makes a nation, to recall Foucault's remarks concerning the old political theology of sovereignty, is—and here he is addressing this "lower layer"—the fact that its members "all have a certain individual relationship—both juridical and physical—with the real, living, and bodily person of the king. It is the body of the king, in his *physical-juridical* relationship with each of his subjects, that creates the body of the nation."[36] The wager of my genealogical argument is that by tracking the passage of *what is compelling* in and about the real, living, and bodily person of the king—of what Kantorowicz elaborated under the heading of the King's Two Bodies—into a new historical epoch, we gain a much better grasp of the powers by which we are really governed, governed where things really matter for the subject, governed, that is, in our subject-matter.

Marx's analysis of the commodity form comes down to showing that one can indeed do sums—*and how*—with "what does not add up in the relationship between the subject and the Other." Marx furthermore wanted to show that the members of modern capitalist societies were coming to be ever more *governed* by what transpires in the production and exchange of commodities, by the fate of those sums. That implies, in turn, that the experts attending to this singular value system amid the differentiated "value-spheres of the rationalized life-world" (Gordon's formulation) had essentially assumed powers previously retained by the sovereign and his councilors in keeping alive, sustaining the vitality of the "physical-juridical relationship" between the king and his subjects. Marx's point, then—and this is precisely what Agamben takes up in his "archaeology of glory"—is that in the new and totalizing capitalist organization of modern societies the subject-matter of this "lower layer" of our social existence had become the subject matter of political economy. But this means that we are ever more governed by a dimension of *Herrlichkeit*—rather than *Herrschaft*—that belongs to the sphere of Value rather than politics proper. We are ever more governed, that is, by our implication in the doxologies of everyday life rather than by way of juridico-political processes and procedures that, of course, themselves have come more and more to serve the glorious self-valorization of Value. We might say that the capital idea of Capital is government not so much by law or decree as by what Adorno et al. called the culture industry, Debord named the society of the spectacle, and I have characterized as the "entertainment" of the life of the flesh that constitutes the doxologies of everyday life that now take place 24/7. These doxologies had, in the medieval and early-modern period, been administered by the "culture industries" dedicated to sustaining and entertaining the King's Two Bodies.

With respect to the concept of paradoxology, I am ready to admit that I have really only offered a sort of promissory note for work still to be done. So yes, it is, indeed, a sort of enigmatic signifier, but one that is also, as I have hoped to have shown, peculiarly self-reflexive. My argument has been that societies put to work what does not work in human life, and they do so to a very large extent *doxologically*. The "effluence of . . . sacramental and liturgical action" that forms the true *subject-matter* of Kantorowicz's *King's Two Bodies* is, in the end, really a sort of sublimated inoperativity. "Paradoxology" is an enigmatic signifier meant to address "from the side" the doxological work individuals and societies do to make add up what does not add up, to convert into glory and splendor those *anstössig*, disturbing remainders left to us, precisely, by our life amid enigmatic signifiers. In the future I hope to explore this new field of theory and practice—one linked, as I have tried to show, to what Bonnie Honig aims at with her notion of "Sabbath-power"—by way of an engagement with, among other works of art, Rainer Maria Rilke's great poetic cycles, *The Duino Elegies* and *The Sonnets to Orpheus*. I see the poems as Rilke's efforts to work through the doxologies of everyday life that had, as Nietzsche had powerfully argued, come to define the life of the European "last man" and to elaborate a new and in some sense unheard of poetics of praise. These efforts, particularly those of the *Elegies*, include a certain wrestling with angels, those doxological beings that have figured so strongly in the liturgical labor sustaining the *oikonomia* of the Church and, for the most part, in hidden ways, the ostensibly disenchanted authority of the global, capitalist economy. I will also try to develop further the few hints offered here concerning the comedic—and more precisely, Kafkan-comedic—aspect of paradoxology, an aspect at home, as it were, in the office. There is a link, that is, between comedy and the dimension I have abbreviated by way of another enigmatic signifier, the *traumamtlich*. To pick up on de Vries's brief remark concerning the relation between paradoxology and Freud's notion of *parapraxis*, we might say that the former aims at cultivating the resources offered by the latter insofar as they interrupt, with an often comedic force, the *liturgical praxis* that sustains the self-valorization of Value. Parapraxis as physical comedy: the *clochard* who turns up and turns out to have always been *unheimlich zu Hause* in the home office.

In this context I'd also like to recall a sentence from Robert Walser's wonderfully strange novel, *Jakob von Gunten*, a work much admired by Kafka. At one point, Jakob, the first-person narrator of the text, tries to characterize the life of his fellow-students at the Institute Benjamenta where they are training to become valets. As if trying to name the purity of their labors as they approach a zero-degree of any meaningful content, Jakob simply writes: *Wir vibrieren*.[37] At this point, not only has their work lost any sense of usefulness; the liturgical-doxological dimension of their labors have also shifted into a sort of quietly sublime—call it *paradoxological*—idling. We might think of it as a form of *idle worship*. At some level, the thrust of this project comes down to the question: What would it look like and what would happen if we all joined in?

A final set of concerns expressed by de Vries here and there throughout his response pertains to my continued assumption that *bodies matter* in the constitution of what I am calling *subject-matter*. Mediatization, virtualization, disincarnation, weightlessness—these are some of the terms that de Vries throws out there to challenge the pertinence of human embodiment as a relevant dimension of analysis especially in the current state of the global economy and technological development. Insofar as such terms pertain to the dimension I have been referring to as spectral, I don't really see where the disagreement is. De Vries perhaps takes the title of my lectures, *The Weight of All Flesh*, too literally. Marx made perfectly clear that what is weighed, in the determination of value, is, precisely something utterly weightless; this is precisely what he was after when he characterized value as "congealed quantities of homogeneous human labor, i.e., of human labor-power expended without regard to the form of its expenditure" (*Capital*, 128). It is this very indifference that renders the commodity—precisely where it *counts*—weightless and spectral. *Gespenstische Gegenständlichkeit* is Marx's name for this sort of weightlessness that nonetheless exercises an enormous gravitational force on everyone and everything. The capitalist cares not about the use-value of his product but only about its contribution to, as I have been putting it here, the greater glory of Value. And it is in the effort to amplify that glory that the capitalist enlists the contribution of labor, offering the worker a chance to participate in this great doxological endeavor.[38] The same might be said, of course, with regard to the king's glorious body. It, too, is weightless in all the gravitas and weightiness of its political effects.

What I do not, however, understand is why any of this would be an argument against the pertinence of human embodiment for social analysis. Perhaps de Vries ultimately has in mind science-fiction fantasies—he mentions *Total Recall,* but I am thinking here of *The Matrix*—in which the self-valorization of Valor—here the self-replication and amplification of the machines—requires from human beings not so much human embodiment as the *fantasy* of human embodiment, a carnal remnant still needed for the production of libidinal energy. At least according to the logic of this film, even where human labor-power is reduced to the status of libidinal battery-power, a (only just barely) living body is still required. If there is a lesson in such fictions, it would seem to be that the attempt to close the gap between bodies and their subject-matter, and to allow the latter to disseminate freely through the ether of virtual reality, leads to the proliferation of the figure of bare life, a figure of reduced and so extreme, even traumatic, embodiment.

I would like to conclude by thanking Bonnie Honig, Peter Gordon, and Hent de Vries for agreeing to engage with my work in the intense and focused way that they did when the lectures were first delivered in April 2014, at Berkeley, and now in more in-depth written form. I am honored and somewhat embarrassed by all this attention, and have lost sleep over the worry that I have no right to demand so much time and effort from friends and colleagues whose work is equally if not more deserving of this sort of attention and who are also, if I might put it that way, some pretty busy bodies. I want to apologize here for burdening them with this surplus labor. I want to assure them that it was all meant paradoxo-logically, for the greater glory of the interrogation of glory. From my point of view there were no wasted efforts here; this collective investigation of the subject-matter of political economy mattered, in my view, in all the right places.

Notes

1. Ernst Kantorowicz, *The King's Two Bodies: A Study in Medieval Political Theology* (Princeton, NJ: Princeton University Press, 1981), 48, 59. As already noted, Kantorowicz's thinking on these matters is in some measure indebted to Henri Cardinal de Lubac, *Corpus Mysticum: The Eucharist and the Church in the Middle Ages,* trans. Gemma Simmonds, Richard Price, and Christopher Stephens (Notre Dame, IN: University of Notre Dame Press, 2006). In his compelling exploration of new forms of ostensibly post-religious spiritual-ity, Richard Kearney has argued that a retrieval and reanimation of the eucharistic imagination can be deployed, precisely, as a modality of critique of the forms of political theology that continue to haunt modernity. See his *Anatheism (Returning to God After God)* (New York: Columbia University Press, 2008). Insofar as political theology lives off of the very eucharistic dimension Kearney offers as a cure, we might ultimately regard the logic of that cure as *homeopathic.* I have elaborated the homoepathic pattern of pro-cesses of mourning in my *Stranded Objects: Mourning, Memory, and Film in Postwar Germany* (Ithaca, NY: Cornell University Press, 1990). The relation-ship between this modality of homeopathy and what I have called "paradoxol-ogy" remains to be explored.

2. As I've argued elsewhere, I think it is helpful to grasp this transfer in conjunction with Jacques Lacan's thinking concerning the shift from the "dis-course" of the master to that of the university. See, for example, my remarks in *On Creaturely Life: Rilke, Benjamin, Sebald* (Chicago: University of Chicago Press, 2006), 82n51.

3. In *Anatheism,* Kearney tries to reappropriate this hum for new ethical and political uses. His project represents, as he puts it, "a call for a new acoustic attuned to the presence of the sacred in flesh and blood" (166). My primary reservations about Kearney's otherwise inspiring work is that he seems not to recognize ways in which secular life is already up to its neck in this "sacred" element, something that Agamben has made it his mission to demonstrate.

Moreover, contemporary materialism—and here Kearney is referring to the ever more abstract nature of production and consumption in contemporary capitalism—does not, as he puts it, "neglect the glory of matter" (159) but, rather, relocates and redistributes it into a quasi-angelic doxology of everyday life. To borrow one of Kearney's key theoretical terms, the "kenosis" he repeatedly invokes to name the process whereby the God of sovereignty abandons himself, "empties himself," into the suffering stranger—a process presupposed, *voraus-gesetzt*, in every revelation, every miraculous epiphany of the stranger qua *neighbor*—needs to be brought to bear on the realm in which the production of the flesh has taken primary residence in modern life, that of political economy. Anatheistic ethics remains, I am suggesting, a series of beautiful, punctual gestures if it fails to be articulated with the emphatic sense of the critique of political economy first proposed by Marx. I am repeating here, to some extent, a critique of my *On the Psychotheology of Everyday Life: Reflections on Freud and Rosenzweig*, articulated by Andrea Roedig in her review of the German translation of that book in "Zu schön, um wahr zu sein," *Neue Zürcher Zeitung*, November 13, 2010, http://www.nzz.ch/aktuell/startseite/zu-schoen-um-wahr-zu-sein-1.8365397.

4. Jacob Rogozinski, *The Ego and the Flesh: An Introduction to Egoanalysis*, trans. Robert Vallier (Stanford, CA: Stanford University Press, 2010). Subsequent page references are made in the text.

5. I explored this gesture in post-structuralist writing in general and in Paul de Man's work in particular in the introductory chapter of my *Stranded Objects: Mourning, Memory, and Film in Postwar Germany* (Ithaca, NY: Cornell University Press, 1990).

6. Sigmund Freud, *An Outline of Psychoanalysis*, in *The Standard Edition of the Complete Psychological Works of Sigmund Freud*, trans. and ed. James Strachey (London: Hogarth Press, 1981), 28: 148.

7. See, in this context, also Gil Anidjar's extended discussion of both *Merchant* and *Moby-Dick* in his *Blood: A Critique of Christianity* (New York: Columbia University Press, 2014).

8. In the Book of Job, Leviathan is characterized as a creature "made without fear": "He beholdeth all high things: he is a king over all the children of pride" (Job 41: 33–34 av).

9. Tony Tanner, "Introduction," to Herman Melville, *Moby-Dick* (Oxford: Oxford University Press, 2008), xxv.

10. That the ship bears the name of an Indian tribe exterminated in the seventeenth century inscribes it from the start in the violent history in and through which the U.S.–American "ship of state" came to establish its own sovereignty and eventual global hegemony.

11. For a detailed and compelling reading of Melville's deep engagement with the Bible and biblical hermeneutics—along with the quasi-biblical aspirations of *Moby-Dick*—see Ilana Pardes, *Melville's Bibles* (Berkeley: University of California Press, 2008). For Pardes, Ahab's hunt for the whale functions as—among other things—a grand version of his namesake's obsession with the possession of Naboth's vineyard, a story invoked by various nineteenth-century critics of American expansionism. In his somewhat different reading of Ahab as a paradigmatically defective king—one, that is, whose defects are seen as emerging from the nature of the office itself—Michael Walzer emphasizes instead Ahab's apparently reasonable efforts to compromise with the Syrian king Ben-hadad. See Walzer, *In God's Shadow: Politics in the Hebrew Bible* (New Haven, CT: Yale University Press, 2012), 67–68. As Walzer notes, Ahab's efforts to engage in "normal politics" as a nation among nations—rather than conduct a holy war in the name of the Israelite God—is characterized by an unnamed prophet as a transgression of Israel's covenantal status as a chosen people standing apart from the normal life and historical time of the nations. In this case it would appear to be Ahab's *lack* of sufficient (religious) monomania—his lack of the single-minded will to exterminate a rival sovereign/Leviathan—that marks him as a defective king. The real precursor to Melville's Ahab would in this instance thus appear to be the prophet rather than the monarch.

12. Herman Melville, *Moby-Dick or, The Whale* (New York: Penguin, 1992), 126. Subsequent page references are made in the text. That the chapter that introduces Starbuck to the reader is called "Knights and Squires" emphasizes the concern with the reimagining of offices and virtues that formerly belonged to the space of royal sovereignty.

13. The tension between the pursuit of vengeance and that of business is, of course, at the heart of Francis Ford Coppola's *The Godfather* (I must confess my ignorance of the novel). In the end it is Michael, the brother for whom the phrase, "it's only business," serves as guiding motto, rather than Sonny, the brother intent on pursuing vengeance for injuries to the family and its honor, who turns out to be the truly demonic figure in the film.

14. Ahab's pursuit of the white whale shares in the predicament already identified by Lacan apropos of Hamlet's "hunt" for Claudius. Ahab, too, must at some level—at some "lower layer"—"strike something other than what's there." See once more Slavoj Žižek, *For They Know Not What They Do: Enjoyment as a Political Factor* (London: Verso, 1991), 256.

15. Here I am indebted to Andrew Delbanco's insights into the socio-psychological dynamics of the episode. See his "Introduction" in the Penguin edition of the novel I have been citing, especially xxii–xxiii.

16. I am tempted to suggest that one of Jacques Louis David's other well-known paintings, the *Oath of the Horatii*, serves as the model for the way in which Ahab groups together first his three mates and then his three harpooners to cross their weapons upon taking the oath. What Melville adds is, once again, the language of electricity or nervous energy: " 'Advance, ye mates! Cross your lances full before me. Well done! Let me touch the axis.' So saying, with extended arm, he grasped the three level, radiating lances at their crossed center; while so doing, *suddenly and nervously twitched them;* meanwhile, glancing intently from Starbuck to Stubb; from Stubb to Flask" (180, my emphasis).

17. This fusion of wills is called into action in the final chase of the white whale: "They were one man, not thirty." Much like the different parts of the ship, "all the individualities of the crew, this man's valor, that man's fear; guilt and guiltlessness, *all varieties were welded into oneness, and were all directed to that fatal goal which Ahab their one lord and keel did point to*" (606, my emphasis).

18. This flux of social substance is represented, in part, as a sonorous or murmuring mass in Melville's last work, *Billy Budd*. Jason Frank's discussion of the novella focuses on the crucial scenes in which an incipient insurrection against authority on the part of the ship's "people" is rendered in its "murmurous indistinctness." See Jason Frank, "The Lyre of Orpheus: Aesthetics and Authority in *Billy Budd*," in Jason Frank, ed., *A Political Companion to Herman Melville* (Lexington: University Press of Kentucky, 2013), 358–85. "In each of these . . . episodes of murmuring," Frank writes, "Melville dwells on an inchoate collective incipience—affective, shifting, episodic—that has not yet been organized as a legible articulation of resistance or subordination . . . a collective defined by affective orientation not yet cohered into the cogency of an articulation or claim. His text lingers on these charged but indefinite moments, registering the subtle empirical contours of a typically unrecognized and ephemeral potentiality before it crosses over into legible experience or registers as an event" (378). As Frank goes on to emphasize, each such state of sonorous flux is, in the novella, finally made to cohere by way of a commanding auditory intervention transmitted by whistle, drum, or voice of authority. In this context one might recall Kantorowicz's portrayal of the acclamation of Charlemagne cited in Lecture 2. What is at issue in each instance is the task of putting this vocal energy to work, to economize or manage the sonorous surplus—the excess over sense—it incarnates.

19. Pardes, for her part, sees even this passage as haunted by the specter of capitalism: "Behind the mirthful nocturnal visions of Ishmael [given the context, we might say: *nocturnal emissions*], however, lies a darker Joban

cry on behalf of human misery. The crew's squeezing of spermaceti at night attests to the dire working conditions aboard the 'sweatshops of the Pacific,' to use Charles Olson's definition for whalers, to the endless work demanded day and night from the hirelings of the whaling industry. Leviathan has an ominous dimension not only as untamed Nature but also as a commodity in an untamed American industry, the nineteenth-century precursor of the globalized industries of today." Pardes, *Melville's Bibles*, 32. In this context it's worth recalling Carl Schmitt's remarks, cited in Lecture 1, concerning the rise of England as a maritime power, an event that for Schmitt signals, precisely, the revolutionary emergence of a new global order in which politics will come to be more and more displaced by economic administration and management: "Measured in terms of the progress toward civilization that the ideal of continental statehood ... signifies, Shakespeare's England still appears to be barbaric, that is, in a pre-state condition. However, measured in terms of the progress toward civilization that the Industrial Revolution ... signifies, Elizabethan England appears to be involved in a phenomenal departure from a terrestrial to a maritime existence—a departure, which, in its outcome, the Industrial Revolution, caused a much deeper and more fundamental revolution than those on the European continent and which far exceeded the overcoming of the 'barbaric Middle Ages' that the continental state achieved." Carl Schmitt, *Hamlet or Hecuba: The Intrusion of the Time into the Play*, trans. David Pan and Jennifer Rust (New York: Telos, 2009), 65.

20. Delbanco, introduction to *Moby-Dick*, xviii.

21. Kantorowicz, *The King's Two Bodies*, 59.

22. There is no doubt much to say about the relation between comedic wastefulness—along with the base materiality over which it "officiates"—and the "economic eroticism" that Freud elaborated apropos of the "anal character," but that is for another occasion. I reserve for another occasion as well further reflections on Kafka as the writer who brings together the dimension I earlier referred to as the *traumamtlich* and the genre of the office comedy.

23. In light of this solidarity between Bartleby and Ishmael, I am tempted to claim that Kafka, an author whose oeuvre has been seen, for the most part, as belonging to the lineage of Bartleby, has left us a prose text that might be read as a minimalist, modernist revision of Melville's epic tale, one in which Ahab's quest for *Moby-Dick* is transformed, is "reduced" in the senses I have been invoking here, into the worries of a bourgeois father concerning another spectral creature to whom Kafka gave the enigmatic name, *Odradek*.

24. For reasons given in Lecture 1, I *prefer not to* equate such kindness with Bennett's notion of "vibrant matter."

25. I develop this thought further in my book, *On Creaturely Life*.

26. I have had another occasion to point out such birthmarks to Gordon. See my critique of his account of Franz Rosenzweig's understanding of Jewish peoplehood in my essay, "Miracles Happen: Benjamin, Rosenzweig, Freud, and the Matter of the Neighbor," in Slavoj Žižek, Eric Santner, and Kenneth Reinhard, *The Neighbor: Three Inquiries in Political Theology* (Chicago: University of Chicago Press, 2005), 106–108. What Gordon misses in his reading of Rosenzweig is what the latter refers to specifically as a kind of second birth, one that is sealed in the contraction of the self around a dimension he characterizes as *metaethical* and infuses with the qualities that Freud, around the same time that Rosenzweig was working on *The Star of Redemption*, would locate in the notion of *das Unheimliche*. Gordon presents his reading in his *Rosenzweig and Heidegger: Between Judaism and German Philosophy* (Berkeley: University of California Press, 2003).

27. I refer the reader, once more, to Crary's concise formulation of the 24/7 economy: "it is like a state of emergency, when a bank of floodlights are suddenly switched on in the middle of the night, seemingly as a response to some extreme circumstances, but which never get turned off and become domesticated into a permanent condition. The planet becomes reimagined as a non-stop work site or an always open shopping mall of infinite choices, tasks, selections, and digressions." See Jonathan Crary, *24/7* (London: Verso, 2013), 17.

28. The cited passages are taken from Karl Marx and Friedrich Engels, "Manifesto of the Communist Party" in Robert C. Tucker, *The Marx-Engels Reader* (New York: Norton, 1978), 476.

29. Jean Laplanche, *New Foundations for Psychoanalysis*, trans. David Macey (Oxford: Basil Blackwell, 1989), 44–45.

30. Franz Kafka, *Beim Bau der chinesischen Mauer und andere Schriften aus dem Nachlaß* (Frankfurt: Fischer, 1992), 235–36.

31. I am referring, of course, to Kant's famous response to the question, "What is Enlightenment?" See *What Is Enlightenment? Eighteenth-Century Answers and Twentieth-Century Questions*, ed. James Schmidt (Berkeley: University of California Press, 1996), 58–64. It is worth recalling that Freud begins his own account of what is aberrant and infantile in human sexuality with a discussion of the partial drives centered on the mouth, on oral sexuality. For Freud, human sexuality begins in primal scenes of *Un-Mundigkeit*, the perverse use of the mouth in excess of its functional use for eating and drinking.

32. Alenka Zupančič, *Why Psychoanalysis? Three Interventions* (Uppsala: NSU Press, 2008), 36. Subsequent page references are made in the text.

33. The dream of Irma's injection, the so-called specimen dream that Freud presents in the second chapter of his *Interpretation of Dreams*, gives us a nice example of what Zupančič means. During the day before he has the dream, Freud runs into a friend and medical colleague who seems to insinuate that one of Freud's patients—Irma—has not been doing as well as she might be—i.e., that Freud's treatment of her might have been in some way deficient. Freud spends the evening writing up the case study and convinces himself that his treatment of Irma has been beyond reproach. With respect to the demands and standards of his ego, he has successfully interpreted the enigmatic signifier conveyed to him by his friend, the remark or tone of voice that had gotten under his skin. The dream that Freud then has—along with the free associations he produces in the course of his later thinking about it—represent, then, the point at which the unconscious continues interpreting from the perspective of its leftover and concomitant *Arbeitsanforderung*.

34. Franz Kafka's insistence that his publisher not try to picture Gregor Samsa on the cover of his *Metamorphosis* must be understood in this context.

35. Much of part II of my *Royal Remains* addresses this very problem: how to picture something that is not there, that doesn't so much *exist* as a positive feature of our common reality as *insist* as its spectral supplement.

36. Michel Foucault, *Society Must Be Defended: Lectures at the Collège de France, 1975-1976*, trans. David Macey (New York: Picador, 2003), 217 (my emphasis).

37. Robert Walser, *Jakob von Gunten* (Frankfurt: Suhrkamp, 1982), 92.

38. For me it remains undecidable whether the Theater of Oklahoma in Kafka's *The Man Who Disappeared*—the novel formerly known as *Amerika*—represents a more radical and purified version of the doxological machine of capitalism or offers, instead, a paradoxological alternative.

Index

Printed in the USA/Agawam, MA
March 5, 2019

698748.007